Zone of Tolerance

ZONE
OF TOLERANCE

The Guaymas Chronicles

DAVID E. STUART

University of New Mexico Press
Albuquerque

09 08 07 06 05   1 2 3 4 5

Library of Congress Cataloging-in-Publication Data

Stuart, David E.
 The Guaymas chronicles. Volume 2, Zone of tolerance /
David E. Stuart.— 1st. ed.
    p. cm.
 ISBN 0-8263-3828-3 (cloth : alk. paper)
 1. Stuart, David E.—Travel—Mexico—Guaymas (Sonora)
2. Prostitution—Mexico—Guaymas (Sonora)—History.
3. Brothels—Mexico—Guaymas (Sonora)—History.
4. Prostitutes—Mexico—Guaymas (Sonora)—History.
5. Guaymas (Sonora, Mexico)—Description and travel.
6. Guaymas (Sonora, Mexico)—Social conditions.
I. Title: Zone of tolerance. II. Title.
 F1391.G985S886 2005
 972'.17—dc22
                              2005008788

Design concept by Robyn Mundy
Book design and composition by Damien Shay
Body type is Janson Text 10.5/14.
Display is Janson Text and AdLib.

Cynthia Morgan Stuart

This book is dedicated to
the *ferrocarrilero's* daughter,
my wife of thirty-four years,
still full of love and joy.

This book is also a gift to
ol' Max Evans, the great
Southwestern writer, who so
ardently urged me to write it.
I finished the first draft on
August 29, 2004,
his eightieth birthday.

contents

illustrations

ix

foreword

A BRIEF PRESENTATION OF SOMETHING VERY SPECIAL

It is a hallmark privilege to read this book and an equally valued one to be allowed a few paragraphs to explain. I was carried eagerly, expectantly, from the magical soul of the first memoir, *The Guaymas Chronicles: La Mandadera*, with such a silken, effortless transition that it seemed to be the same book. Seldom in literature do we find a sequel joined seamlessly even though there are several years separating them. It was a treasure of a pleasure totally unexpected, and an accomplishment of much merit by David Stuart.

The characters he had become so interlocked with—in attitude and in the joys and pains of surviving on the streets, plus the varicolored sights, smells, and tastes of his favorite hotels, bars, eating establishments, and whorehouses permeate the reader's senses so that he or she becomes part of the sea air from one side and the desert winds from the other. The intoxicating breath of the books is so strong that one becomes filled with the essence of life itself.

Stuart has written these works with his heart as a pen. The words coming from his naked and deepest feelings. A great risk taken, with even greater courage.

We discover love lost here and love precariously found. Tears of laughter, loss, and the zest for living is transforming. Rare indeed.

After reading the first book, I had a calling to conjure up nonfiction works from the past that were on a level with David Stuart's creation. It is immensely difficult to write nonfiction as actual literature—that is, a work that has a chance of enduring. Since the average hardback, bookstore shelf life is about six weeks, that gives one a picture of the odds. They grow much longer in nonfiction.

I cannot help but think way back to James Boswell's biography of Dr. Samuel Johnson (1791) and how it impressed itself on me with its uneven but powerful feelings and sharply pointed accuracy of human observation that have stayed with me all these years. Then there is Steinbeck's *Travels with Charley* and Hemingway's *A Moveable Feast*. There are a few others, of course, but among their scarcity I must place *The Guaymas Chronicles*.

All Stuart's deeply felt relationships in Guaymas—most especially those with little Lupita and her aide-de-campe Juanito, the shoe-shine boy—are so heartwarmingly, heartbreakingly told that they become as indelible as the initial view of one's firstborn or of lightning striking a nearby treetop.

With Stuart's return to Guaymas in physical reality, as well as in the words of *Zone of Tolerance*, we have a high-quality continuance of volume one. His hauntingly beautiful feelings for and descriptions of those he loved, and who loved him, in the early Guaymas adventures are only enhanced by his return to search for Marta, the whore who had given him so much earlier, and this and the ectoplasm of little Lupita everywhere he goes are tragicomedy with attitude. The latter is the most difficult of all writing styles.

Stuart's adventures—or reliving his time in the "zone" of bordellos and the main monetary product, the whores—is a true revelation. We meet, and know, the manager, the bouncers, the clients from taxi drivers to powerful elitists and wealthy politicians, all told with precise insight, compassionate observation and the subtle humor of understanding. There is a cleansing forgiveness all the way to his final, fated meeting with Marta.

Since I have always thought of northern Mexico as the southernmost part of our great Southwest, these chronicles endow us with a bone-true classic of that vast and special region of America.

— MAX EVANS, author of *Madam Millie*,
The Hi Lo Country, *The Rounders*,
Xavier's Folly, and others

acknowledgments

It takes "a little help from your friends" to get a book written and published. This book, like the first volume of *The Guaymas Chronicles*, would not exist without the massive transcriptions of tapes and notes undertaken by Gail Wimberly of Tularosa, New Mexico, in 1984. Nor would it have transformed from handwritten legal pads into a finished typescript without Danita Gomez and her meticulous work. Many thanks to both of you!

And without both the ardent urging and support from legendary Southwestern writer Max Evans, it wouldn't even have been written. It's been a tough year—but "ol' Max" knows "tough" too. So his advice and admiration for the first volume helped pump enough adrenaline into me to get the job done. Writing is hard work. Writing well, even harder. So, Max, I truly hope this one meets the standards you have set with your Southwestern classics, like *Hi Lo Country*, *The Rounders*, *Blue-Feather Fellini*, and many others.

A writer needs real readers to "preview" the work before you, the reader, see it in bookstores. Thus many thanks to Kathy Linn,

Kijrstin Bauer, Christine Hatch, Julie Brown, Angelique Paull, and Laura Moser of Albuquerque. And "¡mil gracias!" to author (*A Gathering of Fugitives*) Diana Anhalt of Mexico City who made a number of compelling suggestions. I also had the good fortune to have gotten sage advice from Tim J. Thomen of Albuquerque. A guy with as much courage as anyone depicted in these volumes, Tim is a stunningly voracious reader with the soul of a writer. He was reading the first volume of *The Guaymas Chronicles* when I met him. Hey—you can't ask for more! From the bottom of my heart, "Thank you, Tim!"

Next, my thanks to colleague and friend Luther Wilson, director of the University of New Mexico Press, who is another big supporter of my writing "habit" (addiction, actually). Luther gets things done . . . and I *do* understand what he has done for me on this volume. I won't forget it, either. Now and again time is of the essence. Luther "gets it" without a word being said. Thanks also to Robyn Mundy, Damien Shay, and the design and production team at UNM Press. They produce books with a jewel-like quality. This two-volume set is but one example. I am also grateful to editors Karen Taschek and Maya Allen-Gallegos of UNM Press, who worked to make this a better book.

These days I write my books at the Flying Star coffeehouse on Central Avenue, near the university. The "kids" at the counter treat me well: Kindra, Diane, Erinn, Dominic, Wes, Tanika, Verónica, Jess, Manuel, Jesse, Jessica, Mazen, Mandy, Emily, Paul, Beth, Judah, Jadira, Troy, and Doug—thanks! And the bussers always seem to find me a table where I can write: José, Victor, Jeison, Ariel, and Efraín—*¡Mil gracias!*

Finally, thanks to Steve Spencer of Corrales (born in Guaymas) for his photograph of the municipal graveyard on the Day of the Dead and to Dan (father) and Rachel (daughter) Shaffer of Albuquerque, who journeyed to Guaymas after reading the first volume of these chronicles and took a remarkable

Dan and Rachel Shaffer. (Photo by Dan and Rachel Shaffer © 2004.)

series of photographs. The majority of the photos used here are theirs. I have also used young Rachel's own photo (taken by Dad) for a reason of which she cannot possibly be aware: she looks so much like Mariquita, one of this volume's main characters, that it not only startled me, but transported me backward in time. I've never met Rachel (she's currently a student at Colorado College), but she has inadvertently given the reader an image quite like Mariquita's at about age twenty.

Obviously I don't think it accidental that she and her father took these photos. As I make clear in chapter 2 of this volume, Fate is a silent, invisible, uninvited, often ignored, but ever-present guest in the cycle of life. *¡Así es!*

Infinity
(for Cindy)

Life is first a struggle for identity

Then ... meaning

Many small steps ... taken through the trials of childhood,

adolescence, coming of age.

Awakening the courage to love.

Each stage a quarter turn toward the infinite.

Eventually to discover that infinity

merely folds inward upon itself.

And there is no time left

to start again.

author's note

This book is the second volume of a memoir of life in the port of Guaymas, Mexico, in the late 1960s and early 1970s. Guaymas is on the Sea of Cortez, about four hundred miles due south of Tucson.

It is based largely on journals and tapes made at the time. Augmented by memory, the recollections of others, and some material relayed secondhand, most of the latter is clearly identified by italics or phrases like, "They say *en la calle*"—the oblique way working-class Sonorans generally passed on most rumors, gossip, and news of the day.

Unlike the first volume, *The Guaymas Chronicles: La Mandadera*, which is both a little girl's story and a tale of love told through my eyes, this book is about the "big girls'" stories. It focuses on the girls of the once fabled Club Río Rita in Guaymas's long-gone Zona de Tolerancia (nightclub or red-light district). It is told through their accounts of "how things were."

Thus this story is not about "love" as most of us define it. It is not even about "sex" in the ordinary sense.

Rather it is about the Gordian knot of conflicting needs, wants, realities, fate, passions, and, above all, illusions that formed the core of the *viejas'* ("working" girls') lives. It is at once funny, sad, angry, and poignant. It is also, at times, desperate. Tragic. Occasionally triumphant. Many of you will also find it, and the viejas, surprising.

Since Guaymas, indeed much of Mexico, decided to close most of its Zonas (some well-known border towns excepted) many years ago, I have written this with some trepidation. I fear that some readers will generalize life in the Zona of 1970 to Guaymas today—or worse, stereotype all of Mexico, having once read it.

Yet this story is important, not only for its human and historical context, but precisely because it is a snapshot of a long-gone, little-known world. That world once constituted a narrow but controlled and compartmentalized slice of life in Mexico, now two generations ago. Most Mexican men of my acquaintance have never even visited "the Zona," remembering it only from whispered secondhand rumors passed along in school yards. Well, gents—here you have it.

Had the average unmarried Guaymas female of the 1960s and 1970s been freer with sex, the Zona would never have existed. As this volume makes clear to the careful reader, most dates at the time were still chaperoned, and a stunning percentage of Guaymas's women made it to the altar still virgins. This, then, is not the "good girls'" story—they were 98 percent of Guaymas. Rather, this is the story of the "fallen angels" of the nightclubs. Exotic. Outcasts, yet at once part of the community.

Many quotes in this book are taken directly from transcriptions of my journals made in 1984 by Gail Wimberly of Tularosa, New Mexico. In the instances where I originally recorded only words or sentence fragments, I have fleshed out quotes in the original style of the speakers. Many quotes begin with "Well" and end with "you know." That's not me talking. Those are the ubiquitous speech signatures of ordinary Guaymenses, where so many sentences began with the Spanish *"pues"* and ended with either *"¿sabes?"* (roughly, "you know?") or *"¿comprendes?"* (roughly, "do you get it?").

This volume opens with my return to Guaymas in 1971 to keep a promise. It then flashes back to the Zona as it was in the summer of 1970 while I wait to talk to a former girlfriend. The main story then fast-forwards to chronicling 1971 and beyond as it relates to the Zona girls, whose stories are told. Finally, simply because readers of the first volume have so frequently requested it, part 3 is an epilogue, the "Where are they now?" so many of you asked me to write.

As a memoir permits, in its genre of "creative nonfiction," I have left some events unchronicled, changed names as I pleased, and described people, places, and dates in ways designed to maximize privacy. This has given me enormous liberty to tell the girls' stories as best I can. One can "novelize" a memoir. As in the first volume, I've used that opportunity—a refreshing change from the textbooks I've written in the field of anthropology.

xxi

I love Guaymas, its people and their values. Had I never lived there, my life would have been very different. Guaymas gave me color, taste, smell, friends, compadres, and goddaughters. It also blew through me—once a restless and "angry young man"—like a warm salt breeze from the Sea of Cortez. Clean, fresh, restorative, and full of love. One cannot ask more of any place or of any people.

— DAVID E. STUART
Flying Star Coffee House
Central Avenue / Route 66
Albuquerque, August 29, 2004

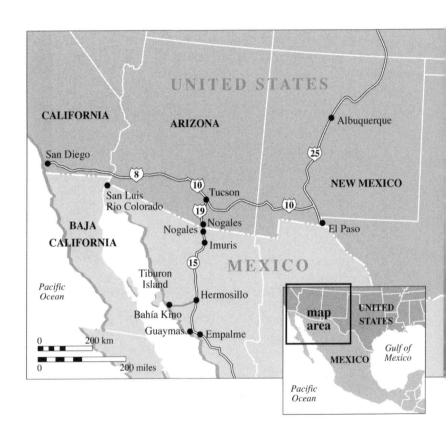

Part One:

RETURN TO GUAYMAS, 1971

chapter one

UNFINISHED BUSINESS

The evening sky was still the same impossibly deep gunmetal blue that I remembered. The limes were still as fragrant, and the wide red clay street that passed in front of the Club Guaymas was still dusty and unpaved. Paradise hadn't changed much during my absence.

But it looked like Marta had. When I first arrived from the States and went looking for her, the cabmen told me she had abandoned her regular downtown hotel clients and gone to work as a taxi dancer out in the red-light district. That was a nasty shock. She had always considered herself a high-class call girl and swore she'd never work in the *Zona*. I simply could not picture her in there, ID number pinned to her blouse, slow dancing with some smelly, sweat-soaked sailor to earn just ten pesos (eighty cents).

And even by the Zona's standards Club Guaymas was a shabby hole. It sure wouldn't be a place she would choose to meet me, her ex-lover. Uncertain, I was about to walk away when "Cocas" Ramírez, a *taxista* from the Sitio del Puerto, drove up in his old white Plymouth and discharged several disheveled male passengers at the door to the club.

I knew Ramírez just well enough to ask for a favor as I pointed and pressed a twenty-peso note into his hand. "Would you please go inside and tell La Flaca (Marta) that you saw me drinking coffee up at the restaurant on the corner?"

"Okay, Güero! Why were you gone all winter, and how was it over on the 'other side'?"

"I went back to school, and it's the same as always, Cocas—bad coffee, cold winters, but lots of blondes." He grinned, made a flamboyant gesture, and disappeared into the club. I turned and headed toward the brightly lit open-front restaurant on the corner and claimed one of the rusting metal chairs outside.

2

The waitress eyed me suspiciously as she took my order for a *café con leche*. Apparently a sober, Spanish-speaking gringo didn't meet her usual customer profile. No matter, I had business to settle with Marta.

Ranchera music blared from the dance hall a few doors away. Still no sign of her. Apparently she was going to let me sweat it out. I had it coming. I'd packed up on about a week's notice and returned to the States when I couldn't sort out the grief that had nearly swallowed me whole after my little sidekick, Lupita, died.

Lupita, my scrawny little *mandadera*, was fun to be with. Our adventures were endlessly absorbing. Her stunning bravado, matched only by her bottomless need for my approval, had pulled me to her like a magnet. She was my business partner, my security agent, my "goddaughter," then "my" child.

Lupita and Marta engaged in an ongoing campaign to get me to choose between them. At the time it seemed silly. One was a nearly unmanageable ten-year-old street kid and the other was a luscious full-grown woman.

When Lupita died, Marta probably thought she had won by fate or by default. But I had tucked my tail between my legs and run back to the emotional safety of the States—a place where you can deny your feelings and everyone thinks you're normal. My run for the border hadn't actually solved much. Lupita's voice still came to me in the long New Mexico nights. Then I'd wake up crying for her.

Just before Christmas, a letter from Marta had come to the Department of Anthropology at the University of New Mexico. In it she said she "loved me"—something she never said when we were together. Then she explained how deeply it had hurt her to realize that Lupita meant more to me dead than she did alive. *You should have been man enough to tell me that to my face*, she wrote. I answered with a denial, but it was bullshit. Marta was right and I hurt her needlessly.

Distressed, I took several deep breaths to relax, enjoying the heady scents of the lime, mixed with chile, coffee, and salt air. About then the coffee arrived. I lit a smoke, took a sip from the coffee, and leaned back. Marta would be okay, I told myself, and drifted into my favorite memories of the first time I ever saw her. . . .

3

The regulars were playing dice and the barman was polishing glasses. Suddenly he stopped, and several of the patrons turned to stare—she must have slipped, unnoticed, through the side door of the hotel bar. Once in, she took a seldom-used stool nearest the glassed patio doors, leaned to the barman, and whispered her order.

Later claiming to have been far too astonished to think clearly, Jesse brought her a shot of Castillo rum and a large tumbler of iced water. Thus Marta was the first to break the daytime taboo on women in the "men's" bar.

Nearly half a century before, the hotel's founder, I was told, had proclaimed his elaborate paneled south bar a sanctuary "for gentlemen only." In those days Guaymas nurtured few men of that class, so the founder's sensible heirs had merely prohibited fighting, spitting on the floor, and wearing huaraches, those distasteful peasant sandals, on the premises.

True, the taboo on women had never been absolute, for at least once weekly a number of the fair sex could be found in the bar. Guaymas gentlemen, successful shrimpmen, even prosperous contrabandistas had always exercised unquestioned rights to the company of their favorite Saturday night whores in the hotel's old sanctuary. But this intrusion was different.

She came late on a brilliant spring afternoon when a dozen regulars had already assembled for games of dice, beer, and talk of the shrimp harvest. Most who were there agree she got away with it partly because don Francisco, owner of the local gasoline station, was at that moment the center of attention.

4

Poised dramatically with the cup of dice, he asked the Blessed Virgin for guidance, then tossed a perfect five aces, decisively ending the game of chingona. Vanquished, the soft-spoken Negro Jacinto turned to Jesse and ordered an obligatory round of drinks. It was then that they saw her.

She was nicely dressed in an unusual gray-striped blouse and knee-length black skirt, not looking at all like the local girls, who went in for bright, tarty colors. Mid-twenties and slender, she tossed a quick, engaging smile to her audience, then drank half her rum in the same fashion.

Someone, it may have been the credulous Enrique, uttered an awed, "¡Madre de Dios!" This embarrassed everyone, but she turned again and retorted with perfect ease, "No, señor, you have mistaken me for another; my name is Marta." This voice was fascinating—in stunning contrast to her subdued appearance, it was throaty, rich, and bawdy. At once, a dozen men wanted her—and her legs. Mother of God, she had wonderful legs and wore a scent dominated by vanilla! She finished her drink, smiled again, and, without another word, left as quietly as she had come. I watched her go, curious at the taste of vanilla that filled my mouth....

Bar Rubi, 2004, with bicyclist. (Photo by Dan and Rachel Shaffer © 2004.)

I was becoming aroused by the memories of her when a honking horn and shouting jolted me back into the real world. "Güero! I heard you came back last night. Have you eaten?" It was El Burro, my part-time business partner and favorite taxista from the Sitio Rubi.

Some things never change—he was wearing the same plaid shirt and driving the same beat-up Chevy taxi. I loved the little hustler. The two of us, with Lupita's help, had sold a boatload of "imported" fans and blenders on the streets of Guaymas before I went back to the States.

"No, I haven't eaten, Burro, join me?" "¡Claro, 'mano! (Certainly, brother!)" He pulled in, jerked to a stop, then jumped out in one smooth move. Burro hopped up onto the concrete "patio" of the restaurant, kissed me on the cheek, and gave me

a long bear hug before sitting down. The waitress gaped and went into frazzled mode.

Burro noticed and, arms spread in supplication, shot her a good one. "What's the matter with you, *chula*? (honey?) Haven't you ever seen a taxista wearing a plaid shirt before?" As always, Burro cackled hysterically at his own ironic brand of humor.

That exchange brought the owner out front. Scowling, he waved his waitress away and took Burro's order. "Rice, refried beans, thin breaded steaks smothered in onions, freshly made salsa—just the way my compadre, Güero, likes it." Immediately the owner was contrite. "Certainly, Burro—I didn't recognize El Güero when he first came in... the boots."

"Not your fault." Burro beamed, then looked at my feet, scolding, "Your boots look like brown turds, brother. No wonder they didn't recognize you. I'll bring Juanito to the hotel tomorrow. He'll shine them up for you—he's still the best shoe-shine boy in town. You've gained weight and your hair is thinner. The States aren't good for you. You belong here." He paused, then

Guaymas graveyard, taken
on the Day of the Dead.
(Photo by Steven Spencer
© 2003.)

asked, a hopeful tone in his voice, "Have you come back to stay?
It will be hot again this summer. Good for business, no?"

"No, Burro. I have come to baptize Mercedes' baby as I promised last September. Perhaps you remember her? She waitressed
at the Colmenar Restaurant downtown."

"Oh yes. Juanito speaks of her. She still gives him a bowl of
soup now and again, and he still shines shoes in front of the
restaurant."

"That's the one, Burro. She had a baby girl on November
25 and named her Olga. We are to baptize the child on Sunday
at San Fernando Church on the plaza."

"Good! Baptisms are happy things and you will have a *comadre*
(co-parent) here as well as a goddaughter. All the more reason
to stay!"

"Thanks, Burro. But I'm just here to finish up some old
business."

"Don't let that business make you sad, Güero. Juanito and I
can take you to the *panteón* (graveyard) to see Lupita tomorrow,

if you wish. Her grave is nice. Juanito and I visited her, ate, and left yellow chrysanthemums for her in November on the Dia de los Muertos.

"We went again at Holy Week. Juanito was afraid at first, but it has been good for him to accept her death and visit her. Now he is happier and spends most nights at La Gorda's. His mother has declined, and old Gorda is good for Juanito, just like a grandmother."

"*Gracias*, Burro! I'll take you up on your offer of the panteón—but *after* the baptism. I don't know how it will be to go there." He nodded and the food came before I had to explain further. It tasted great. Nothing on earth tastes better than freshly prepared Mexican food. My little steak had that distinctive, almost gamey flavor characteristic of range-fed, un-aged, un-adulterated Sonoran beef.

As we ate and Burro brought me up to date on the local news, I stole glances at the Club Guaymas's front door, hoping Marta would appear so I could get it over with.

About the third time I did that, Burro said softly, "If she does not come out to see you tonight, you should wait to return for her until after the baptism. You will not like what you see."

"Is she drinking?" I asked. Without looking up, he nodded, looking sad.

"What happened to her little boy, Burro? She didn't just leave him, did she?" Burro shook his head, looked away, and shrugged. Uh-oh! That's how disaster had begun for little Lupita—a mom gone off whoring, leaving her to her fate. By then I had a sick feeling in my gut, worrying about her and her son.

We finished eating. Still no Marta. It had been more than two hours since Ramírez went in to let her know I was here, and the club was filling up with revelers. Burro urged me to accept a ride back to the Hotel Rubi before its bar closed. He suggested a nightcap. I waffled.

Port of Guaymas boulevard (Photo by Dan and Rachel Shaffer © 2004.)

I really wanted to resolve things with Marta and get that out of the way. It had been eating at me all winter. Now it seemed even worse than I'd feared. But in Mexico, things don't necessarily happen on gringo time.

I accepted the ride. Within two minutes we rolled into the darkened neighborhoods of the poor but respectable folks who lived in the little, widely spaced houses that lined the dirt lanes between the Zona and Guaymas proper. In ten minutes we were back onto the broad, tree-lined boulevards, bright lights, buses, and clusters of late-night taco carts that announced the port of Guaymas.

To my right, lights sparkled off the harbor's rippling waters as Burro's taxi passed the lamppost where little Lupita once waited in vain nearly every night for the missing mother who would never return for her. My heart raced as we went past. Mercifully, Burro kept chattering until he pulled up to the rear of the taxi line at the Sitio Rubi and ushered me into the bar.

It was cheerful inside. Just what I needed! I was in paradise once again and only three days away from a baptism. I wondered what little Olga would look like and her mom, sweet Mercedes, for that matter.

As Enrique poured me a Bohemia, I decided to concentrate on the baptism and not on the fact that one I had loved was in a grave and the other now in the Zona. I told myself that "shit happens... even in paradise," and raised my glass for the first taste of good beer I'd had in eight months.

I chatted with Enrique, the bartender, catching up on news of the hotel's regulars. He was as immaculately dressed as ever and still dating the same girl he planned to marry one day. The only thing different was that he wasn't smoking in the bar. I wondered if he had quit. I'd been waiting all winter to witness what I called his curbside "smoking dance." When he smoked, he rocked back and forth on his heels, rhythmically flicking cigarette ashes behind him between puffs. Once you had seen him do it, you could spot him two blocks away.

When the bar closed about eleven, I stood on the corner to shoot the breeze and pitch twenty-centavo coins with the Hotel Rubi's taxistas. My friends Burro and Mateo questioned me about the States. When Enrique came out from closing up, he lit up a cigarette and did his little dance right on cue. I grinned and Burro winked at me.

Everybody loved Enrique—he was young, likable, clean-cut, and reliable. In a word, *simpático*. Most of the crowd there, including me, had to work at being simpático, but for Enrique it was a natural state of grace.

When Enrique left, I climbed the lobby stairs to the hotel's open-air balcony, overlooking the harbor and shrimp fleet. I pulled one of the huge, old-fashioned rockers to the front railing where

I could watch the moon set behind the low, rugged mountains that fell into the Sea of Cortez. I settled in and rocked.

At first it was peaceful and beautiful, the shrimp boats bobbing on their moorings. The moonlight reflected from harborside rooftops and swaying palms. Then the memories came flooding back. I rocked harder, trying to concentrate on the moon and the baptism. But it wasn't easy, so I lit a smoke and inhaled deeply. No good. I was only twenty yards from the roof of the shrimp-packing plant where Lupita had called to me during a lull in the storm.

That horrible night clawed at me, trying to tear me open again and again, as if it were a wild beast instead of just a moment in time. "Stop!" I told myself. "The kid is dead. You can't change it."

But I could baptize little Olga and watch over her. I was being granted another chance. I would not waste it, I promised myself.

The clawing sensations eased. Feeling better, I went downstairs to room 21. They saved it for me, just as I had left it. I sipped an Orange Crush, then tried to sleep. I had arranged to meet Mercedes at the rectory at 10 a.m. The baptismal registry to sign. A church "class" for compadres to attend. A baby girl to hold in my arms...

chapter two

"TO FATE," SHE SAID

Mercifully, I slept and morning came gently. I awakened about nine to the insistent ringing of the taxi stand's call box and slamming taxi doors just fifty feet from my window. It sounded like business was good.

I loved Guaymas in the morning—clear, turquoise blue sky, a warm breeze spiced by salt water, creosote smells from the shrimp fleet out front, and the sounds of children playing. Children! I had slept late and needed to be at the church on the plaza in less than an hour.

A tepid shower, a quick shave, then a fifteen-minute stop in the Rubi's bar for a café con leche with *panes dulces* (sweet rolls) from the hotel's kitchen and I was off, walking up the main street toward the plaza.

Simply walking Avenida Serdan was an experience. Kids, taxi drivers, beggars, cops, food carts—*life*, vibrancy, community, all rolled up into one. The only places I'd experienced anything like it were in some of New York's livelier ethnic neighborhoods, the

Quarter in New Orleans and San Francisco's Chinatown. But the Serdan was my "home turf." I'd almost forgotten how much it excited me. The Serdan and Guaymas had given me a sense of power—I *was* someone here—identity is intoxicating.

As I passed, I waved to the taxistas on the Sitio Rubi's corner and headed uptown. I felt good until I neared Lupita's lamppost a few yards past Calle 28. I could still picture her standing watch under it night after night, totally oblivious to the world around her. She always stared across the harbor, waiting for her mother to come back to the spot where she left Lupita at age five, promising to return from a "vacation" with a new "boyfriend" she'd met. That never happened. Poor kid.

When I reached the lamppost, I stopped, picturing her with her shaggy mop of hair and big eyes. She grinned at me almost as if she were real, then vanished.

I wanted desperately to reach out and touch her, but she was gone. So I walked up to the lamppost, hugged it, and told her I'd bring Juanito and visit her at the graveyard as soon as the baptism was over. My imagination treated me to another brief, shadowy glimpse of her, smiling and nodding in anticipation.

I touched her tenderly and brushed against her warm cheek. Apparently I got lost in the moment. A cop tapping me on the shoulder and asking in heavily accented English if I was okay startled me back into the real world. In the States caressing a lamppost and talking to an imaginary friend would have required an elaborate, plausible, but bullshit explanation—unless of course you actually wanted an obligatory "psychological evaluation" and jail cot, courtesy of city hall.

But I was in Mexico again, where struggling with the human condition isn't a dirty little secret. So I answered in Spanish, "I was remembering someone who used to stand here before she died. I miss her!" He nodded, patted me gently on the shoulder, and walked on. I said goodbye to Lupita and walked on up to the plaza.

Mercedes was waiting outside the old stone rectory at the edge of the square. She looked radiant, about twenty-two, five feet, three inches tall, medium build, freckled, and with long brown hair. Her smile could light up a concert hall. As I stepped up and gave her a hug, she gave me her best. I absorbed the radiance and my mood brightened considerably.

My favorite waitress and comadre-to-be motioned me into the building where her friend, Leobarda, was valiantly holding on to a squirming, splotchy, screaming infant girl. Little Olga was already nearly six months old. I got a briefing. She had been underweight at birth after a difficult pregnancy and had struggled to thrive. So Mercedes had been anxious about Olga and the baptism.

We stepped up to the counter and were ushered into a larger room where a dozen couples were awaiting church instructions for the next day's (Sunday's) baptismal ceremony. They handed us printed copies of the service so we'd know our parts and gave general instructions on how to conduct ourselves as co-parents (*compadres*).

Thirty minutes later we moved on to yet another room with a long counter and folding chairs. We waited our turn, little Olga raising hell until Mercedes handed her to me in desperation.

Miraculously she went silent, tried to focus on me, and finally quit squirming. Hot to the touch, she smelled good, like the freshly changed baby she was. I rocked her in my arms and she made gurgling, cooing noises. Mercedes rolled her eyes and Leobarda giggled.

For one moment I felt a satisfying fatherly omnipotence, then my goddaughter-to-be went back into her normal squirming, screaming mode. We got called to the counter just as I began to panic. Mercedes' eyes twinkled as I quickly handed Olga back to her and stepped forward to face the church's clerk, who reminded me of my sixth-grade Latin teacher.

It was question time: "Are you the father?"

"No, godfather. The father will not be present at the ceremony." That answer brought both a nod and a pause. My gringo-accented Spanish brought the next question, "Are you baptized?"

"Yes."

"*¿Cristiano?* (Christian?)"

"Of course!" Another pause and nod. "Do you promise to raise this child in the Catholic faith should the mother die and you become the guardian?"

"Absolutely!"

"Are you married?"

"No, *soltero* (single)."

"Residence?"

"I move between Guaymas and New Mexico, where I have employment as an anthropologist."

"Full name, please."

"David Edward Stuart," as I handed her my University of New Mexico business card so she'd get the spellings correct.

She paused again, reading the card slowly and carefully. That made me nervous, so I asked, "*¿Hay problemas?* (Are there problems?)" She looked up and actually cracked a smile.

"I studied anthropology in Guadalajara many years ago—an interesting field." She pushed the registry toward me and, relieved, I signed. Leobarda followed.

Done for the day, we walked six blocks up to the Colmenar Restaurant, where Mercedes waitressed. The Colmenar was tucked into a modern brick-and-tile passageway leading back from the main drag to the street behind. The restaurant was small but clean and modern. Tiled floor, long counter to the right. Several wooden tables out front. Tall floor-model fans provided some relief from the heat of the late-May afternoon.

One of Mercedes' sisters was waiting for us as we breezed in. She had Mercedes' oldest daughter, Martha Aurora, with her.

About three years old, the kid was inquisitive and had big eyes. Just as Lupita had done the first time she saw me, little Martha watched me intently from a safe distance.

The owner, Maximino Flores, was young, simpático, and delightful. In the summer of 1970, I'd first seen Lupita out in this very passageway, watching over Juanito, the crippled shoe-shine boy who relied on her for protection on the street.

Even though bittersweet memories flooded back, I was happy to be in the Colmenar (Beehive) again. The food was nicely priced, and they brought your meal just the way you liked it. I'd spent many afternoons seated at the tables out front in the passage, enjoying the street life and surrounded by the congeniality of the restaurant's regulars.

My coffee and steamed milk (café con leche) arrived at the table just as I preferred it—two-thirds hot milk and one-third dark roast coffee. Then came a bowl of tortilla soup with fresh sliced limes... and they say you can't go home again.

That may be true in the States, but in Mexico, if you could magically arise from your coffin five years after your death and march right into your favorite restaurant, not only would your food arrive just as you had once ordered it, but folks would be delighted to see you again.

I was halfway into my bowl of soup and adjusting pretty well to the squealing, ever-squirming infant we were going to baptize on Sunday when an insistent rapping on the front window caught my attention. Juanito!

The little guy was out front with his wooden shoe-shine box, motioning me out. Like the other street kids, he wasn't allowed inside—Mercy! I'd forgotten just how lopsided he was. I went out and gave him a big hug. He looked good, didn't smell bad, and had even gained a couple of pounds. Miraculously his clothes were pretty clean. Old Gorda must have taken good care of him. His mom certainly never had.

No improvement on the gobs of snot he continually exuded or his appalling speech impediment, but it didn't matter. Juanito was family. He not only supported his mean drunken mother but had waded through flooded streets in the midst of last year's worst cyclone to find a doctor for Lupita. The doctor hadn't arrived in time to save her, but it was no small feat for a kid born largely paralyzed on one side.

He considered himself a failure because she died. But I considered him a hero. Guaymas taught me that in the real world, it isn't winning—but trying—that counts. And Juanito *had* found a doctor.

Juanito pointed to my boots and motioned me to sit. I smoked while he worked. Just like old times. The year before he had given my oil-tanned Red Wings an amazing two-tone treatment. The bottoms sported a rich burgundy patent-leather shine, while the tops were a subdued oil-tanned brown. Striking!

Those boots had attracted lots of attention. On the street, people knew me by them and my fair complexion. Now they looked old and beat-up. Undaunted, Juanito went to work on them as if they were the ceiling of the Sistine Chapel. The nuances of leather were his chosen canvas.

He chattered as he worked. The food at Gorda's was good . . . and "miraculously," he marveled, the bigger shoe-shine boys no longer stole from him.

He also ragged me about my weight and thinning hair. "Another year on the other side and they will call you "*pelón* (baldy)!" Just as had happened when my father died in '67, I'd lost brushfuls of hair after Lupita's funeral. I wasn't good at crying—emotions too bottled up, I suppose. So I simply shed hair instead of tears. Mentally you can deny grief, but your body knows the real score.

Finished, I tousled Juanito's hair, handed him a twenty-peso note, and told him to let Jimmy Kiami know I'd like to have coffee with him right here at the Colmenar on Monday afternoon.

Heading uptown on the Serdan. City hall's dome on left. (Photo by Dan and Rachel Shaffer © 2004.)

Kiami owned the boutique on the opposite corner and had helped me arrange for Juanito's safety after Lupita died. He was a delightful guy and I was anxious to see him again.

Juanito gone, I stepped back inside, settled the final baptismal arrangements with Mercedes, and said my goodbyes, little Martha Aurora still watching me intently from a safe distance. Now to do a slow stroll back down Avenida Serdan, the main drag, and renew old acquaintances.

First stop was the Sitio Medrano. Handshakes, ritual *abrazos* (stylized hugs), and a quick briefing on the purpose of my visit, then I was on my way.

Working the street and maintaining relationships was an important part of life in Mexico. I loved the custom and invested heavily in it while I lived in Guaymas. Since the main street was Avenida Serdan (named after a minor revolutionary/shoemaker who captured the republic's imagination in the 1920s), working the Serdan was known as "*Serdaneando.*"

My next stop was the Sitio Centenario, several blocks farther on, then the Chapultepec, on the waterfront a few blocks from the Hotel Rubi. About an hour had passed before I made it back to the Rubi's taxi stand to talk to some of the *veteranos* on the day shift. Burro, Manuel Mejias, and old Mateo were among them. The taxistas and barmen on the Serdan had been my lifeline during hard times. Subsequently I repaid their favors when my luck turned. We had history.

I passed out coveted Pall Mall Reds and updated the taxistas on my winter in Albuquerque. Things were going okay for me at the university, but North American food still sucked...several who had worked as *braceros* laughed and nodded knowingly...and I'd met a girl. "*¿Una rubia?* (A blonde?)," interrupted a young, clean-cut guy I didn't know. Old Mateo shushed him up and asked, "What kind of girl, Güero?"

"Tall, slender, wavy brown hair. Great smile, warm...and very smart—she just finished her degree in anthropology." "*¡A todo madre!* (The whole nine yards!)," someone else exclaimed. Mateo shushed that one too, asking, "*¿De la gente fina?* (Upper class?)"

"*No*, Mateo, *es la hija de un ferrocarrilero. Buena gente.* (She is the daughter of a railroad man. Good people.)" Mateo nodded approvingly, but Burro was worried. "*¿Güera o Chicana?* (roughly, Anglo or Chicana?)"

"*Güera*, Burro, I should have mentioned this last night when we ate, but I had my mind on other things."

He nodded knowingly but mercifully left my business in the Zona unmentioned. Then the conversation turned to the ordinary—business, the shrimp harvest, who had done what (or who) over the winter.

Several had also heard about the upcoming baptism and wanted to know more about my comadre, Mercedes. I filled them in. Several knew her vaguely from the restaurant. Everyone approved. Extending one's relationships through work, marriage, friends, baptisms, and favors was a national occupation.

In the States wealth is measured in "things"—cars, houses, stocks, TV. In Mexico most measure it in friends and relationships.

We were just finishing the conversation when Jesse, the Rubi's legendary bartender, came strolling up, cheerful. "¡Ándale, Davíd! I heard you arrived late Thursday night after the bar had closed."

"You look good, Canelo ("Cinnamon," his widely used street name).

I grinned and gave him an abrazo. "And how is Jacinto?"

"Fine, compadre, he'll join us when the bar closes tonight—Chang will have a good table for us at the Río Rita." The other taxistas laughed.

Everyone envied the clubbing the three of us used to do on Saturday nights. Frankly, I missed it but told him I'd have to be in bed by 2 a.m., given the Sunday baptism. "¡Propio! (Proper!) But you'll need a taxi to return." He chuckled, reminding me that Mariquita would be dancing. That meant a late night for him and Negro.

Mariquita was young, radiantly sensual, and had a figure that would have sent any supermodel into spasms of self-hatred. I teased, "What did she do—lower her price enough that the two of you could share her?"

"No such luck, Davíd, but she likes you. Maybe you could ask her about a group rate."

"Include us!" shouted one of the taxistas. Everyone whistled and laughed. In reality none of us there was ever going to have the money to spend a night with her. A pity—any one of us would have appreciated her far more than the rich guys who banged her for ten thousand pesos a night ($800 US in 1971)—more than a year's rent!

But whoring isn't about appreciation—in spite of the undertones of anger and self-destruction—it's about being paid. Or power.

As the laughter subsided, Canelo pulled me aside, looking concerned. "Some things have changed, Davíd. I'm not sure how to tell you." Then he panicked—at a loss for words. . . . I waited. He stuttered. Finally I broke in. "¿La Marta?," I asked. He nodded gravely. "It's okay, Canelo. Old Mateo told me where she was and I went looking for her last night."

"Did you talk?"

"No, I waited two hours for her, but she never came out."

"Perhaps it's better that way, Davíd, *qúe no*?"

"Perhaps, but I'll try again after the baptism, compadre. I owe it to her." He nodded, pulling out his comb to redo his signature James Dean hairdo and regain his cool. "Time to go to work, Davíd. See you later."

I followed him into the hotel lobby and watched him walk down the long hallway to the bar, head high and that distinctive rolling stride characteristic of powerful men.

Back in my room, just like old times, I wrote in my journals and listened to the rhythmic sounds of the taxi stand outside. First the call box would ring, followed by a shouted order to the first in line. Then a slamming car door and the growl of an engine starting. Moments later came the low grunts and whooshing noise of the next taxi being manually pushed to the front of the line. Mexican efficiency in motion—it wasted gasoline and wore out engines to restart them incessantly as the taxi lines moved forward. Ring. Shout. Slam. Crank. Grunt. Whoosh. The endless rhythm of a Mexican *sitio*. There one never hears engines idling. Idling taxis are a gringo extravagance.

An hour later I drifted upstairs to the big balcony overlooking the harbor. I worried about Marta, deeply upset. I didn't even know what our relationship had been. Need? Sex? Perhaps both,

Sitio Rubi call box.
(Photo by Dan and
Rachel Shaffer © 2004.)

but certainly not love. It was Lupita, not my girlfriend, who first taught me the true meaning of love.

A cold Orange Crush and a Pall Mall Red kept me company while I watched another sunset in creation. As boiling heat waves rose from the pavement, the sky rippled like an immense azure canvas while an unseen hand added stroke upon stroke of brilliant peach and crimson. Each new brushstroke flowed upward from the horizon in long, sweeping arcs, a divine reward for those who had survived the day.

But the roof of the packing plant was too close for me. I wanted Lupita desperately. Did the same unseen hand that painted the sky each evening caress Lupita when she was lonely? Was she with her mom in heaven as I had promised on the day of her funeral? I was filled with doubt. Never very spiritual when I was in the States, Guaymas—and Lupita—always seemed to bring this out in me. Confused, I left, Serdaneando my way up to the Copa de Leche Restaurant, overlooking the harbor.

A bowl of soup and a café con leche on the roof picked up my spirits until I found myself staring out across the harbor— just as Lupita had.

Later, unsettled by the memories, I walked through the city market district, enjoying the breeze, gunmetal blue evening sky, and rich scents of the evening meal being prepared in shaded court-yards, hidden from view. About 10 p.m. I drifted back to the Rubi bar to drink an Orange Crush and played dice with the regulars.

The bar bustled with activity. Each evening locals dropped in to nurse a beer, exchange gossip, and shoot dice till Canelo closed. The long mahogany bar, dark paneling, and subdued lighting pro-vided a haven from the June heat, noise, and chaos of the port.

Air-conditioning, still uncommon at the time, was a huge draw in the hot season. Vintage Hunter fans turned slowly while an elaborate old Wurlitzer jukebox belted out rancheras, punctu-ated by sounds of laughter, clicking dice, and dominos.

Eva came in about ten-thirty. One of the few women who came to the bar, she was warm, pretty, and, like many hookers, world-wise. Simply watching her move was a sensual delight. Catching sight of me, she glided over, studied me for a moment, a worried look on her face, then leaned over to kiss me on the forehead, whispering, "Some things have changed, Davíd."

I reached out and caressed her cheek. "I know, Eva. I have already heard about Marta." She nodded, apparently continuing her appraisal. "You've aged, Davíd."

"*Sí*, Burro said the same thing. He told me the States were bad for me." She laughed. "You should listen to your friends, Davíd! Have you come back to live? Burro and Juanito need you. You have *raíces* (roots) here."

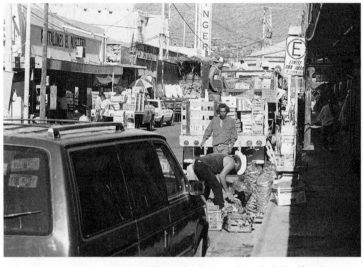

Street scene near city market. (Photo by Dan and Rachel Shaffer © 2004.)

"No, Eva, I'm here for a baptism and will return to the other side in about ten days." Palm up, she stopped me. "But Davíd, there is *nothing* over there for you." I reached out, touched her hand, and explained, "Now there *might* be—I met a girl. She's warm, kind, smart. I'm going to marry her."

"A gringa?"

"Yes and no, Eva—if it works out, you can judge for yourself. I'll bring her to meet all of you."

"Is that a promise, Davíd?"

"Yes!"

She frowned. Silent... I waited. "So many of them are cold and greedy. I hope she is right for you."

"She's right, Eva—I'm sure of it. I was sitting at a table talking to friends and looked up. There she was. I almost turned away, then glanced into her eyes and felt the greatest warmth and joy I've ever known."

"*¡Ay, Dios! ¿El hado?* (Oh, Lord! Fate?)"

"I think so, Eva."

"I've always wondered what that might feel like, Davíd . . . and with a gringa!"

"Haven't you ever felt it, Eva—not even once?" I asked.

"*Pues*, I thought I felt it once when I was fourteen. There was a boy I watched and smiled at on the plaza every Sunday afternoon. Carlos was tall and handsome. One Sunday he asked me to walk around the plaza with him. I thought I was in love. But my oldest cousin became jealous. He and a friend caught me on the way home from school several days later. The big one held me down while my cousin raped me. Then the other took his turn. They hurt me. I was a virgin and still a child.

"The next Sunday when I went to the plaza, I tried to pretend nothing had happened and I saw Carlitos and smiled. He walked up to me, angry, and called me a little *puta* in front of everyone. Then spat on me and turned away. I never saw him again.

26

"My mother insisted I had disgraced them, so a few days later I ran away. I decided I'd give men what they wanted and make them pay me. So now all I feel is *la monda* (penis) while I ride them and think of my bastard cousin. The quicker I make them come, the better I feel. But it's not warmth, Davíd. I tell myself it is only a 120-peso ride on a smelly old burro. The smell washes off."

"But Eva, you didn't seem to treat *me* like that!"

"At first it was the same as always, Davíd, but suddenly the image of my cousin disappeared and I actually felt sorry for you— you seemed so lonely. So I spoke to you and you told me your dreams had turned to *mierda*, just as mine had when I was a girl." She shook her head, looking wistful. I interrupted her thoughts, shocked at what she had just so casually told me. . . .

"Do you still see your cousin's face when you are with a client?"

"Once in a while, Davíd, but not like before. Now I dream of running a club and leaving the screwing to the others. I'd even like to have a child someday."

"You—married!" I blurted out, incredulous. "No! *¡Baboso!* (Drooling idiot!)" She laughed—a vieja knows where to find good sperm when she needs it! Still laughing, Eva turned and took her post at the end of the bar.

As I watched her take her stool, Enrique brought me a fresh Bohemia I hadn't ordered. "Compliments of La Eva, Davíd. *'Al Hado,' me dijó.*" ("To Fate," she said.) So Mexican—"Fate" would provide me the answers!

Even if it didn't, the beer itself was an unusual gesture. Mexican hookers never buy their clients, current or former, anything. It is rule one of their sisterhood. My hundred-peso assignation of the year before had just been officially erased. It never happened.

This was the second act of absolution I'd received from a *vieja* in Guaymas. The first one had come from Francisca a few days before I left Guaymas in 1970. Eva smiled from the other end of the bar and I blew her a kiss. She left with a client a few minutes later and Canelo began to close for the evening.

chapter three

A SATURDAY NIGHT

Like most events in Guaymas, even everyday ones, closing the bar at the Hotel Rubi was a ritual with its own sacred rhythm.

First, Canelo regaled the remaining patrons with stories while Enrique collected glasses and cleaned tables. As usual, this phase of the ritual was formally announced when Canelo stepped out from behind the bar and touched up his Hollywood-perfect James Dean hairdo in preparation for the gentle "goodbye."

As he moved forward that Saturday night, I was transported backward in time. His ritual had the emotional impact of an old movie reel—an important image etched forever into the folds of my brain. Though Canelo is seventy-two years old as I write this, his image lives in my mind as the powerful young lion he was. Imposing. Perfectly pressed blue-striped Van Heusen dress shirt, tails worn out. Spotless khakis and brilliantly polished penny loafers. A confidently distinctive style in working-class Guaymas.

Then he assumed the pose. One elegant burgundy loafer on the second rung of the tall bar stool, leaning forward, a Winston cigarette behind his ear. Heavily muscled arms folded casually over the loafer-supported knee. The effect enhanced by his fair complexion and amazing cinnamon-colored mane.

The jokes always began in a conspiratorial whisper. As he leaned toward the assembled, bar stools swiveled and rapt patrons, like beer-stained sunflowers, turned to bask in his radiance. Then came the deep voice, resonant with the merest hint of a stutter. "*El pinche périco dice* ... (the frigging parrot says ...)"

Canelo was, possibly, northern Mexico's greatest fountain of "parrot" jokes. Nearly all were sexual or social commentary with short hilarious plots and gut-busting punch lines. Parrot jokes were the bartending world's equivalent of Mexican *corridos*—street stories in word rather than in song.

The deepest appeal of the "parrot" format came from the fact that it met Mexico's instinctive social need to be oblique and indirect with sensitive commentary so as never to offend. If a patron were to be offended, it would be attributed to the third-party persona of the parrot, not the teller.

As the parrot finished "his" tale, Canelo would pull the Winston from behind his ear, light it, and inhale deeply. This was the ritual signal for the patrons to abandon their stools and glide out into the night.

Next came the floor mopping, or "*trapeando*," so named since most Mexican mops of the day were but long rags wound through a wire hook at the end of an ordinary handle. It would not have been dignified for Canelo, the lion and lord of the Rubi bar, to be seen doing the floors while patrons watched.

Enrique, Canelo, and often Jacinto and I all mopped. It made us equal—and time was of the essence. At 11:15 p.m. it was only forty-five minutes till the main floor show began at the Río Rita nightclub in the Zona. After the feverish mopping, Canelo tallied the register, personally chalk-marked the fill level of all the liquor bottles, and prepared the cash box for delivery to the Rubi's huge, old-fashioned safe behind the registration counter in the hotel's main lobby.

That lobby was about 250 feet down a long hallway, one allegedly haunted by the ghost of the owner's grandfather.

This stage of the ritual was signaled by the gathering of all but Canelo at the tiled hallway's door to the bar. Then Canelo, just in front of us, ducked into a seldom-used side door to throw the main power switch, which fed electricity to that wing of the hotel kitchen.

Cash box tucked under his arm like a quarterback carrying a football, Canelo would emerge in front of us, triggering a mad dash down the inky-black hallway toward the lobby. Canelo detested the dark. He feared *espantos* (ghosts) even more. The object of that dash was to successfully evade the ghost of the hotel's founder and make it, unharmed, into the light and safety of the lobby.

We usually formed a flying wedge before frantically driving the cash box downfield, deep into the bowels of opposing territory. Protecting the quarterback, Enrique, the youngest and fastest, took the point. Jacinto and I brought up the rear. Once the year before, Jacinto goosed Canelo from behind to heighten the experience. Canelo let out an extraordinarily impressive "ooh!" and took off like a bat out of hell. I'll say this—the big man could really move. Not a prayer that Elway could have matched him downfield.

That Saturday night Jacinto and Enrique laughed uncontrollably while Canelo made strange whooping noises as we ran. But as always, we made it to the lobby unscathed, where Canelo delivered the cash box to the safe. Then he compulsively recombed his James Dean to perfection. Restoring his "cool"!

Nearly everyone, both in our team and the desk crew, laughed hysterically and snickered as the nightly ritual ended. But I never laughed quite like the others since I had actually seen the ghost of the old man as clear as day the year before. My sightings had subsequently contributed considerably to the bar-closing drama.

The first sighting began innocently enough. I lived in the hotel, room 21, and so had slipped into the bar one quiet mid-afternoon in July of 1970 as the dour, brooding day shift barman known as "El Pelón" was getting ready for Canelo's arrival.

Just as I entered, an old man dressed in a dark suit got up from a corner table and shuffled out through the rarely used glass patio doors at the rear of the bar. El Pelón was, at that moment, facing the bar's mirrored wall and chalking liquor bottles to mark the end of his shift. He turned, surprised, saw me, and grunted. I ordered an Orange Crush. I wouldn't even have remembered that glimpse of the old boy at the patio door had I not seen him again several days later.

It was fairly late on a wickedly hot Friday night, the bar nearly full. Canelo and Enrique were both busy, hoping the evening rush would peak before the supply of ice-cold beer in the big old-fashioned cooler boxes ran out.

I'd been playing dice and telling embellished stories about a recent road trip to Tucson during which I'd smuggled a new set of tires for Burro's taxi into Mexico, mounted on my old gray '62 Rambler. I may be a gringo, but I'd certainly put the *chingas* on a certain Mexican federal customs official!

In truth, little Lupita always handled the *mordidas* (bribes), but hell, my BS was good enough for a free Bohemia from one of the many local haters of *los pinches federales* (the frigging federal police).

As I turned to pour my well-earned beer, I glanced toward the still-empty rear corner of the bar nearest the old patio doors. There sat the old boy again. All alone and dressed in a dark, old-fashioned suit and black-striped vest, sporting an impressive gold watch chain, he seemed a half century out of date.

That in itself wasn't amazing since some of Guaymas's grand old geezers occasionally still dressed in 1930s style and wore their heirloom pocket watches—like badges of the old order. But that was usually in the winter. That summer night the temperature was still at least a hundred degrees Fahrenheit outside. Impressed, I studied him briefly.

He leaned forward as if he were drinking a beer, elbows on the table, a cigar in one hand, apparently oblivious to the world around him. As several new customers drifted in and headed toward his corner hideaway, he struggled to his feet and once again shuffled toward the glass patio doors. Short, squat, and thick, his gait was distinctive. He opened one patio door, apparently irritated—slamming it as he went out—and disappeared into the night.

Startled, Canelo froze when the door slammed. So did a number of the regulars. It was one of those weird, silent moments full of social suspense as if someone had farted loudly during a papal audience or the moment in the summer of 2004 after U.S. vice president Cheney snarled, "Fuck you!" to Senator Leahy on the floor of the U.S. Senate. At such moments the cosmos shudders briefly, its rhythm perturbed.

And the slamming patio door had clearly created such a disturbance. Canelo also stuttered, "W-What was that? Did someone go out the patio doors? They aren't suppose to be used!"

It was quiet for another second or two, then I answered, "Yes, Canelo, an old man just walked out onto the patio. Is it safe out there?"

Canelo was stressed. "No! It's all glass, littered with broken equipment and garbage. It hasn't been used in years." He motioned Enrique out onto the patio to check it out. Apparently there was no sign that anyone had walked out there because Enrique came back in, eyes wide, shaking his head no.

Canelo, looking expectant, exclaimed, "¿Y? (And?)" "¡Nada! (Nothing!)," confirmed Enrique.

Next Canelo turned to me, acting strange, and asked, "Well, did you really get a look at this guy?" I shrugged. "Well, I glanced at him once or twice." Stuttering, Canelo pressed, "W-Where was he? I didn't see *un viejo* in here."

I clarified, pointing. "Well, he was over at that table, the one between the glass doors and the air conditioner." That particular table was seldom used. I had never seen the bar full enough to notice anyone there.

Canelo wanted more information, so I described this guy as about five feet four, rather heavyset, maybe 190 pounds, prominent jowls, and wearing an old-fashioned striped vest with gold watch chain, baggy unpressed pants, and smoking a *puro* (cigar). Canelo, now really rattled, was beyond more questions.

Enrique took over. "Well, did you notice anything else about him?" I nodded. "He walked funny. He waddled, like a duck. What's the big deal?"

Enrique explained—I had just given a stunningly accurate description of the hotel's founder. By then long dead, he had been a well-known and colorful figure in Guaymas. Every evening he came to his bar, sat at that very table, drank a beer, smoked his Veracruz puro, and then went out through the patio doors, which once led to the narrow pathway that ended at the lovely, wooden Victorian house his descendant and current owner, don Hector Morales, then inhabited with his charming family.

Later others questioned me on what I had seen. Everyone concluded that their resident gringo had definitely seen the espanto of the founder. Since Mexico is inhabited by many ghosts, the only real amazement was that a gringo had seen the old man.

Nonetheless, the incident created a bit of a legend. Canelo had apparently long been spooky about ghosts in the old wing of the hotel. This event convinced him that it was truly haunted. My sightings and the slamming patio door confirmed it. Hence the heightened urgency of the mad dash down the hall every night at closing time.

I still don't know what to make of my sightings, but one hot night several weeks later I was certain I smelled cigar smoke as we ran through the darkened hallway. I said nothing at the time. Perhaps it was only a lingering illusion—the result of self-suggestion. But Canelo made impressive gurgling noises that night, so perhaps there really was the scent of cigar smoke.

After the momentary panic of our "reunion" dash down the hallway, we piled into Jacinto's turquoise-and-black Ford Crown Victoria and headed for the Club Río Rita. Just nineteen minutes till "showtime!"

The trip out to the Club Río Rita also had its own rhythm, coupled with a sense of anticipation. The Zona wasn't just a cluster of cathouses, nightclubs, and restaurants—it was the very sepulcher of Guaymas's secret life. Its doors opened each night like the petals of a great, jet-black flower, emitting the luxurious scent of sin. An antidote to both the grueling six-day workweeks and the guilt-laden shadow of Catholicism, which shaped the sex lives of the entire community. To go to the Zona was at once both defiant and exhilarating.

In the Zona, one walked not through the valley of the shadow of death but through the valley of mortal sin. Drink and gambling on the left, the vibrant flesh of Babylon on the right. Sodom and Gomorrah re-created on earth and right in front of you.

You had but to walk through the front door, sit down, and order a drink... the devil's forked tail slicing through the heavy night air just behind you as you entered. And if one listened carefully, one might occasionally even hear him lick his fetid chops, anticipating the capture of yet another soul.

And souls were captured in the Zona. The drunks, sex addicts, psychological freaks, and predators were tangible proof of that. Some would claim that it was most of all the viejas, the hookers, who had surely been claimed by the evil one. That might have been true of some among them. But this was Mexico—and the viejas, true to the core of Mexican culture, played dual roles.

In their flesh, which they offered up for a price, they were at least momentarily active agents of sin. But in their hearts and souls, they were redeemers—saving countless young Catholic señoritas in *el centro* from the taint of consummated sex. The whores' nightly sacrifices saved virgins for marriage...and Mexico, in those days, demanded virgins at the altar.

In Mexico's spiritual and social food chain, the Zona was essential, a part of the community, and the viejas were but fallen angels whose ministrations preserved at least the illusion that once separated female Mexico into "good" girls (marriageable but innocent and untainted) and "bad" girls (accessible and voracious, for a price). The good girls were bred to become the "mother of my children." The bad girls, like Eva, were accidents of fate or misfortune.

In Guaymas the "good" girls *hated* the viejas. They simply neither appreciated nor forgave the fleshly sacrifices made on their behalf. After all, the viejas were their sexual competition. The Zona's hookers were the ones who moaned, writhed in feigned ecstasy, and told the señoritas' fiancés how big, hard, and hot they were. Things a "good" girl could never say and do, even after marriage.

But that, too, was an illusion. The mechanical sacrifice of paid flesh was real enough. But nearly all else was a pantomime. Ironically, the devil only claimed those who actually believed in the illusions.

Our trips to the Zona were not like most men's trips to an ugly border town's "Boystown." Unlike those truly captured by illusion, our trips combined male bonding with the excitement of facing the most treasured of male fantasies. Fully enjoying the illusions, yet walking away with our souls intact. Toes over the precipice of every hormone-driven male urge, yet the groundedness of character not to leap headlong into the abyss, the vortex of that flickering tail.

Among the three of us, only I had stepped out over the edge. And it was the viejas themselves who had twice pulled me back with admonitions to "find a nice girl, get married, and have babies." Thus I became one of their group redemptive projects in the summer of 1970.

So I felt a kinship with a number of them in ways that are hard to describe. I saw goodness where others saw only the damaged wings of the fallen. Too often I saw the pain of my own childhood reflected in their lovely dark eyes. And I often took them places they could never have gone without me—protecting them from the "good" girls downtown, who almost always demanded that restaurant and store managers immediately eject them. Just as with the bartenders and taxi men, I had history with the girls at the Río Rita.

Jacinto's Crown Vic slipped away from town through June's warm night air, floating along quiet, unmarked dirt lanes lined with the darkened houses of Guaymas's working poor. No pavement, city water, streetlights, or garbage collection were to be had in the residential district out there.

If one wished to enter the Zona itself—the sepulcher doors to the town's secret life—one must purposefully seek it out. Tucked away in a dusty bowl, hidden by rocky hills, the clandestine location also allowed decent, downtown Guaymas folks to pretend if they chose that the Zona simply did not exist. For some the Zona was but another of the secret compartments so common in Mexican society.

Despite such precautions, rumors about the Zona traveled in hushed whispers through much of polite Guaymas society—the stuff of local myth and mystery. But we were greeted with shouts, not whispers, as Negro's turquoise-and-black Ford emerged from the dark and pulled up to the brilliantly lit Río Rita's front porch.

Recognizing the car, a number of the girls waved, yelled, or wiggled their butts, shouting "*¡Desgraciados!*" ("Unfortunate wretch!") to celebrate Canelo and Negro's arrival. Both were local working-class legends. Besides, they treated the viejas with friendly respect, always paid their bar bills, and were good tippers.

When I stepped out unexpectedly and started up the steps, the catcalls stopped and someone ran inside shouting, "*Regresa Davíd*—tell Chang!"

I actually got a rush from that. True, it wasn't equal to, "Ladies and gentlemen . . . the president of the United States," but it wasn't just, "Here comes another pinche gringo looking for cheap *carne!*" either. I still had respect here—a veteran who had once swum in the scented pools of that black flower, yet had later become "a friend of the house." The girls' very own pet gringo. Not bad for a clueless twenty-five-year-old guy.

Hell, I got more respect from the girls in the Zona for what I hadn't done than from the professors in the States who were soon to award me a doctorate for what I had done.

That had seemed weird at the time. But looking back on it, I thought perhaps it was the way it should have been. Getting a Ph.D. wasn't particularly easy—write an interesting two hundred pages, successfully engage in "Academic Ego Management 101," and bingo, you're suddenly "Doctor Somebody." Real work, but doable.

But not pulling out a hundred-peso note ($8.00 US in 1970) and diving headlong into the hard nipples and gorgeous, soft brown flesh of the Zona every time you got testosterone fever was a real test.

No one knew that better than the viejas themselves, who earned their livings from clients who flunked out—or worse, but even more lucratively, had totally confused the pantomime of sex for affection. Those guys did get laid—but they got neither respect nor affection. Miraculously, I eventually earned both from the girls. Seven minutes to "showtime"!

As we crossed the tiled porch to enter, Chang, the Río Rita's bubbly, rotund manager, stepped out to give me an abrazo, then personally ushered us in, seating us at a prized front table.

Our customary drinks appeared moments later. No order necessary—a Coke with lime for me, long-necked Corona beers for Canelo and Negro, and a mysterious fourth drink in a highball glass placed in front of the empty chair to my right. Was Chang actually going to sit with us...? Wow! That would have been like Frank Sinatra stepping off the stage to have a beer with his fans.

Canelo raised his eyebrows and shrugged. He had no clue either. As he pulled out his comb to work on the James Dean, the announcer strode onto the stage. "Showtime! *Damas, caballeros...y viejas*—*bienvenidos* (welcome) to the Río Rita's Saturday Evening Spectacular! *¡Lo mejor de Sonora!* (The Best in Sonora!)...and tonight La Mariquita dances...." Instantly the room erupted in testosterone-driven applause, just as someone's hand brushed my arm...Francisca!

She had slipped quietly onto the chair next to mine. Tall and elegant in her little black dress, silver pumps, and matching belt, Francisca once rocked me in her arms, crying with me, after Lupita died—my first grant of absolution from a hooker in Guaymas.

Now she smiled gently, a noncommittal tone in her voice. "So did you actually go back to the university, Davíd?"

"Yes, Francisca, I didn't know what else to do...and thank you again for—" She cut me off quickly with a grin and toss of her head. "Let's watch the floor show. We can chat after!"

The floor show had begun, as always, with several sultry female singers setting the mood. Like French cabaret, risqué but not coarse. Just like Jane Monheit or Diana Krall singing "Peel Me a Grape," their eyes and voices ignited one's sensual imagination, prying open portals to private places in the listener's psyche. Setup for the illusions to come.

 Rachel Shaffer in *gafas*. (Photo by Dan Shaffer © 2004.)

40

The main illusion was, of course, the now legendary Mariquita herself. Still several acts away, Francisca nodded toward the main door. "I'd like some fresh air. Would you escort me, Davíd?"

"Of course, Francisca, honored." Canelo and Negro nodded in approval. Francisca on my arm, we headed for the colonnaded terrace out front.

Once outside, I lit her smoke, then tapped a Pall Mall on my thumbnail. She lit it for me. "*Mira*, Davíd—La Marta is in the Club Guaymas and the taxistas say you have been looking for her. You cannot save her, Davíd."

"But Francisca—I owe it to her to at least talk. After I returned to the other side, she wrote me that she loved me."

Rolling her eyes and wagging her cigarette at me for emphasis, she gave it to me with slow determination. "*No* ... Davíd. It's *not* ... like Lupita! Lupita loved you. You are now merely Marta's excuse for having abandoned her family and come to the Zona. Must I always protect you?" She paused, pouting. "And you *never* take my advice."

The lecture over, she smiled again, touching my shoulder. I gave her a little squeeze, then started to escort her back inside. She resisted, whispering in my ear, so close that the tip of her tongue gently brushed my earlobe. "Wrong direction, Davíd. Would you like to spend the night with me across the street—a coming home gift?"

Oh, Lord! I already had an erection from the earlobe bit, was bright red, and didn't know what to say.... She was waiting, looking amused, then whispered, "So...?"

Now it was my turn to stutter like Canelo. "Oh, Francisca! I'd love to, but I can't. Truly! I have a fiancée on the 'other side' and I promised her I'd be faithful! I hope you understand! I don't mean to offend you...."

She paused, absolutely no hint of emotion in her face. Shit! She actually had me sweating. I fumbled with my blue bandana, wiping my forehead. Apparently she was satisfied; her face came alive again, her huge eyes suddenly moist and glittering. "So its true, *cabrón*, you really are going to be married on the other side. And to a university girl! I am angry that you did not tell *me* first!"

"Does everyone in this town know everything, Francisca?" I shrugged, exasperated. "No, Davíd—only the taxistas know everything. But the girls here know *almost* everything."

"Are you angry with me, Francisca?"

"No—I am delighted! When are you to be married?"

"On June fourteenth—just nine days."

"And La Marta—are you waiting to talk to her tonight?" I shook my head, no.

Francisca smiled. "Good! Now let's go inside and see if La Mariquita can shake your resolve!"

Mariquita was spectacular, but even she couldn't get my mind off Marta. Back in my room at the Hotel Rubi, I tried to sleep while vivid memories of Marta flashed through me like dry lightning on a summer's night....

chapter four

MARTA, 1970

Marta had always been compli-
cated, yet intoxicating. When I first saw her in the Hotel Rubi's
bar in the spring of '69, she had scattered rich fantasies of sexual pandemonium in her wake. Like shards of broken glass on a
beach, those fantasies shimmered in the sunlight of desire—but
their jagged edges could cut deeply if one was not careful. It had
taken her only twenty minutes to own a piece of nearly every mas-
culine soul in the bar—specifically that part of a man's psyche
that is joined like Siamese twins to the sexual realm in his brain.

None likely succumbed more quickly than I. Having been
raised in a sexually repressed social environment, soaked in aus-
tere Calvinism, I once fretted that I might have been *the* last guy
of my generation to actually get laid.

The pain of seemingly unending virginity was enhanced by
the curse of my innate sensuality and earthiness. These were dangerous "character flaws" that my family both discussed and tried
valiantly but unsuccessfully to root out and extirpate. By the mid-
'60s, the virginity issue resolved, my sensuality had been fully

unleashed. Yet it sometimes spiraled in eccentric directions. Okay—foolish ones, too!

So as Marta first walked out of the Rubi's bar, it was I who had fatally inhaled the scent of her vanilla, savoring it like fine, aged brandy. And the glittering, crystalline shards of her sexuality later haunted my fantasies in the Ecuadorian Andes.

Of course, I should have been fantasizing about Iliana, my fiancée from Empalme—just several miles south of Guaymas. That troubled me, but I had no practical control over it at the time.

It took me a long time to figure it out. I could have decent, even rich emotional relationships with women I wasn't screwing. Or I could (though still too infrequently) have knockout sex with women who didn't fully engage me emotionally. But I had never managed both at the same time. So I had loved Iliana. But needed Marta.

Since part of me was nearly always emotionally guarded, protective, expecting disaster at any moment, I both survived the breakup of my engagement more easily than I should have, then fell quickly into the vortex of Marta's glittering sexuality—the ease of it enhanced by the lack of deep emotional attachment, which she actually insisted upon!

Marta was 105 pounds of sleek, dark, gorgeous, big-eyed, but emotionally inaccessible sexuality—perfect! And the drop-dead pair of legs that she teasingly squeezed chilled limes over as I slowly licked the juice from her soft skin were one hell of a bonus—an antidote to the hot Guaymas nights. The last icy lime always saved for her own favorite fantasy.

She came to my room every Sunday night, staying for a few hours. Like a trained rat, I'd have an anticipatory hard-on two hours in advance, already fantasizing. Cool limes. Legs. Hard nipples, vanilla! And she openly demanded that I not fall in love with her.

Free of guilt and emotionally safe, I imagined, she consumed me each Sunday. Once a week I bathed in the epicenter of a full five megatons of turbulent sex. I reacted like I'd won the Mexican national lottery.

Yes, I should have known better. I knew she was a part-time hotel hooker. Even my friend Negro had warned me. And there were the times when she'd get drunk, *pistiada* (smashed), and sway back and forth, cursing. Those were nasty rages when her throaty voice transformed into a coarse rasp, which cut as deep as any cabinetmaker's tool.

But both our needs and our flaws allowed us to treat our relationship as if it were an Argentinian tango. Addictive. Dramatic, stylish, filled with exotic contrasts—light flesh against dark, Spanish and English. Lime and vanilla. Turbulent, then calm.... The tango ended each Sunday night when the music stopped.

Had it not been for Lupita, my *mandadera*, the first to actually get past my emotional safeguards—those ancient vellum walls I'd so carefully erected during childhood and adolescence to protect my inner self—our agonizingly flawed tango might have gone on for years. Trapped in our own pantomime, our souls lost in the vortex of our own need-driven illusions.

Frankly, it stunned me when Marta's letter came to the States in the fall of 1970, telling me she "loved" me. Real or bullshit, that had slapped my Calvinistic guilt back onto the table. The guilt loomed in front of me like a pair of aces turned up on the three-card flop of community cards in Texas Hold 'em. Dangerous if you don't have an ace in your own two-card hand, since someone else surely will.

When the letter came, I had only known the ferrocarrilero's daughter for several months. The relationship was still young, tentative, like holding a pair of tens. Good. But not a lock, given aces on the board. Just like poker, my choices were to fold the tens and go back to Mexico. Or take a chance and go all in. You either win—or lose such hands *big*. Nothing in between.

Had it not been for Lupita, I would have folded the pair of tens at Christmas break at the University of New Mexico and returned to Guaymas to see Marta. Instead I went "all in" and asked the güera to marry me.

She said no. Twice! Jesus. That had scared the bejeebers out of me. But I could taste the pot! If I could win it, I just might get a shot at love, romance, friendship, sensuality all rolled up into a whole, healing relationship—my secret dream of dreams!

But this dream also required that I shed my protective layers of fear about closeness. Those layers had been added one by one, like a tree's telltale growth rings, through the course of my life to protect my soul from pain. Reality. After Lupita's death I realized that those layers trapped me as much as they protected me.

So I had written Marta before Christmas that I'd visit in May, then waited. I'd already decided that it was marriage to the ferrocarrilero's daughter or permanent bachelorhood.

I came to that position in an odd way. One early December evening in Albuquerque, I dreamed of Lupita. Sometimes I'd wake up, cheeks wet from those dreams, calling to her in vain. But that night she walked right up to me and smiled, nodding yes. Then vanished.

That dream had come several days after Cynthia's second "not" and request that we "just be friends." "Just friends" was the kiss of death. I had declined the "just friends" proposition, telling her again that I loved her deeply. She left, silent. And I hadn't seen her in several days.

Then came the dream. I became calm. It was all or nothing. Clear. And Lupita agreed! My roommate, John Bröster, suggested I not press for a while.

"Give her some rope," he urged. I did, and it worked. I went to Pennsylvania to meet her parents at Christmas, still no promise of marriage. But the cards were in play; another ten had come up on the "turn." I was holding a decent full house and my odds had skyrocketed.

The guilt over Marta tugged at me, but not deeply enough to change course. Still, it was deep enough to repeatedly rivet me to a table, drinking coffee in the Zona, only ten days before my wedding. Every vieja in local whoredom was counting the hours of my penance and humiliation.

Shit! Marta was becoming the Boo Radley of the Zona. There were probably even modest betting pools among both the viejas and the taxistas over whether, or when, she might emerge.

It would have taken a stunning talent for denial, the kind only senior politicians and Jimmy Swaggert types seem able to summon, for me to believe no one noticed my situation. I was both the featured entertainment and a living morality play—"Honor" versus "Humiliation." The mystical balance between those two was already teetering precariously. Hence my friends' concerns.

47

In the States a poor or merely jobless man is a nobody. In Mexico a man too deeply humiliated also ceases to exist. So I took the evening off on Tuesday. I ate dinner at the Colmenar, then went out to the Hotel Miramar and talked to Negro. He got me a front table in the dinner club, where I danced with several of the tourist women. We flirted. Negro passed by and winked. Approval.

Later an early a.m. snack at the Almita Restaurant and a long talk with the night manager Ana Maria López really picked me up. It was almost like old times. She was bubbly, her expressive almond-shaped eyes and crinkly nose constantly punctuating the conversation. At nearly 2 a.m., I stepped out of the brightly lit restaurant directly across from the old city market, turned left, and headed toward the Rubi. As I passed the narrow, darkened passageway to the tortilla factory, I had another unsettling "Lupita" moment.

Little Lupita had emerged from that very passageway the year before to "sell" me on the idea of *negócios* in fans and blenders.

That was the start of the small-time *fayuca* (contraband) operations that had both drawn us together and put food on the table. How can you miss a kid who wasn't really "yours" so much?

Slow, deep breathing got me to the next corner—where I crossed the Serdan, then walked straight up Avenida 15 to the rear of the Hotel Rubi so I wouldn't suffer another "Lupita" moment while passing her lamppost.

I sensed her presence so vividly that I ached for her again. She seemed to be everywhere, just beyond sight. Exactly as she had so often been in real life. Following Güero's moves. Stalking her prey. Hustling for a meal. "*Metido en negócios* (engaged in business deals)."

Did the gatekeeper in heaven let kids like her out every now and then? As I finished a slow smoke on the Rubi's upstairs terrace, I watched the roof of the packing plant, half hoping she would materialize—even if only for a moment.

And oh, Lord! How she and Marta had hissed at each other over my attention. Love? Validation? Unmet needs? I don't think any of us really knew as the course of events propelled us into a complicated triangle of uncertainty.

And Marta was mercurial. Sweet and gentle one moment. Man-eater another. Proud and confident one day. Frightened and insecure the next. Sexually in control one Sunday, emotionally inaccessible the next.

It should have driven me crazy, but "crazy" was a state I could understand and deal with. I was a veteran at not knowing what to expect. In fact, I was raised on it. At least Marta was living proof that some woman, somewhere, wanted me, even if only on Sunday nights.

But it was her drinking that worried me the most. She always wanted me to drink with her. That damned Castillo rum she absorbed like a sponge turned her mean and angry, fueling her self-destructive streak. She'd get smashed, go whoring with one of the bar's regulars, a middle-aged "engineer" I knew only as El Alemán (the German).

One weeknight in 1970 after a drunken argument with me over Lupita, she walked out of the Rubi bar with him right in front of me! Making certain that her negotiations were loud enough that others overhead. And her agreement had been sensational.

Enrique let it slip that she was going to give him a "*buena culeada*" (anal sex)! Whispers of forbidden sex rippled through the clientele. Some of the regulars glanced nervously at me. Payback for her screwed-up, drunken fantasies that I had a sexual relationship going with Lupita, who was about ten or eleven.

The whole episode was designed to wound my pride, drive me mad with sexual jealousy over the kind of sex we'd never shared, and if possible pound a stake through my "*pinche gringo corazón*" ("frigging gringo heart"—her words).

It did hurt, *bad*, but I feigned calm. After pondering the situation for several minutes, I walked over to Enrique and asked him to call the front desk to find out if they had taken a room in the hotel. He hesitated. The mood was very tense. In Mexico, this is "revenge" time—¡*La venganza!* Guys sometimes grab knives or pistols and settle the score. Then and there.

So I assured Enrique I didn't want the room number but merely wished to send a fresh bottle of Castillo rum as a "gift" before I left for the Río Rita.

He was still motionless, so I reached for my wallet. "Here, let me pay you for the bottle in advance. I've got to get out to the Río Rita. If the bottle is deliverable, take care of it for me. If not, you can credit my account. Thanks, compadre!"

He nodded. "I'll see you tomorrow, Davíd. If Negro comes in, I'll let him know you went to see Chang."

"*Bueno*," I said. Then turned to the regulars, nodded, and tossed everyone a breezy "¡*Buenas noches!*" stepping out into the

49

night as several of the veteranos nodded back. They heard me crank up my old gray Rambler and head up the Serdan.

Canelo had understood the move perfectly but simply couldn't explain it to Enrique in front of everyone. I *needed* to do something to save my honor in front of the regulars. Mexican working-class society demanded it . . . and a bottle of booze sent to the "bridal couple" was a gesture of contempt, sufficient to meet that need.

I didn't have to cut on Marta or break into the room in a rage to redeem my dignity. If she was going to play *perra* (bitch), I was certainly entitled to send them the booze as a *chingadazo* (screw you, too!).

According to Enrique, Canelo merely delivered the bottle and glasses to the shelf under the front desk of the hotel, returned to the bar with the empty tray, and said, "*¡Hecho!*" then combed his James Dean and began telling parrot jokes.

The regulars were satisfied, one, according to Enrique, actually pronouncing my response as "*muy Mexicano. Frío pero digno* (very Mexican—cold, but dignified)." Canelo never said another word to me about it. Nor did any of the regulars.

To my surprise, the brotherhood of the staff and regulars had apparently decided that cool and nonchalant had its merits. For days no one paid any attention to Marta when she came to the bar. That drove her absolutely nuts!

I'd begun to actually process, and didn't like, the fact that the primary way she related to men was through sex. There just weren't any other consistent dimensions to her. And I was going along with it. Not good.

She displayed flashes of kindness and warmth, which I encouraged. Then hastily retreated behind her wall of sexuality and the medium of sexual favors. Marta understood sex but neither herself nor other male needs. In relationships she was monolingual. Sex was her only true means of communication.

Meanwhile I had begun to give, and get, the genuine warmth I craved through my relationship with Lupita and, to a lesser extent, from other friends. Gradually I discovered that these emotions, resonances, and daily interchanges were "love."

I had always wondered what *love* was. Trying to define it so I would know "it" if I ever found it. Ironically, in the summer of 1970 the puzzle of it was slowly being solved, day by day.

It was revealed to me, frame by frame, like a flickering black-and-white movie, which made no sense until the reel came up to speed, stunning one with the action hidden in separate small, almost imperceptible individual actions and emotions, each like a single frame on the celluloid. Love—the mystery of small motions.

Marta was not at all pleased by this awakening in me. She sensed it, obsessed about it, feared it... and had taken extreme measures with Alemán to break me of it. But it took on a life of its own. A sexual picnic was no longer a substitute for love. Not even a five-megaton one. Thus began her spiral downward even before I realized it or understood the cause.

51

That spiral had pulled her from the hotels to the Zona in less than nine months.

chapter five

THE BAPTISM

I had not slept well—turgid, confusing visions of Francisca, Marta, Mariquita, and my bride-to-be all collided in my dreams. Flashes of brilliant sensuality, followed by blind panic. My subconscious had obviously waltzed onto a Stanley Kubrick movie set! Or perhaps it was merely a consequence of sleeping in the very same bed where I once made love to Marta each Sunday night...

At one point they were all right there together shouting at each other—arguing about sex, love, marriage, babies, and *me*. Spanish and English were all jumbled up in disconnected fragments like a bad Picasso sketch. And women love to imagine that it's just so easy to be a young man!

Thankfully, the sitio's phone box was ringing off the hook fifty feet from my window at the Rubi and wakened me from the nightmares. The early Mass calls for the town's aging widows. Dressed in formidable black, resigned grandchildren in tow, early Mass spared them both the heat of the day and having to rub elbows with any real sinners.

The genuine articles were still groggy from Saturday night's revelry and choking on their flaming-hot *chilaquiles*, a hangover cure of tortilla strips, tomatoes, and high octane chile sauce, and tumblers of lemon water. The most pious among them never made it before noon mass. The least pious never showed up until their age and health made mortality a day-to-day adventure.

I showered, carefully laid out my good clothes for the baptism at 2 p.m., and hustled out to the Rubi's small dining room for café con leche and scrambled eggs. Juanito did my boots again while I ate.

I asked him to get me fifty pesos' worth of coins in a paper bag—five- and ten-centavo pieces—then to go to the plaza by San Fernando's front doors around 2 p.m. and wait for me to come out of the church. He nodded, pocketed the banknotes I handed him, and took off with his shoe-shine box.

Breakfast over, I went to the roof terrace again, smoked, and rocked, the mid-morning breeze from the harbor warm but fresh. After working up the courage, I turned the rocker toward the roof of the shrimp-packing plant, facing Lupita's hideaway, and asked her for permission to baptize little Olga and watch over her. I received no signal that she heard me, but at least I'd asked.

Then I prayed that Lupita was safe, at peace and in her mom's arms. Her mother magically restored to the lovely young woman she must have once been before she fell into the vortex of *el ambiente* (prostitution). That mom had given Lupita enough love as an infant that the kid had still been capable of bonding to both me and Juanito after all her harrowing years alone on the street.

I didn't know if God heard guys like me . . . and still don't. But I desperately needed to believe that Lupita had finally found her mother. It was noon when I descended to dress.

I headed for the plaza at 1 p.m., wearing a white shirt, black dress pants, and mirror-bright Red Wing boots—nervous but well

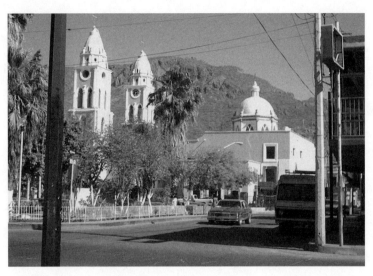

San Fernando church and plaza. Serdan to right one-half block. (Photo by Dan and Rachel Shaffer © 2004.)

turned out. I stopped briefly at each sitio on the way up, the Rubi, Chapultepec, and Centenario. At the corner of Calle 22 and the Serdan, I angled left past the rectory and sat on a bench at the edge of the plaza, lit a Pall Mall, and waited for Mercedes.

The little plaza was alive with activity. A mere one hundred paces from the harbor, its iron benches, shady trees with white-washed trunks, immaculate Victorian bandstand, and towering church formed the heart of old Guaymas. Marriages, baptisms, funerals, novenas, speeches, dances, ice cream vendors, shoe-shine boys, lovers, old men playing checkers, old women praying.

One chamber of the city's heart consisted of the square itself; the other was formed by the imposing whitewashed church of San Fernando de Guaymas.

As those chambers pulsated, the social and spiritual essences of Guaymas's lifeblood flowed through its arteries, the avenues.

Returning through its veins, the narrow side streets, to be oxygenated by the harbor's moist salt air before pulsing through the plaza once again.

Juanito showed up first. Limping up to me with a big lopsided grin, he displayed the sack of coins. "Good job! Juanito—now go to the steps of the church and guard the bag till I step out after the ceremony. Hand me the bag from the left as I pass—I'll wait a moment before I throw the money."

Juanito confided, "I have a surprise for you, Güero—you'll see when you come out of the church!"

I tipped him twenty pesos. He shuffled off toward the church, dripping huge gobs of snot as always. As I watched him, Mercedes arrived with Leobarda, the *madrina*-to-be (godmother), and little Olga, sparkling in a white baptismal dress but splotchy and squirming.

We entered San Fernando, joining another half-dozen nervous groups waiting for the priest. He appeared punctually at two. Fortunately two groups were called ahead of us—a chance to observe the drill and one more opportunity to mentally rehearse the mimeographed lines of the ritual (in Spanish), which had been handed out at the godparents' orientation session in the rectory.

Our turn. Whoa! I was nervous but elated. In my earlier pool-shooting days it would have been described as "feeling tight, but good," like the nervous elation that often came just before a big money game.

Mercedes—always a calming influence—was radiant; her big eyes, freckles, and genuine warmth were infectious. You somehow knew that God himself took a moment to smile as Mercedes walked me toward the baptismal font.

This was a moment focused on the meaning of life itself—warmth, love, hope. All invested in a new generation. A fresh life to be lived—a life yet untainted by folly and misadventure.

Then the priest asked if the father was present. Mercedes hesitated, nervous. He had never been mentioned, so I assumed his existence was a cipher. Mercedes glanced at me, uncertain. My cue, I assumed. I butted in, "Padre, the father will not be present today. I am here in his place and I understand my obligations fully." The priest nodded, smiled ever so slightly, perhaps curious about the story behind our unusual baptismal assemblage, then proceeded.

Olga raised cain as the priest poured holy water on her and I bobbled one of my lines in the ceremony, but a squirming still-innocent soul was at last consecrated to the Almighty. Mercedes was relieved.

In Catholic Mexico you do not want anything to happen to an unbaptized child, and Olga was now six-and-a-half months old. In turn, I was elated—Guaymas had taken my fictive goddaughter, Lupita, then granted me a real one to ease the pain. My second chance was now a reality.

My right arm around sweet Mercedes' waist, Olga cradled in her arms and drooling copiously on my starched white shirt, the three of us marched back to the church's front door and stepped out to face the crowd gathered on the plaza. While the remaining couples assembled behind us, Juanito sidled up from his post, ready to hand me the sack of coins.

As cameras clicked, Mercedes handed Olga to me. I raised her high, as did the other fathers and *padrinos*—presenting the children to old Guaymas and giving them their first full view of the plaza where they would one day play, make friends, go to confirmation, meet sweethearts, marry, baptize their own children…and, in the fullness of time, have their funeral masses recited.

As I handed Olga back to Mercedes, Juanito jammed the sack into my hand and hustled down the steps expectantly. The shoe-shine boys and younger children surged forward out of

57

the crowd as the contents of six bags of coins were thrown, like rice at a wedding party, into the squealing tide of kids competing for the money.

The tradition—*tirando las bolas* (throwing the "shines")—both brought luck to the baptized child and created a ritual obligation that set in motion the great wheel of reciprocity that drove the core of Mexican society.

As a gringo, I needed to be careful—if I threw too much money, poorer baptismal families might be humiliated. If I threw too little, little Olga's star of fortune might not be appeased. As in most important matters, I consulted Eva—she thought fifty pesos (four dollars) about right. Burro later agreed—fifty pesos was an average day's wages, respectable but not arrogant. Hey, hookers and taxistas knew everything, so I went with it.

As the coins disappeared, Juanito's "surprise" emerged from the gaggle of now squabbling kids—"La Gorda!" The old woman who had once fed Lupita and now cared for Juanito. She folded me in her arms and squeezed me tight—no ritual abrazo for El Güero! She rarely strayed from her big corner room with the tall, barred windows a few blocks away. I was honored!

She asked me to come by for coffee later that evening after the baptismal dinner with "my family" ended. Oh, how sweet it sounded to have Mercedes, Olga, her sisters, and her brother, Raúl, who were now gathering, referred to as "my family"!

Then Gorda shuffled away, leaning on her cane, Juanito parting the crowd for his fictive "nana" (grandma).

I watched her go—remembering her together with Lupita. A poor, shapeless old widow to the casual observer, she embodied every wonderful aspect of the Mexican character: kind, generous, frugal, honest, respectful, dignified, and able to love without a trace of cynicism.

After a few photos, we walked down to Sr. Efrén Preciado's house—the home of Mercedes' brother-in-law and sister Aurora.

Preciado house porch. Mercedes (center) and family, 1994. Olga, her daughter (second from right), is the author's goddaughter. Mercedes was carrying her when the author left Guaymas. (Photo by D. Stuart © 1994.)

Just a block from the church, its front veranda was shady, full of flowers.

Its swirled mosaic-tiled floor fascinated little Olga, who had begun her first attempts to crawl. Something about the floor's pattern apparently frustrated her. Still trying to focus on the pink and gray swirls, she began screaming.

I gathered her up, cradled her in my arms, and rocked her, hypnotized by the feel of her. The luxury of it all! Meanwhile Mercedes' oldest daughter, Martha Aurora (then about two years old), watched from a safe distance—her expressive eyes fixed on my every move.

She was curious, as at the Colmenar Restaurant. Natural, since most gringos not only look different—lighter skin and odd clothes—they also sound different. They form unexpected "words"—almost but not quite Spanish. The rhythm and tones of their voices are different—harder, more urgent, forebodingly abrupt. So different from the gentle, calming musical cadence of the other adults around them. Even more curious, they don't even know how to speak local "baby talk"!

And perhaps most important to a child, gringos smell different. Their clothes smell foreign, no hints of the subtle but ever-present local scents of corn oil and tortillas. No minuscule undertones of garlic or chile in their sweat. Even their boots, purses, and leather watchbands smell exotic—different tanning processes. Different soaps, shaving lotion, perfume!

Two-year-old children still have all their "primitive" instincts intact. I may have been accepted in working-class Guaymas as nearly one of their own, but little Martha knew I was an unfamiliar species. She checked me out, eyes wide and nostrils flared, like a wolf pup testing the wind for scents of danger.

In this respect she reminded me of Lupita—who survived by clinging to every primitive instinct she had been born with. Most of us eventually lose broad realms of those natural senses. If fortune smiles, we learn that the world is "safe" in infancy and become incorporated into a nurturing human family. Then we let go of our protective animal capacities to see, hear, and smell everything around us. We test the winds against the layers of social and cultural conventions we have learned—not with eyes, ears, and flared nostrils.

That day began my fascination with Martha. I stared intently at her for a moment, then smiled. She met my gaze for a full two seconds—not bad. The kid had spirit! But one quick flash of a half smile was all she could manage before she darted off and hid behind the Preciado family sofa.

Dinner followed. Steaming tamales, rich with scents of corn, pork, and red chile, *sopa seca de arroz* (Spanish rice), and a cake for little Olga. The cake, and bottles of Coke I'd provided, brought more children to the house's front terrace—neighbors? Cousins? Strangers? I couldn't tell . . . and in Mexico, it doesn't matter.

None of us had the money for a lengthy celebration, so after cradling Olga again, I drifted away several hours later, shaking hands all around and formally bidding goodbye to my "comadre."

Mercedes, in public, was no longer "Mercedes." She was "comadre" and it was proper for me to use the formal "*usted*" with her. She always cut me slack on the "usted"—and continued to indulge me in calling her "Mercedes" in private, but on the street, the formal greetings let others know of the relationship.

Had she died, it would have been both my legal and sacred obligation to take Olga in, raise her as my own, and ensure that she was brought up in the Catholic faith. Because of the legal obligation for a godfather (padrino) to raise a godchild (*ahijado*) in place of deceased parents, it was then extraordinary for a foreigner to be asked, or legally permitted, the honor. As I ambled down the street, waving over my shoulder, I was amazed and elated.

Leaving the Preciados, I turned right down Avenida 15 toward Gorda's and the Hotel Rubi. Directly to my left was the Café Combate store—its wondrous smell and dark yellow facade beckoned. I stuck my head in, bought a half kilo of their best dark roast, and headed on down to Gorda's.

The huge colonial-style house where she lived had been broken up into "apartments" for nearly a dozen families. Her room was on the corner—one immense, iron-barred window faced Avenida 15, the other a narrow, shady side street.

I shouted a greeting and rattled the bars. Gorda shuffled over and I passed her the sack of coffee through the bars, asking, "When should I return for coffee, Gorda? What hour is convenient for you?"

"*A las nueve, Güero, cuando es fresquecíto. ¿Sirve?* (About 9 p.m., Güero, when it is cooler. Does that work?)" I nodded.

Gorda's house district. (Photo by Dan and Rachel Shaffer © 2004.)

"*¡Perfecto, hasta las nueve!* (Perfect! Till nine!)," I said, then walked on down to the Rubi.

On a Sunday evening the Rubi's bar was closed, so I briefed the taxistas at the sitio, who wanted a report on the baptism. Versions of my account likely began spreading *en la calle* the minute the first taxi in line pulled out to pick up the next fare.

Tired from the day's excitement, I went to the roof terrace, lit a smoke, and rocked, enjoying the solitude. In the States solitude is pervasive. In Mexico it is precious.

The aura surrounding the shrimp-packing plant had somehow softened and I relaxed, actually dozing, until awakened by a car horn below, honking insistently. Then came the cursing. "*¡Pinche peón, apúrate!* (Move it, you frigging peasant!)" Rude. Wow!

I leaned over the railing to check out the action below. Brand-new white pickup truck. Extra roof-mounted lights.

Sinaloa plates. Whoops! Drug money—probably a mid-level narco...and some poor bastard's hot dog cart was momentarily blocking his truck.

Several of the taxistas from the Rubi's sitio were already heading toward the truck, pissed off, as I hissed from the railing, "**Psst!**," then yelled, "*¡Sinaloense!*" as loud as I could. Sinaloa State was, even then, Mexico's drug export capital.

As folks on the street below processed "Sinaloan," everything seemed to go into reverse mode and the waters of the Serdan quickly parted to let the rude bastard and his truck pass without incident.

Mr. Pickup might have been nothing more than a rude but prosperous rancher from the Mochis or Guasave area, but there wasn't a speck of red dust on that truck! So it was far more likely that he was one of those dyed-in-the-wool drug trade SOBs from Culiacán who always carried at least two loaded Browning Hi-Powers and often an Israeli Uzi for good measure.

Guaymas's taxistas were certainly not wimps. Among them they had sent their fair share of nineteen-year-old drunken switchblade-wielding "badasses" home to their mommas with both fat lips and newfound respect for men who actually worked for a living.

But the taxistas could also figure the odds on most any event as accurately as Jimmy the Greek. Showroom-clean truck. Bad attitude. Sinaloa plates. The odds sucked. "*¡Ni modo!*"—the prick from Sinaloa got a free pass—and Guaymas returned to the gentle rhythm of another Sunday evening in paradise.

It was nearly nine when I went to my room—ditched the afternoon's dress clothes and strolled up to Gorda's in Levis and a short-sleeved shirt.

The street behind the Rubi was shady and green, punctuated by shockingly bright splashes of *buganvilla* that cascaded over the garden walls of aging architectural gems. Like Gorda's

63

Bougainvillea/walls. (Photo by Dan and Rachel Shaffer © 2004.)

place, these once housed the rich, entrepreneurial merchant families who had developed the port of Guaymas—the Iberris, Morales, Zaragozas, Iñigos, Fourcades, Uribes, and others.

Still grand when Steinbeck wrote his *Log of the Sea of Cortez* in the 1920s, most of those houses had eventually faded as the great families moved out to the Miramar colony to build new compounds fifty feet from the soft, tan beaches.

I rattled the bars at Gorda's. As she cackled and plugged in her floor fan for my comfort, the distinctive scent of her dark Mexican coffee prepared with a hint of chocolate washed over me. Oh, Gorda! How your old man must have loved Sunday evenings with you before he died! Snot still dripping, Juanito admitted me through the main courtyard door, curious at the package tucked under my arm.

Inside, her large corner room was as before, except for the addition of Juanito's small burlap cot in the corner near the eight-foot-tall, barred east window, which looked down Avenida 15 toward the Rubi. A pegboard over the cot held his change of clothes, his precious shoe-shine box stowed neatly underneath.

As I surveyed the scene, its familiarity ignited a deep sense of calm. Gorda had that effect. She was as solid and as deeply rooted as the ancient trees outside.

On the north wall's high altar her painted tin Virgin of Guadalupe shimmered in the soft, flickering light of three votive candles. One for her deceased husband and another for Lupita. But the third one was a mystery. She watched me out of the corner of her eye as I inquired, "¿*Gorda, ha pasada otra tragedia?* (Has another tragedy come to pass?)"

"No, Guëro—it is something between the Virgin and me. Private." She motioned me to sit.

Her plain wooden table was set with a plate of panes dulces, five unmatched coffee mugs, spoons, and a chipped bowl full of dark, chunky sugar—the kind one shaved from blocks of unrefined cane, called *raspadura*. She filled our three cups, then splashed a bit in each of the other two. This ritual not obvious, I was trying to figure it out—it must have shown in my face.

Juanito, watching me, finally spilled the beans—the *tazas* (cups) were for his "*abuelo*" (his deceased, fictive granddad—Gorda's husband) and La Lupita! She shushed him, bowed her head in prayer, and thanked the Virgin that her family was together again. Saints come in unexpected guises—in my book, La Gorda was the Mother Teresa of Avenida 15.

After coffee, I set my brown paper parcel in the center of Gorda's table, handed my Buck knife to her, and invited her to open it. Two smaller packages emerged—one for Gorda and the other for Juanito. Juanito gurgled, "¿*Régalo?* (Gift?)," and in his excitement choked up a gob of snot that would have made the *Guinness Book of World Records*.

He swallowed it unselfconsciously while extracting his prize—a modest jackknife. Gorda's eyes flickered with delight—her very own built-in votive candles.

Gorda's turn. As she opened her package, she laughed and cackled in total delight—the forgotten four pairs of genuine, made-in-the-USA men's cotton jockey shorts—size 44! Lupita and I had promised her those since our very first "buying trip" to the border in 1970. Hey—a year late was better than never! Tucked inside was a five-hundred-peso note for Juanito's maintenance. She grabbed the note, then rubbed the soft jockeys on her face. Inhaling the scent of fresh, Stateside cotton, she blurted out a peremptory, "*¡Con permiso!* (By your leave!)," and disappeared.

Meanwhile Juanito tried out his new jackknife on a pan dulce, cutting it into impossibly narrow slices. Satisfied, he tucked the knife away in his pocket, systematically eating the paper-thin pastry's fingers. He offered me one, but I declined—fear of stray snot, you know.

A few minutes later Gorda returned, redolent with the scent of baby powder, looking blissful. After a big hug, she commented on "the luxury of North American cotton—heavenly!" That's when I told her I would be getting married on the other side in a fortnight. She already knew. *"En la calle dicen es la hija de un ferrocarrilero. ¿Es la verdad?"*

"Yes, she's the daughter of a railroad man. Is that good, Gorda?"

"Yes—she will make you a fine wife! Railroad men work hard and are reliable. My husband laid track—El Pacífico. Thirty-seven years. A hard worker." She nodded toward his flickering votive candle and made the sign of the cross, looking wistful.

I touched her shoulder gently, thanked her for watching over Juanito, and took my leave. As I passed the grate to her front

Rubi terrace, sitio, Cabezón. (Photo by Dan and Rachel Shaffer © 2004.)

window, she leaned to the bars and thanked me again. "It was a grand evening, Güero! Almost like Christmas when I was a girl!" I kissed her forehead through the wide bars, tousled Juanito's hair, and turned toward the Rubi.

Four pairs of cotton underpants and a jackknife! The real world. In the States tossing a set of keys to a brand-new black Mercedes wouldn't have created as much joy.

As I turned to look back into the brightly lit room, Juanito was balancing on a stool under Gorda's altar, blowing out the third candle. A prayer answered? My soul? The underpants? Forty bucks? It didn't matter. Like she said, it was between her and the Virgin.

In the States we pray for fame, fortune, beauty—big things. Then doubt the existence of God when we don't get everything. In ordinary Mexico the formula worked in reverse—smaller prayers. More frequently answered.

I rocked on the Rubi's upstairs terrace, watching the lights twinkle in the harbor. I lit a smoke, at peace, enjoying the echoed whispers of young lovers hidden below in the shadows.

For a moment I thought about praying too—asking God that the ferrocarrilero's daughter would still be waiting when I returned to the "other side." Then I decided against it. Greedy. Too pushy. I'd already been granted a perfect Sunday.

68

chapter six

BETWEEN WORLDS AGAIN

By noon Monday, I was already immersed in the business of being a compadre. Visits. Gifts. Abrazos. My heartbeat had already slowed to match the rhythm of the Serdan, and the States began to seem distant, unreal. Guaymas was so self-contained that virtually nothing beyond one's vision mattered. From La Cantera hill above the grave-yard one could see Baja on a clear day, but even it was hazy and indistinct.

If the entire world beyond had magically disappeared, Guaymas would have gone on, only moderately inconvenienced by the lack of some imported items. Just as it had sustained itself during its first two centuries of existence.

That ability had formed the Guaymenses' basic character. Patient. Solid. Reliable, inventive, durable, and warm, like the sun-soaked Sonoran landscape. And the surrounding region was bountiful...

The Sierra provided stone, timber, venison, herbs, gold. The deserts yielded nopal, cactus fiber for cordage, ironwood, charcoal, more herbals, and the fruits of exotic succulents. Even now cactus candy is still sold in the old city market.

The coastal bays provided conch, limpets, crabs, clams, oysters, red snapper, and mullet. The sea provided shrimp, a huge variety of fish, seaweed, whale meat and oil, ambergris, seal, and sea lion. Great green turtles that weighed two hundred pounds, octopus, squid.

Nature's variety was endless in this land where the Sierra's great pine groves overlooked the surprising collision of cactus-studded mountains, emerald-watered mangrove lagoons, shallow rivers, narrow beaches, and the Sea of Cortez.

Had the rest of the world simply disappeared that afternoon as I walked the Serdan, I would still be there. Whole. At peace. True, I might yet be wistful at losing the railroad man's daughter—the unfulfilled hopes for that relationship a lingering question about "what might have been."

But I would have been blessed with food, a roof, true friends, perhaps one day even a lover who would put her lips to my ear and whisper, "Make me a baby!"

Guaymas offered the circle of life—and a calming, permanent community to sustain both body and soul were mine for the taking. I had but to pretend the States no longer existed. Toss my passport into the nearest *basurero* (trash bin) and walk on. The immortality of a genuine community is seductive. And Guaymas was a social Gibraltar—the bedrock upon which Sonora's foundation had been built.

Thus Monday was a day fraught with metaphysical pitfalls. The warmth and joy that had radiated from my "gringa" fiancée's eyes was compelling. But was it real? If not, would Guaymas really take me in again?

Or was that too an illusion, like the mystery of sex/love/pantomime in the Zona? An illusion that might actually trap my

Shrimp boats, Guaymas South Harbor. (Photo by Dan and Rachel Shaffer © 2004.)

soul in some twisted netherworld—a special compartment in limbo reserved exclusively for confused gringos?

And I *was* a confused gringo—still frightened by the specter of a real commitment. Haunted by the possibility that my fiancée, and my feelings, were both as ephemeral as the transitory shadows cast by a summer afternoon's drifting clouds, I thought again about staying in Guaymas. Can the love of a place be as powerful as the love for another person?

If so, did I risk self-imposed exile in Guaymas only to find myself surrounded by other *norteamericanos* "searching for meaning" and indulging themselves in endless e. e. cummings–style stream-of-consciousness analyses of their neuroses? And all in breathless, nonstop English? No thanks! Not a solution.

As I reached the Colmenar Restaurant, shaking off the truly ugly possibility of a "gringo wannabe limbo," it struck me that I had never actually left Guaymas. At least, not emotionally.

I'd merely taken a mental vacation from it—and from Lupita's death—in the States.

I had a true dilemma in front of me. Guaymas was real. So was my American fiancée, Cynthia. The community I wanted was in one place. The love I needed in another. And then there was Marta. . . . Decisions. Shit!

Mercedes, back at work behind the counter after only the morning off, grinned, eyes twinkling, and brought me a café con leche. "*¿Cómo anda, compadre?* (How are you doing, compadre?)"

Since it was a real question, I answered, "Confused today, comadre; my heart is divided between Guaymas and my *prometida* on the other side!"

"Life is a battle, Davíd—that is what makes us human. We decide so little. Usually it is Fate that guides our souls. Do not fret."

So simple! If only Fate would sit down at the table and brief me.

Still radiant, Mercedes brought me a bowl of *sopa de fideo*, with lime and corn tortillas. Juanito appeared moments later, so I moved out to a table in the passage while he touched up my boots. Jimmy Kiami came by a few minutes later, asking about the baptism. He had been the one who managed "Chingón"—the badass of the Serdan's *boleadores* (shoe-shine boys)—ensuring Juanito's safety during my absence.

Actually Kiami managed everything well—English, Spanish, people, businesses, his family. I admired him and asked, "Any problems with Chingón, Sr. Kiami?"

"None, Davíd. He has settled down. I explained to him after you left that protecting Juanito was not only an obligation but would make him a *patrón* en la calle. It appealed to his need for power. He should be by any minute now."

"You are a pinche genius, Kiami!" I blurted out. Jimmy was still laughing as Chingón entered the passageway. Badass still looked like an overgrown feral rat, but his former swagger wasn't in evidence—hmm?

"¡*Buenas tardes, don Santiago!* Y-You wished to see me?" stuttered Chingón.

"Yes, Berto. I wanted you to thank Sr. Stuart for financing the *carga* (community responsibility) that you undertook to protect Juanito." Jesus! The boss prick among the boleadores actually had a name and wasn't sneering? He actually called Kiami "don Santiago," like a real humanoid! I was stunned.

Chingón, docile but confused, stammered again, "¿*S-Señor Estuar*...?"

Kiami, nodding at me, explained. "Yes, Berto. Sr. Stuart— El Güero." Chingón hesitated, then thanked me respectfully. Okay. I was amazed. So I stood up and shook his limp, sweaty hand. Made eye contact. But given last year's threats to make him "disappear" if he preyed on Juanito, the eye contact was a bit too much for Chingón.

73

He stuttered, worse now. "*C-c-con sus p-permisos*..." Kiami smiled. "¡*Propio!*" As I nodded in assent, Chingón squirted out of the passageway like a blob of grease ejected from an overheated rear axle.

Kiami grinned. "Progress, no?"

"Actually, amazing," I offered.

"Not really," Jimmy went on. "He wants something—badly. There is an auto upholstery course beginning next month in Hermosillo. He wants to apprentice and repair taxi seats when he returns to Guaymas. The cost for the program is three thousand pesos ($250 US) plus meals. Shall we send him?"

"Jimmy, I think it's a great idea—he won't be beating up the littler shoe-shine boys for money anymore. But I'm nearly broke and am getting married on the fourteenth."

"Good, you agree, so I'll send him for both of us, just as you financed Juanito's 'project.' It will be good for Guaymas.

One more productive citizen, and you and I will be *a manos* (even-steven)."

"But Jimmy," I protested, "I only put up five hundred pesos."

"Yes, but you had less to give. I'll arrange Berto's *matriculación*—he can pay us fifty pesos a week once his earnings start. Learn to be a Guaymense. Good! That is settled.... Now tell me about the ferrocarrilero's daughter...!"

"Jimmy" Santiago (St. James) Kiami. Businessman, community benefactor, psychologist, redeemer of lost souls, and reader of tea leaves already knew about my upcoming wedding. So I gave another of Guaymas's part-time saints the briefing: "College degree. Smart, warm, kind, attractive..."

"Good!...And her personality?"

"Honest, direct, *poquita brava* (assertive), independent, lots of *corazón*! What do you think, Jimmy?"

74

"Why are you asking *me*, Davíd...and how *smart*?"

"Very, Jimmy!"

"And how independent? Will she tell you to screw yourself if you take her for granted?"

"Yeah, already has!" I laughed uneasily. He grinned, too knowingly for comfort. "So why do you hesitate, Davíd? She is perfect for you! She has corazón, brains, and self-esteem. You need a woman who will stand up to you. One you will respect!"

"Well, it's about Mexico, Jimmy...."

"Oh, Davíd, you are not...pues...ordinary. I do not mean to offend—but you *need* an extraordinary woman. Else you will drift. Fans, blenders—*las movidas*—will all eventually bore you. You will not lose Guaymas if you marry her. You will gain direction. Meaning. Trust me!"

I sighed. He went on, "When you rejoin her on the other side and first look into her eyes, you will know. If you see only Guaymas in her eyes, then perhaps your doubts have merit. But if you see love, joy, corazón reflected back to you, marry her without another thought!"

I grinned. "You are persuasive, don Santiago!"

"Yes, I know—it's my job!" Jimmy beamed. As he drained his coffee cup and stood up, looking mighty satisfied with himself, I took a parting shot—"So . . . you know everything?"

He answered offhandedly, amused, shaking his head. "No, only the taxistas know everything, Davíd."

His last footfalls still echoing in the tiled passageway, I said my goodbyes to Mercedes and worked my way back to the Hotel Rubi.

Baptismal briefings over, I took time for abrazos and jokes at every sitio along the way. Then roof time. Rocking. Thinking. Later I nursed a beer in the Rubi bar, talking to Enrique, but left early.

I still had business in the Zona. Marta. Fondness? Guilt? Sense of obligation? All of them mixed together? I wasn't certain.

Marta hadn't forced me to sort out our previous relationship. She had simply showed up unexpectedly in my room at the Hotel Rubi one Sunday night the year before—exuding her "come take me" sexuality. An hour later I was "in a relationship" I neither understood nor analyzed until much later. At first I saw her as powerful, confident, and in control of her world. Later, when I saw beneath the surface, I didn't like myself and felt sorry for her.

Looking back on it now, I reckon that we were both victims of childhood circumstances. But that Monday evening, after rocking and thinking, I merely lay on my bed at the Rubi, smoking, while my gut churned ominously. Guilt. Yes, guilt. Unsettled business meant somehow "setting things right." But how? Get her to leave the Zona? Hmmm. No solution except to go out there again and have another go at it. It was Monday night and the Zona would be all but abandoned. No sense in waiting, so I grabbed a cab at the Chapultepec.

I didn't know it then, but I'd spend a number of evenings waiting on the porch of the Río Rita before I would see her again. That waiting game brought back lots of memories of the Zona and of the viejas' exotic daily lives.

76

Part Two:

WAITING FOR MARTA

(Memories of the Zona, 1970)

chapter seven

COMPARTMENTS

Monday evenings were always slow in the Zona. Most of the regular clientele, to put it indelicately, had already shot their wad, or wads, on Saturday night. By Sundays, known as "the day of trapped husbands" in Mexico, most "clients" were both broke and in deep shit with their wives.

That meant penance. Noon Mass on Sunday and forced *paseos* (walks) around the plaza in the afternoon. Kids in tow, one could actually see the hysteria reflected in the errant men's puffy, bloodshot eyes.

Extra starch in their white shirts to enhance the misery of a ninety-eight-degree Guaymas afternoon, the wives always "preferred" to walk in the sun: "But it's so 'fresh' out today, *mi amor*! The "mi amor" intoned in a sweet, singsong voice poisoned with sarcasm.

Every drop of fear-soaked sweat glistened like the beads of a pale amber rosary before cascading to the pavement as the women's eyes glittered in revenge. Momentary control—if only for four hours on a Sunday afternoon.

View of San Fernando south of plaza. (Photo by Dan and
Rachel Shaffer © 2004.)

Sometimes I imagined the poor bastards endlessly circling
the plaza, reciting the Zona's version of a "Hail Mary" as each
bead of sweat fell. "Hail Mary, full of grace. Got to keep my 'chile'
in its proper place!"

And silly theologians actually argue the metaphysical "reality" of hell! The live version was once a pantomime acted out on
plazas throughout Mexico each Sunday afternoon, courtesy of
righteously pissed-off wives.

Then came Monday, when the penitent men slunk off to
work and their Saturday night viejas slunk off to the obligatory
medical clinic's back door. Blood tests, the search for syphilitic
genital sores or the milky, pink thrush of gonorrhea in an indiscreet throat. Each girl found "clean" and healthy had her hooker's
card restamped. In those days the stamp was sometimes humor-
ously referred to as "*el CA*," for "*Carne Aprobada*" (certificate of
government-approved meat).

Those that didn't pass got clinic time/treatment at their expense, of course, and no card. If they were found working in the Zona without card or date stamp, it was jail time. Money nearly always resolved that problem, but if you were broke or had no powerful benefactor, such a vieja was doomed to screw and blow a fair number of cops before being released. The federales were, of course, considered a girl's worst fate. They made occasional and unpredictable sweeps of the Zona.

Those raids had two purposes—free sex and letting the local cops know just how pathetically low they ranked in Mexico's law-enforcement food chain. According to the viejas, true to their alleged penchant for dominance in all matters, girls that the federales took sometimes never reappeared. Dead? Snuff films? Locked away as sex slaves? All these "girl's worst fate" scenarios, real or imagined, haunted the viejas.

The luckier ones who did eventually get released were widely rumored to have been both sodomized and filmed as the price of their freedom. The porn flicks later sold for hard cash. Anal sex was the most forbidden of all sex acts . . . you couldn't buy it in the Zona for any price.

I don't know if any of these federales stories was true, but the girls I knew in the Río Rita believed them as forcefully as they believed in the cheap, framed prints of Mexico's patron saint, Guadalupe, who watched over every "working" bed, protecting them from freaks.

So, fraught with risk, reality, and uncertainty, Monday evenings in the Zona were quiet and tentative, the black flower's petals still not quite fully opened from its Sunday rest. Even its distinctive scent was thin and ephemeral on Monday.

Still waiting for Marta to come out, I took advantage of the quiet interlude and posted myself in front of Club Guaymas. Almost 8 p.m. As a small gaggle of the club's girls stepped out of the fifty-centavo local bus that stopped at the Zona's far corner, I jotted a note for Marta on my pocket pad.

When the girls strolled past, an older one glanced at me. I motioned her over—folded note and ten pesos in hand. "Can you deliver this to La Marta, 'La Flaca,' for me, señorita?" A pause, then I asked, "*¿Está ella en residencia todavía?* (Is she still in residence here?)"

The plain, already-shopworn courtesan smiled slightly at the gracious "señorita" and looked down to check my boots. Utterly devoid of expression, she snatched the note and money, turned, and disappeared inside. Time for coffee again at the corner restaurant.

My café con leche appeared magically, the waitress all smiles. I tipped her well and settled in for the wait. Two hours later, the evening sky already its dark, gunmetal blue, I gave up. There were no taxis in sight, so I walked a half block up to the Río Rita, which dominated the Zona's northeast corner. It was the only club important enough to have its own but "unofficial" taxi rank. Chang came out almost immediately and invited me to sit on the porch with him. Unusual.

Brigido, the club's "security" man, brought out a table and several chairs. One trip was all he needed—big wooden table in one hand, two chairs in the other, he was an immense moody dark-skinned presence. Hideously marred by smallpox scars; they were so deep that you could have hidden nickels in the craters of his face. The size of an NFL defenseman, he towered over me, nodding almost imperceptibly in greeting.

Dressed head to ankles in flat black, Brigido wore a pair of shocking white Keds tennis shoes. Once in the summer of 1970 a drunken sailor had snickered and pointed at them—a huge mistake. Thereafter the white tops became respected as "a rare import item necessary for his work." He weighed about 270 pounds but was as light on his feet as a cat. Constantly stalking the hallways of the working cribs to make certain none of the girls were hurt or abused, like a gloomy, intense avenging angel.

Río Rita ruins in the 1980s. (Photo by D. Stuart © 1989.)

Screwing with Brigido was roughly equivalent to standing in the middle of I-10 and giving the finger to a Mack truck as it bore down on you. Defiance or not, you were roadkill. The federales never entered the Río Rita—probably not confident that their pearl-handled Colt 38 Super automatics would drop him before he rolled over several of them. Their caution perhaps enhanced by the legend that Brigido had come to the Zona many years before, after a singularly unfortunate incident.

Over the years I heard several different versions of it—in all of them some guy had raped and savagely cut (a) his sister, (b) his cousin, or (c) the only girlfriend of his life. The victim varied, but all versions agreed on the outcome—Brigido had grabbed the knife hand, thrown the bastard to the ground, then torn off his arm, knife and all, before walking away with his bloody trophy as the perpetrator bled to death, screaming, right there in the dirt street!

Fleeing the consequences, Brigido had allegedly found his way to the Zona, seeking asylum and doing a self-imposed sentence of sorts. Protecting the viejas from that special brand of sexual predator who needed their victims' screams to heighten the pleasure. I always suspected the story to have been mostly apocryphal, but I never had the balls to ask. Apparently the local federales hadn't either.

Chang waved Brigido away and invited me to pull up a chair. The arcaded porch caught gentle gusts of the evening breeze, the rich smell of tortilla soup and limes wafting up from the restaurant below, where I again waited for Marta.

Unlike Sr. Kiami, Chang came from a less elevated, thus more oblique social stratum. He was breezy and cheerful. I was honored to sit there with him—and told him so. He appreciated the respect but had actually earned it the old-fashioned way. The girls in his care always went to clinic escorted by Brigido and a well-tipped local cop. The Río Rita's girls never disappeared or spent a full night in jail. And no *federal* had ever laid hands on one. Not on Chang's watch.

The Río Rita's girls didn't even have to "take clients" if they found that distasteful. They could pay their rent and drink tea water at cocktail prices with the customers and remain "virgins," at least in the commercial sense, if they chose.

And a number I knew had taken that route. Decorative, amusing, good dancers, but no tail for sale. Those girls were off-limits to "clients," unless of course one actually wanted a macro-camera lense's close-up view of Brigido's smallpox scars. There were no takers that I knew of.

After the obligatory twenty minutes of courteous chitchat before getting down to business, Chang briefed me on *my* trip. "Well, Davíd, I heard the baptism went very well. Now you have true *raíces en el centro*—and you are still a special friend of the house here. I am happy for you. It is a good thing that your roots are now in el centro—and not here with one of the little angels of the Zona. It is a sign of your maturity... and I hear rumors of a prometida on the other side...."

"Has El Burro briefed *everyone*, Chang?" I queried, exasperated. "No, Davíd—only those who care for you. He loves you like a brother and does not want to lose you to the other side. Do not be angry with him for consulting his friends."

"And your advice, Chang?"

"If you marry, be faithful, Davíd. Meanwhile do not drink too much coffee down below—the coffee is not that good there." I took his shoulder in my hand and squeezed. "Another gentle lesson in disguise for me?"

"You learned the last one well, Davíd—and this one may matter even more."

"Okay, Chang, no more than another evening of coffee down below."

"Careful, Davíd! Burned coffee can be very bitter."

Then, in classic Chang style, he turned to casual jokes, laughing and recalling the peak of last year's season. A huge shrimp harvest, a sudden unexplained abundance of affordable fans and blenders. I laughed with him until an empty taxi pulled up. As I stood up to grab the taxi, Chang held me back "Reserved, Davíd. Some private negotiations inside." Ah! That explained the unusual alfresco seating.

About five minutes later the governor of a Mexican state (pick any you choose) emerged with two burly bodyguards and quickly stepped into the taxi, which had an Hermosillo sitio sticker. Natural, since that city also had the only airport then serviced by jets. Chang grinned.

Moments later the Sonoran parties to the "negotiations" emerged as a private driver pulled up. Seeing me, they hurried past. I pretended not to notice.

The promise of silence was one of the Zona's most cherished virtues. And a source of enormous hidden power. "What happens in the Zona stays in the Zona" had been a well-known and iron-clad rule in most of Mexico for six decades before Las Vegas appropriated "its" version for their TV ad campaign.

Students of American "pop" culture, please note that this campy ad campaign and the "in" Corona long-neck beers with lime on toothpicks both made it straight from Mexico's venerable nightclub Zonas to upper-middle-class America. Ironic, no?

After the big shots left, Chang went inside again and a few regulars drifted in for a beer, cards, dominos. Monday's clientele were mostly lonely guys *matando un rato* (killing time) to avoid the solitude of their bachelor quarters. Others were bargain hunters—on clinic day prices started at eighty pesos—a 20 percent discount! I hung out on the porch, waiting for a taxi, surveying the scene.

It was almost 10 p.m. The stars were out and the night sky had subtly transformed from evening's gunmetal blue to the darker hues of a lowrider's bottomless, hand-rubbed indigo lacquer.

Signs of life announced the black flower's furtively reopening petals. Jukeboxes had been turned on in a half-dozen cabarets. Laughter and swearing floated up from several different locations nearby. The visceral *braap!* of an old diesel bus punctuated the night from a block below. Bright splashes of light from open-front "restaurants" and nearby clubs created a shocking contrast to the darkened, makeshift "residential barrios" that abutted the Zona but still had no electrical service.

Most of the encircling barrio's residents made their living by servicing the Zona's diverse needs—tobacco, tacos, fruit carts, charcoal, laundry, seamstresses who made the girls costumes and frocks, cleaning women. Handymen. Trash collectors. Beer and grocery can recyclers.

There were also the countless mom-and-pop vendors whose front rooms served as impromptu "7-Elevens," selling cigarettes,

Cokes, lipstick, Kotex, Vaseline, rubbers, candy, and herbals to make a guy "bigger," "harder," "last longer"—all to get his money's worth in the clubs above. It surprised me that six-year-olds in the poor nearby barrio bought penny candies from the same hand-made shelves on the wall that also displayed "French ticklers." Bet they didn't have a clue what those were.

On the other hand, many of the children in that barrio were the older viejas' own kids. Mexico's genuine "*hijos de putas.*" One of the reasons that actually using this epithet in Mexico has always been considered so socially toxic is that there really are a few "sons or daughters of whores" sprinkled among many sizable working-class crowds.

At the time there certainly were plenty of those kids in the surrounding barrio. But there were also many more poor kids whose parents made humble but "respectable" livings from hard work and front-room mini-marts.

Even more socially complicated was the fact that a number of the viejas had sisters, comadres, girlfriends, aunts, uncles, even parents with whom they shared modest, nearby houses, "off campus," so to speak. Most were female-focused households. Those other females' kids and the hookers' kids were all raised under one roof with a comadre, older sister, even an impoverished, widowed grandmother serving as "mom." Thus if you use "*hijo de . . .*" in any of its variants on the street in Mexico, you will not be considered "cool."

As I sat on the Río Rita's porch, still waiting for a taxi, La Blanca—slender, light-complected, and one of the club's veterans—came out to chat. Then she suggested we walk down to Eva's (of the Rubi). Till that moment, I hadn't known that they knew each other. This explained how Francisca knew about Lupita and how she came to comfort me in my grief!

Most houses in the barrio, like Eva's, were modest six-hundred- to eight-hundred-square-foot structures cobbled together from cast-off plywood, lumber from wooden pallets, cardboard, recycled Stateside garage doors from the Nogales dump—all covered by a variety of roofs.

A barrio roof might be made of real galvanized (uptown!) steel, semi-opaque fiberglass panels, rolled tar-paper roofing, even the fish-scale-like "shingles" made from recycled lids and bottoms of number-10 restaurant-sized tin cans of beans, chiles, other vegetables.

At the time those cans came from nearby Empalme, where a family team of recyclers gathered them from every possible source—expertly cutting each into four pieces. Tops and bottoms became the "fish scales" for the poorest folks. The body was split into two metal "tiles." Rows of these can halves were then hand-laid into a long concave, troughlike wooden mold and shaped into wider, shallower finished "tiles" by clamping a long rounded post into the trough for the reshaping.

These homemade tiles were then laid on the roofs of the slightly more prosperous householders among the working poor.

Like hand-pushing taxis at the downtown *sitios*, this recycling, whatever the material, was another form of Mexican efficiency and provided housing for perhaps 30 percent of the nation's families. Almost all of this "useless" material—wood, cans, plastic—would have been thrown away in the States and bulldozed into landfills.

In the summer of 1970 most households in the Zona's barrio did not yet have running water. So outhouses and water barrels were ubiquitous, as were kerosene lanterns.

The finest barrio homes had both concrete floors and an indoor toss-in-the-water toilet housed in a concrete stall leading to a rudimentary septic tank. One or two plastic or metal buckets (often five-gallon paint cans) were found next to nearly every toilet in working-class houses. One bucket was nearly always partly full of tightly folded toilet paper "packages" that

Hilly barrio and old car still in use. (Photo by Dan and
Rachel Shaffer © 2004.)

looked like little squares or rosettes. This is where you tossed
after you wiped. Not in the toilet. Never in the toilet. If there
was a second nearby bucket partially filled with water (usually
collected from the roof), that was there for the "flush."

For me, the toilet ritual was initially the single greatest mystery of these households. In other respects, especially in the
female-focused extended families, they were delightful and surprisingly "normal." Family life functioned pretty well.

Even though a stone's throw from the Zona and largely sustained by it, the homes beyond the four wide, dirt streets that
clearly defined the Zona were outside of it. Not of the Zona or
its magical compartment within Mexican society. That compartment not only confined the Zona's dangerous scent of sin, it
allowed one beyond its perimeter but in sight of it to ignore its
very existence.

A fifty-foot-wide dirt street actually had transformative powers! As La Blanca stepped off the porch of the Río Rita and crossed it into the barrio, suggesting I follow to see if Eva might be home, we morphed from "hooker" and "potential client" engulfed by the aura of sin to a "fair-skinned couple" innocently making our way to visit old friends.

In the Zona, La Blanca was a vieja. At Eva's house, only two long blocks away, she was "Tía Blanca," who worked in the "entertainment" industry. In households like Eva's, "mom worked at a hotel downtown." Her female colleagues/friends were "artists," "entertainers," "*bailarinas*," "hostesses," "singers," or "in tourism."

Eva's household contained four adult females, Eva, a friend (sister? Lover? Comadre?) named Alicia, another whose name I do not remember, and another older lady much like Gorda, who the half-dozen kids all called "Nana."

I assumed that Eva, from her comments, was childless but never really knew who had produced just which kids or what genealogical and sociological relationships had initially formed the extended household. One did not ask.

As we approached her house, the next-door neighbors sitting outside to catch the evening breeze nodded. We waved, tossed them a casual "*buenas noches*," and I tipped my hat. "*¿Está la Eva en casa?* (Is Eva at home; i.e., 'receiving guests'?)" One of the kids sailed off to Eva's, next door, announcing the news. Predictable.

Twenty feet beyond, a creaky door suddenly jerked open and Eva waved us in with a shout of, "*¡Pasales! Vienen 'tú Tia Blanca' y Señor Davíd!* (Come in! Your aunt Blanca and David are here)" (locally few could pronounce "Stuart" except Kiami and don Francisco). The announcement was for the benefit of both those inside and the neighbors.

The house itself was a bit larger than most. Front room with two tattered sofas and half a dozen folding aluminum picnic chairs, an impromptu coffee table in front of the best sofa.

90

A two-burner propane stove, cast concrete sink, and shelves for dishes dominated the opposite wall. Nails in the wall above the sink secured large pots.

The dining room table consisted of an old door, fitted with locally made legs recycled from wooden pallets, then covered by a white-and-red plastic checkerboard tacked down underneath. The concrete floor and adjacent concrete toilet/shower cubicle with another checkerboard plastic "door" for privacy announced relative prosperity.

To the rear, a second large room contained wobbly beds lined up on each wall. This served as the dormitory. Eva's newer double bed to the front, nearest the bathroom, was the only sign of her rank.

The younger kids took turns sleeping with her, and several were already squabbling over just whose turn it was as Eva and Alicia prepared coffee for us. The third woman disappeared into the back room and one of the older kids was sent running down the block to fetch panes dulces from an impromptu "store" on the corner.

We had been chatting about Guaymas, people, the States, "news" for fifteen or twenty minutes when a little girl named Rosa stuck her head out from the sheet that separated the dormitory from the *sala* (front room), asking if I would bring my daughter, Lupita, to play with her again before going to a ball game—just as we had done the year before. There was a moment of stunned silence—another of those moments when the universe stutters and skips a beat.

Eva's "kids" obviously had been briefed long ago never to mention Lupita. With Burro, we had gone to several ball games after my mandadera died and not a word was said. But Rosa was just a tot at that time, probably remembering only that Lupita had taken a shine to her, played with her and gave her candy.

I was tearing up and Eva was obviously ready to scold the kid when La Blanca stooped over, gathered Rosa onto her lap, rocked her, and explained, "La Lupita became very ill and suc-cumbed. So she went to heaven, where all children go when they die. Tonight you can say 'hello' to her in your bedtime prayers—Lupita will hear you." Pause . . . Rosa looking concerned, Blanca explained, "Heaven for children is a happy place—ice cream, ball games, *dulces* (candies)."

"Is that like my *abuelo*?" asked Rosa. "Yes, honey, except he was a grown man so he gets cold beer and all the cigarettes he wants."

"So, like Grandpa, I can't visit Lupita when I want to, either."

"No, baby. God makes us wait our turn to visit."

By then the sweet rolls had arrived. Eva, now teared up her-self, caressed little Rosa's cheek and crossed to the "kitchen," where she carefully divided the four sweet rolls into little wedges for all the kids, asking if I minded. I didn't.

La Blanca took the plate in one arm, Rosita in the other, and disappeared into the dormitory. I walked over and wiped Eva's face. "*El abuelo*—your dad?" I asked. "*Padrastro* (stepfather), *mas o menos* (sort of)." She sniffled. "*Al fin me aceptó como soy.* (At the end he accepted me as I was.)"

When La Blanca came out, smiling gently, she put in the final word. "*¿La vida es una batalla maldita, verdad? Pero, seguimos batallando. Raro, no?* (Life is a cursed struggle, but we just keep on fighting back. Strange, isn't it?)"

I passed out some of my precious Pall Mall Reds and we drank cafés con leche out front, watching the stars. Alicia didn't smoke, but Granny came out, drawn to the creamy, exotic smell of my long-leaf Virginia tobacco.

I gave her one and lit it for her. Flattered, she winked, took a long drag, observing that it was the smoking that had killed her man, Rosita's "abuelo." After a pause to exhale, she went on dreamily, "*Pero estos son tan suaves que no hagan daño!* (But these are so smooth they wouldn't hurt you!)" Then came her social commentary.

The universal struggling-class Mexican illusion, "If I could just afford the food, cars, booze, cigarettes, doctors...that the rich cabrones have, my life would be easy. We'd look good and live just as long as those bastards—who never seem to die, especially since the eldest son nearly always carries the same name ('Los Juniors,' in Mexico), and the dynasties of the rich go on, darkly immortal." Just like hockey-masked Jason in the gringo horror flicks.

"The bastards screw you. Then they screw your daughters, then your daughters' daughters and still look good into their eighties when they screw you, economically, one final time, only to arise from the grave in the persona of their eldest sons to start the cycle of screwing anew." These weren't the exact words of Granny's speech, but close.

For a few brief moments the imported Virginia tobacco apparently worked its magic on Granny. It may even have given her the momentary illusion of being in power—the screwer instead of merely the screwee. I fancy this since she referred to that cigarette when I visited the house again in '72 and in '75. Face it, we all have such illusions at times.

In Mexico those who put the "chingas" on the working poor are pretty easy to identify. Their public conversations nearly always begin with the phrase "*se trata de principios* (it's about principles)." Yeah, right! When you talk about the little people's principles, oblivious to your own bodyguards, private planes and limos, mansions and businesses everywhere, not to mention the Swiss bank accounts—it's never about "principles." It's about money, position, power.

We have the equivalent in the States these days too—only our conversations usually begin with, "The Founding Fathers..." Sometimes its variant, "family values." That means your values, of course—not theirs. You know the drill.

After sitting out front enjoying the breeze, stars, and chitchat, devoid of reference to the Zona, La Blanca heard the

93

last diesel bus of the evening slowly working its way up the hill. She suggested I walk her back partway to her "apartment" so I could catch the bus.

Handshakes, a hug from Eva, and a couple of kids giggling and hollering, "*Buenas noches*," from the unglassed dormitory window (a wooden flap, actually) and we were off, crunching along in the red gravel and dust. We stopped below, just as the brightly lit bus turned a corner and came into view. As it groaned up the hill toward me, La Blanca blew me a kiss, leaving me to meet the bus alone. Discretion, you know.

By the time the bus door opened for me, she was already across the wide street, mounting the steps to the Río Rita— transformed once again from "Tía Blanca" into the slender, fair-skinned hooker "La Blanca," whose sexual persona catered to those dark Mexican men who would never have otherwise had the chance to bed a *güera* (white chick). That was the illusion she sold to her "clients."

That illusion had put both money in the bank and property in her portfolio. She owned two modest houses on the block where Eva lived. To paraphrase one of her many clever sayings about *el ambiente*, "Sometimes in order to get ahead, a girl's got to give a little behind." "Tía Blanca"; "La Blanca," the vieja; "patrona"/landlady. Three personas, each in its own distinct compartment. So Mexico!

As the bus turned back downhill for its final run to the port, I got one quick glimpse of the Club Guaymas's aging facade, beginning to wonder if Marta would ever come out.

chapter eight

THE ZONA

On Wednesday afternoon after
the baptism, I walked down in the old San Vicente neighborhood, where Marta once lived with her aunt and uncle and her
son—just a kid. Heart pounding, I actually worked up the nerve
to bang on the door. It opened. Strangers! I asked about Marta's
family. They knew only that the prior tenants "had moved
away." I even asked directly about Marta. No good. Shrugs.
"¿ . . . *Sabe?* (Who knows?)"

So I returned to the Zona again on Wednesday evening,
mindful of Chang's warning about "bitter coffee." Instead of going
either to the corner restaurant or the Río Rita, I took a more subtle approach and stopped for a drink at the B-47 club next door.

Though a pale shadow of the Río Rita, the B-47 had been a
powerhouse in its day. Built partly into the side of a hill to the
west of the Río Rita, one stepped down from the street onto the
main room's elaborate tiled floors going in. The entire interior
styling appeared to be some local architect's loose interpretation
of the Alhambra in Spain.

The Río Rita was crowded, boisterous, lively, even bubbly, like Chang. Its color scheme was red, green, and orange. In contrast the B-47 was subdued, rarely full, had only a few "hostesses," and no longer featured major floor shows. Its color scheme was cool white, with touches of Arabic blue tiling. Somber, even a touch spooky. It didn't radiate the warm vibes of the Río Rita.

The bartender there was a friend of Canelo and Negro's. Tall, lean, penciled-on mustache and a "Fonzie" hairdo, he looked like someone Hollywood had invented for the role. I ordered a Bohemia, chatted, tipped him, and asked a favor. "Could you ask one of the girls to go down to the Club Guaymas and check on a friend for me?" No problem—the same charge as "*un ratito*," the fifteen or twenty minutes with a client that it usually took the girls to get the job done.

I handed him a hundred-peso note (he took twenty for the house) and one of the older girls, in tight skirt and spiked heels, came over. She was pleasant and about thirty, the veteran, I assumed. I described my "friend," slender, dark, usually a gray-striped blouse, black skirt, wore flats. . . . She paused, then asked, "*¿La Flaca?*"

"Yes, that is she." I nodded. She smiled. "So there really is a *norteamericano novio* (boyfriend)."

"*¡Amigo!* (Friend!)," I emphasized. "A discreet inquiry, please!"

She understood, went out the door, and wandered down the block.

About twenty minutes later she returned, animated. "She's there! Number 19. I did not talk to her directly, as you asked, but I spotted her and one of her colleagues said she has not been well. Indisposed."

"How does she look?" I asked. She broke eye contact, wagging her hand vertically from side to side. In Mexico that meant "so-so." I thanked her, shook hands all around, then went to the Río Rita's porch. Asking for a chair out front, I sipped a Coke with lime.

Still mid-evening, the sky was majestic. High, flat-layered clouds stacked up like white pancakes, illuminating irridescent peach, pink and pastel orange streamers as they floated up into an inky blue zenith. Love songs played on the big jukebox inside. "Cuando Calienta el Sol" hit me hard, triggering a wave of emotions.

I felt bad for Marta. Why had she finally come to the Zona? And if the Zona, why a hole like Club Guaymas and not the Río Rita? She had always been defiant and unruly, in the literal sense of the word. But the Zona was about rules, structure, custom. In many ways it was as demanding and as stylized as Kabuki theater.

The physical structure of it was the first clue. Laid out in a great slanting square carved from a sloping mountainous bowl, its four wide dirt perimeters formally, legally, socially—even spiritually—defined it. Clubs were scattered along the outside of the square, each side roughly two ordinary city blocks in length.

But what should have been its plaza with bandstand was a huge jumble of adobe and plaster structures—laundries, restaurants, and "sex food" vendors—eggs, liver, *ceviche*. Cheap dance clubs, a billiard hall.

Behind the store fronts were bodegas (storehouses) for the beer, liquor, and other mass supplies needed by the clubs. Four-foot-wide open storefronts, wedged between the nondescript bodegas, sold rubbers, toilet paper, Vaseline, Kotex. The essentials.

In Guaymas the "Zone of Tolerance" was defined by law, custom, and social expectations—not merely by mordidas (bribes) and *not* like a wide-open border town meat market, bare-breasted teenagers sitting on the bar. Live sex shows in back rooms. None of that.

If the scent of the black flower was inevitable and Mexico understood that it was, by the saints, that flower's scent was going to be contained. Ritualized. Controlled.

Hence there was no "plaza" for "the people" in the center of the "town" square. A total inversion of old Spanish, then Mexican town structure already a thousand years old.

Whores were *not* going to be doing Sunday evening *paseos* on some plaza. Those paseos were ritualized boy-meets-girl events as old as Mexico. At them, opposing circles of slow-walking teenagers made eyes and passed notes.

No public bandstand, benches, and trees for the viejas! They weren't citizens of Guaymas in the ordinary sense. They had no *public* life. Their lives, their "business" was *private*. They existed behind thick walls, beyond huge iron-studded doors. Their diversions took place in hidden, interior courtyards.

And unlike real, public towns, there was no "church" on the plaza, either. The evil one ruled within the four broad dirt streets that formed his spiritual cage. So the nearest "chapel" was a shrine only big enough for a dozen girls to stand in front of the three-foot statue of Guadalupe and light candles after saying their rosaries. It was perched on a rocky hill above the Zona, beyond the confines of the devil's cage. Part of it was still there in 1994, a fading blue-and-white concrete shell, its walls crumbling and its statue of the Virgin, like the girls, already long gone.

Inside the clubs like the Río Rita, there were even more rules. "Proper" dress. Skirts, blouses, party gowns, "little party dresses"— in every color of the spectrum. Red, "She's hot!" Black, "refined, dangerous"; emerald green, "She might give you head if you paid enough." Silver, "Guess! Cowboy," and all the rest that implied nothing at all—bright yellow, "Wow!" (smashing against dark skin), pastel lime ("'cause I like it"), purple ("my favorite"), moss green (sedate). But only one girl was awarded each distinctive color, or outfit, on the floor at a time. No white. Never white.

One can't go confusing the customers who knew you only as "the tall one in black with the silver belt and stiletto heels (La Francisca). Or "silver gray, with sequins, very light-skinned

(La Blanca). Bare bellies, miniskirts, or too much boob sticking out. Not here in the Río Rita, you don't!

You want "anal"—go to Tijuana or Juárez, cabrón! You want a "donkey show"? The city bus station is just three miles away; can we get a cab for you?

You want *two* girls? Maybe they have that someplace nasty like Piedras Negras. It's about a thirteen-hour drive. We hear the Texans like that stuff. In fact, we hear they got everything on the Texas border. Then muttered "lowlifes" or "*degenerados*" as the disappointed shoppers walked away.

When you walked into the Río Rita and other clubs like it, you got cold beer, an efficient waiter, courtesy. Even respect, if you behaved respectably. A hostess if you wanted to flirt and dance.

Your cost was the inflated price of the beers and the "*cócteles*" (cocktails) she drank. She got a token, or *ficha*, for each drink, real or tea water, that you bought. On a slow night twenty pesos was an appropriate "tip" for an hour of her time at your table and a few dances. She cashed in her fichas at the end of the night.

You were expected to be clean, recently bathed. Dress shirt, or traditional *guayabera*, and dark pants with polished shoes were the commonest urban male uniform. Cheap, shimmering nylon shirts of any hue and dark pants also were common among the younger men.

The country boys and ranchers wore Sonora's straw cowboy hats (many really were vaqueros), Western boots, and braided horsehair belts with outrageous buckles. These guys often wore the dark pants, but Wranglers and Levis (pressed) were acceptable with the boots and hat.

In my weeknight garb of blue-striped dress shirt, pressed Wranglers, polished Red Wing Wellington boots, and Panama hat, I was but a subset of the vaqueros, albeit a gringo subset.

On Saturday nights for the main floor show, even I dressed in white or striped Van Heusen shirts and black dress pants (still wore the Red Wings, though), the blue bandana folded around the back of my neck protecting the shirt collar from sweat.

One addressed the viejas as "señorita." If someone started shouting the *p* word (*puta*), it was "show the customer to the door" time. You *invited* the girls to sit with you. You *asked* if they "wished" to dance with you. They *always* accepted the first dance unless you stank, were already knee-walking drunk, or behaved like a shithead, calling them names.

If they chose not to have a second dance, they'd say, "Señor or *jovén* (young man), thank you! But I promised my girlfriends I'd be right back." Your cue to graciously back off. Further negotiations out of the question.

If you were sitting alone or simply perhaps too shy to ask for a dance, one of the "little angels" might show up, a "girlfriend" on her arm, and *ask* if you'd like company. If you nodded, she sat and chatted you up. If you thanked her after one drink and said you appreciated her time—she'd thank you, stand up, often shake your hand or touch you on the shoulder, then be off.

If a girl came up to you and you weren't interested, you simply stood up partway and said, "No, but thank you for asking!" then sat down again. Off the hook. She might ask if any of her "colleagues" or the "other hostesses" had caught your eye. If you nodded yes and pointed one out (the dress, always the dress), that girl might drift over.

Or you might say, "Last time I was here, I met a 'señorita' wearing a bright yellow dress. Is she still here?" That would often get prompt action—repeat business could lead to regular "clients."

Regulars were the best customers. Many were single. Mexico also has its share of nerds, often the nicest, shyest, and loneliest guys (stereotypes notwithstanding) who never seem to get laid, either. And there was no risk of "bait and switch" on "The Bright Yellow Dress."

Girls owned their costumes while they were on a club's "team," just like professional athletes owned their numbers. If a regular in yellow had retired, her dress color might be recycled (perhaps even the dress itself), but you would be told. No young thing, however hot, could simply waltz in and take over a veteran's color or persona. Not even the legendary *"artista"* (stripper) Mariquita.

Onstage Mariquita wore a little plaid skirt, kneesocks, ruffled shirt, and plaid tie. Black-and-white lace-up shoes—a Catholic girl's school uniform, so close to forbidden that it was considered the Zona's most flamboyant display.

And she was the only one I knew of in the Zona who ever stripped to bare breasts. In the early days she'd even turn away from the audience and ditch her G-string onstage as the lights blacked out.

That, her honey blond hair, tiny waist, light eyes, and stunning, muscled figure had made her a legend. It rained money on Saturday nights when she danced. At one point in 1970 you could occasionally even find flyers stapled to highway-side electric poles:

Club Río Rita Floor Show
Sabado, 15 de Agosto
¡La Mariquita Baila!
Medianoche en punto.
Guaymas, Sonora (Cubierta, 50–100 pesos)

(Club Río Rita Floor Show. Saturday, August 15. THE Mariquita dances at midnight! Cover, 50–100 pesos)

But off the stage and again "on the floor" after her dances, the schoolgirl uniform was considered too risqué. And she couldn't get the jet-black and silver that Francisca owned. So she wore the uniform's shirt and tie with a flowing blue-print sarong that daringly exposed one thigh. This had been a compromise with Chang over the boobs-covered, mid-thigh rule. Tight was legal; thin silk worth its weight in gold, but on the floor, no nipples "accidentally" popped out of low-cut dresses on Chang's watch.

A contemporary party group of Stateside high schoolers would have been bored to tears in the Río Rita of 1970, out of there for someplace "exciting" in fifteen minutes. Ironically, a number of those Stateside girls wouldn't have been dressed to acceptable local standards of the time, their thongs, bare bellies, and band tops simply too outré for Zona society.

Yes, they would probably have been seated. Guaymas catered to tourists, treated them well, and put up with their shorts, sneakers, fishing hats, and swimsuit-covering wrap skirts. But the locals didn't really approve. Their standards of public attire were simply more modest and more formal.

The Zona was staid by contemporary Stateside standards—both sexually and socially. And unlike the American sex trade, there was a structure, standards of treatment and behavior that would be totally alien to our drug-driven sexual underground.

The sex for sale, among those girls who actually offered it, was plain old-fashioned conventional sex. A bit of foreplay and verbal cooing and teasing to get things going. Then three simple variations: missionary, doggy style, and "vieja on top," the girls' favorite since they had much more control.

Several of the girls in any large club might go further. Oral sex for a client. They were known as "*bomberas*" (fire pumpers) in the trade. Most were older, a bit less attractive, or were in denial that they were truly viejas since they'd not yet sold the real thing.

Whatever their motives, whatever their rationalizations, the price was higher than these girls would have otherwise commanded. A surcharge, of sorts. The day-to-day bomberas were the equivalent of the lower middle class in the hierarchy of local whoredom.

For that reason, most of the girls who gave head to their rich, regular clients usually made them pay the *salida* (exit fee), so the "date" was off campus. Just like some married guys in the States who insist that getting a blow job from a hooker or girlfriend isn't really "cheating" on their wives, off-campus oral high jinks didn't count against a vieja, either.

A few of the younger, prettier, and higher-priced girls might do an expensive Saturday night "*combinacíon*" (combo) every now and then for a classy or rich client. A bit of oral treat first (never to completion), then straight sex. That's about as wild as it got "on campus."

Of the nearly two hundred girls who cycled though the Río Rita on a big week, only about half actually were active "sex workers." The other half were temporarily "indisposed"—their periods (*traendo caballo*, in Mexican slang) or were singers or hostesses (known as *ficheras* from the drink tokens they cashed in at the bar each night). There were also several exotic dancers in the floor show, artistas who *never* sold tail.

Yet others were hairdressers, makeup, and wardrobe girls who worked the dressing rooms. Eventually some of these girls got desensitized and crossed over into el ambiente, but most did not.

Finally, there were the stars. Francisca, for her class, looks, and education. She would occasionally serve drinks or bring snacks to the big-time politicos and businessmen who engaged the Río Rita for the several hours necessary to "private negotiations."

Such meetings were arranged by the agents of powerful men who were "public" enemies. These guys simply couldn't do business or politics with one another where reporters, cameras, or the indiscreet might actually see them together. Francisca, from Mexico City, spoke their kind of Spanish, understood their world.

Francisca was reserved for one regular client, a certain don Francisco. She also fulfilled those other "house" assignments. High-class hush-hush stuff. Occasionally she took a client on ordinary fiscal terms, "cheating on" don Francisco, for both her own amusement and some extra cash.

Francisca, then in her late twenties (a guess), liked young stuff, which the girls referred to as "*ternera*" (veal). Clean-cut guys in their late teens to mid-twenties, she once told me, turned her on.

If those guys went down on her, "*pegándome una buena lenguada*" (laying some good tongue on me!), she once confided on a rare occasion when she'd drunk a bit too much, they could bed her for the basic hundred-peso fee till the "roosters crowed."

The viejas, at least the straight ones, almost never got oral sex. In Mexico's male sexual realm, giving head, as opposed to getting it, made one submissive, controlled. Not good. Besides, most of those viejas' vaginas were high mileage. Medically unwise.

The difference with Francisca is that she not only could have stepped off the porch of the Río Rita and onto the front cover of *Vogue* in her ordinary Saturday night persona, but she was a low-mileage model. Most weeks she was only with one man for a few hours—rich, aging don Francisco.

The other viejas envied her looks, class, purported bank account, easy schedule, and secret missions but most of all getting it on with cute, clean-cut, upper-class twenty-year-olds. In the words of one who resented her, "The bitch has it made."

And she had once been a nurse. Because she took so few clients, she was at a premium. The downside was that she had to take birth control measures, unlike the girls who took dozens of customers a week. The hot, fast chicks with lots of customers rarely got pregnant. Even those who didn't slow down for the "rhythm" days were at low risk if they had lots of clients.

The less desirable girls—too skinny, too plain, too bitchy, too arrogant, or too desperate—far more often got pregnant. At the time this seemed counterintuitive, the Zona's equivalent of an urban myth. But a few years ago I read a book called *Sperm Wars*. The viejas had it right.

In short, life was no fairer in the Zona than beyond its confines. You made big money, took lots of clients, looked good, went to clinic religiously, and didn't even wind up with a fat tummy and swelling breasts. And if you were Francisca, you even got head once or twice a month instead of gave it. "*¡Ni modo!* (Whatcha gonna do!)"

What most of the girls never grasped was that the most important organ that made Francisca successful was her brain. She was smart and in control most of the time. Most of her earnings were safely in the bank. She collected deposit slips like the other girls collected jewelry and cosmetics.

But the Zona system itself, as practiced by the Río Rita and similar clubs, was fairer and more benign than you might imagine. Most of the girls weren't like Francisca, but her behavior was a model that the system actually encouraged.

Girls paid rent to the house, some daily, most monthly, at prices about 30 percent above the commercial rate for the same quality of room downtown. About forty girls were "in residence" at any one time. Their private sleeping rooms were either in the far rear of the club itself (oldest and cheapest) or across and down the street in *pensiones* (boardinghouses) owned by the club. Known as "*las residencias*" among the girls, there were two nearby Río Rita pensiones. The cheaper one had clean, modest rooms, tile floors, and bathrooms down the hall—rather like a Stateside college dorm in room size and quality.

A second, newer room block had larger, high-ceilinged studio-style rooms, each with private bath. I described Francisca's bright, airy private quarters in volume 1 of the *Guaymas Chronicles: La Mandadera*. These were not "working" rooms.

True, a girl might occasionally take a "guest" to her private quarters, with the house's (Chang's) permission, during club hours, but that was pretty rare. The residencia room's rental value and therefore the house's profit margin depended on a fairly high level of normalcy and tranquility. Not to mention security.

So the detached residence halls weren't noteworthy. Most clients and tourists wouldn't even have noticed them, as the entrances were to the rear, away from the street. They were virtually all single occupancy, save an occasional girl with an unweaned infant. Those girls (I only remember two) were housed in the far end of the older residencia room block, and both had older "nannies" (probably related to them) living with them in the summer of 1970.

While the house made lovely profit margins from the rooms, especially since occupancy was 100 percent, with a waiting list—its take on the beers and, even the sodas, was astronomical by ordinary downtown standards. Exactly like buying a "brat and a beer" at a Big League baseball game in the States, you were in for roughly double, even triple, the ordinary street price.

The house also made money from the rows of small rooms in the club where sex was the commodity sold. In those days almost everything in Mexico had a minimum standard price—minimum taxi fare was ten pesos—didn't matter whether it was for ten feet or ten blocks. The same minimum applied to the working rooms where girls met their "clients" once their "colleagues" vacated them.

Since the girls sold sex at a hundred-peso minimum, the most efficient ones got their gents in and out in fifteen minutes. The average ones took twenty-five minutes or so. On a Saturday night when Mariquita danced, really hot viejas got five to six clients—at one hundred pesos and up.

Mariquita's midnight dance usually drove prices up to two hundred minimum for un ratito between midnight and 2 a.m. The house got ten pesos on its working rooms every time a girl entered. There were sixteen such rooms, I was told.

Friday and Saturday, full floor show nights, alone brought the house about three thousand pesos weekly from the "working" room fees. But that was chicken feed compared to the drinks and cover charges for the floor show. Snacks brought in even more. Horny guys are hungry guys.

Then there were the salidas. When the working rooms were full, the waiting order based on seniority among the girls, often a client's only way to get laid *now* with the newest "little angel" in the house he had fixated on was to pay her for an hour (about three hundred pesos) or about five hundred "for the night," plus an exit fee (the salida) for the loss of her commerce during club hours (usually 8 p.m. to 2:30 a.m.). Pay the salida, hail a cab, and get a motel room out by the airport.

The house got 50 percent of the salida—the girl the other half. This could be big money. Mariquita's first salida was set at ten thousand pesos ($800 US cash). This was about an average year's wages in working-class Guaymas.

Her first client paid that sum, plus five thousand pesos for an overnight date at San Carlos. In the Río Rita on a Saturday night, you could get into big money quickly if your testosterone trashed your brain after processing Mariquita's hard nipples and dilated pupils.

And what made this system work so well as it did? No pimps! True, a number of the girls had no-account "boyfriends" who lived off of them—off premises, of course. But there were no hotshots with strings of girls, fancy cars, bags of coke working the street and pulling girls into the Zona. There were no stone-cold control freaks "turning them out" and kicking their asses if they didn't make enough money.

Why? First—being a pimp was not "cool" at that time in Mexico. In fact, it was absolutely reviled. Low. "*Padrote*" (pimp) was not a name/profession one aspired to. Even no-account "boyfriends" were widely reviled, especially those who were actually with the women long enough to have formed a "*unión libre*," Mexico's version of common law marriage.

For such men to watch their women take a bus to the Zona while they lounged on a porch was the equivalent of committing a "*cabronada*" (now morphed into "*cabronismo*")—prostituting your wife, the mother of your children. In the States, these guys would have enjoyed roughly the same social status as pedophiles.

And the Río Rita's girls didn't need pimps. They were free, if of legal age, to walk into the club and apply for work. Those "in residence" were obligated on the floor Wednesdays, Fridays, and Saturdays. Hence the salida if they left.

After the working room fee and tips to the ladies who changed sheets, they had only monthly rent (about one thousand pesos—$80 US in 1970), meals, and incidentals as baseline costs. Those in residence, Mariquita and Francisca the exceptions, could count on at least four thousand pesos a month in earnings. Of this, they could bank half after all expenses if they were careful. And they were free to leave and "retire" or take vacations during the slow season—usually mid-fall.

108

The girls not in residence got to keep a higher percentage of a much smaller take. They didn't get preference on the most desirable shifts. Weren't usually given hostess roles at the expensive front tables, got the leftover clients and the quiet Monday, Tuesday, and Thursday nights.

Some made decent money on big Saturdays, especially when Mariquita danced. But most of these part-timers were already saddled with too many kids or a useless "significant other" and so were not candidates for the residence arrangements. A disadvantage.

The viejas in residence were often in safer and cleaner surroundings and much better fed than many had been in the prior lives that brought them to the Zona in the first place.

And why wasn't "The House" more oppressive with them? Simple—the big money was in the booze, food, and cover charges. The presence of the girls was an important attraction, both those who sold sex and those who provided merely titillating decoration. Pissed-off, beat-up girls were simply not attractive to the clientele that the better clubs relied on.

Zona de Tolerancia itself meant that there were customs, standards, regulations. Many of those redounded to the "little angels'" benefit. Finally, in the Río Rita and similar clubs, the male staff, waiters, security, bartenders, and managers were forbidden to sample the merchandise. The guys around you were not hitting on you. It stays "in your pants or you go out the door" was the rule of employment. Period.

That sexual distance maintained professional relationships and was core to the idea of "colleague," "management," "friends of the house." Sexual distance promoted respect, allowed illusions of normalcy to flourish, and protected the social-psychological compartments in Guaymas's society.

And the clients? Their motives, backgrounds, and characters were rather diverse. Since I knew the girls much better than most of the patrons, I can only give a broad impression from my own observations—the girls rarely talked about their own clients. Most of what I learned came as "the girls say" or "at the club down the street, it is said that… " Part of the basic contract.

109

Camaraderie, male bonding, and the excitement of a big club with good music, girls who wouldn't refuse a first dance, and a floor show, though tame by Stateside standards, were the biggest client draws.

A huge percentage of the Río Rita's floor show clients left quickly when the show was over, rushing home, fantasies afire, three or four drinks under their belts, to finish off the night with their wives or older, divorced "girlfriends."

Another group of guys simply liked the intrigue and defiance of the surroundings. Drinking, grabbing a snack, telling stories, ogling the hostesses, *"matando un rato en un ambiente suave"* (killing time someplace cool). Think restaurant chain Hooters. Boys' night out, even if not refined.

But there were other types of clients. The innocents sent by their dads, sometimes accompanied by dad, age sixteen or so, to get their first lay. An old upper-class Mexican tradition, then already fading.

Message from dad: "Screw the maids (known as '*gateando*') or the hookers, *not* my associates' daughters!" mixed with, "Now you are a man!" The girls fought for these clients. Thursday night trade, which brought both good money and rich little virgins to them. Sweet!

The problem, of course, was that a fair percentage of these young upper-class guys imprinted on hooker sex as the real thing, later in life to be seriously disappointed in that performance aspect of their pretty, young, nicely raised, but often sexually fearful wives.

These guys, as they aged, made up the hooker's bread and butter: Saturday night regulars whose married lives must have been seriously marred. I considered this the hooker's metaphysical revenge on those upper-class kids who bought into the Zona fantasy.

Next were the sailors, unmarried laborers, and vaqueros—most away from home and away from women. They just wanted to get high, get laid, spend half a month's wages, then go back to their tough, lonely lifestyles. Some were trouble, but Brigido took care of that. Others needed a bath. They could get one in a public shower across the street and come back if they cleaned up okay. They were trade a girl couldn't count on.

Yes, there were also the sex addicts and freaks. The sex addicts could be good, trouble-free business. But among them were the squirrelly bastards who thought that if a girl winked at them from across the room, they "owned the bitch." These guys could be trouble. Some were emotionally flat and creepy—the dreamy-eyed and very dangerous "watchers."

Others were those noisy pricks with a chip on their shoulders the size of Chihuahua, known as "*pelados*" (plucked ones) in working-class Mexico. They were insecure, often mean. Always outwardly worrying about their pride and dignity.

Brigido didn't like either of these two types and, along with the veteran male waiters, watched them like hawks. These guys often wound up escorted, quietly if possible, off premises.

Finally, there were the rest of us. Occasional tourists, local working-class legends, like Canelo and Negro, who weren't clients but tipped well and held court on weekend nights. The true big shots who occasionally needed the privacy envelope in which to conduct their business unseen and... me... El Güero, lost child, screwed over by a local fiancée, friend of the house—an exotic, Spanish-speaking gringo pet that many of the girls sought to transform and "save" even as others used me as their confessor.

111

chapter nine

WOMEN AT THE CENTER

The tone of social life for the girls at the Río Rita was set not by the men who worked there or even the owner, the never seen "Pepe X." Rather, their world revolved around the personalities and power of half a dozen rather remarkable female colleagues.

They were Francisca, La Blanca, La Negra, La Chuleta, La Indita, and La Mariquita.

Francisca had enormous influence because of her formal education, clear thinking, and refinement. She was someone that the rest of the girls could respect and emulate since most had little formal schooling. I was certainly not the only one whose life she tried to plan. "Davíd, marry a nice girl, have babies with her, get a real job, settle down!"

Francisca had an uncanny ability to assess people, their needs... even hopes, then plot a practical path by which that person's life could be fulfilled. Because of that, some girls, especially among the wanna be part-timers, went back to school. Others became seamstresses, making a living of sorts sewing for the girls outfits and costumes for the floor show rather than taking clients.

Each newcomer met with Francisca. Unofficially, she was the chief "human resources officer" for Chang. The convener of occasional but necessary meetings to sort out tensions among "the female staff."

If after a day or two Francisca judged a newcomer as either too "*tierna*" (tender, vulnerable) or too "*cabróna*" or "*sangróna*" (bitchy, more or less), that girl was soon to leave, not because Francisca capriciously ordered it, but because Chang relied on her for advice. Chang was the boss, Francisca his counselor.

That role probably made Francisca the most powerful *veterana* in the house. Like a number of the hookers, she was into power, refined, oblique, and subdued by comparison to Mexican male interpretations of power but power nonetheless.

114

Her status was enhanced by her reliable prestige client, don Francisco, her looks, her whispered bank account, her "secret assignments," and her "sport fucking" the clean-cut, young upperclass guys, who paid well and occasionally delivered even those envied sexual treats.

Francisca only associated with clean-cut, high-class, or powerful men. Never the sailors and field hands. No exceptions at any price. The Zona provided disenfranchised women one of Mexico's few routes to power and Francisca played it like a violin.

The other role that made her powerful was her nursing skills—invaluable. She knew when to send for a doctor, order a remedy from an all-night pharmacy, and teach girls how to remain "clean."

She also taught the girls how to casually squeeze a suspicious client's penis for signs of gonorrheal discharge, to identify syphilitic sores, venereal warts, pimples, and the like during foreplay. That meant either "end of assignation" or "here are your necessary *profilácticos*, señor."

Francisca's knowledge benefited both the house—less clinic time for the girls who attracted a regular following—and the girls. By sex trade standards of the day, the Río Rita was a fairly well-educated, risk-averse, well-run, even respectable platform for an outcast girl's career.

La Blanca, then in her early thirties, was another member of the "central committee." Her status derived partly from the fact that she was white-skinned—actually pale and washed out by my standards. But she was a genuine veteran in every sense of the word.

Actually born in the famously infamous Club del Bosque in Torreón, Mexico, across the Sierra, she was the only girl at the Río Rita to have been raised in a cathouse. Raised in "the life," La Blanca was as institutionalized to it as any lifer at Sing Sing. Or any kid raised entirely in an orphanage. Or, for that matter, like so many university professors who never left school. The outside world has little attraction for such folks, and they often do poorly in it. But La Blanca knew everything about her trade that Francisca did and then some.

She advised the girls on "*coqueteando*" (flirting). Making a guy *terminar* (finish) quickly. "Ask him to marry you if he can't get hard or takes too long. This usually works," she would advise the young ones.

"If you specialize in sailors, you'll spend the rest of your life screwing them. They are disease-prone, unreliable, and don't give you return business. *Always* make them use a *condón* (rubber)." Her advice on sailors was prodigious. "Give them a small discount (knock off ten pesos) if they whine, and don't waste your time with them on Saturday nights unless they pay you double.

"If you do take sailors as clients, the Chinese and Japanese guys are best—they have little pricks and go simply crazy if you have big boobs. They'll pay extra for that. Their women are flat-chested. Let them tongue your nipples—once they feel real tits, they come in ten minutes and rarely make trouble."

"If you screw tourists, beware of the *tejanos* (stereotype Texans) who dress like our vaqueros. They are rarely vaqueros. To be certain, check their boots first—they are almost never scarred from the spur straps. If they have no calluses on their hands or broken fingers, they are often mean mama's boys who screw us to prove they are men. Superior. Always do them on top so they don't hurt you. Some of them really do have big dicks—and these bastards always remember the pinche Alamo!

"If they have big noses, they often have big *macanas* (clubs). Don't kiss them if you can avoid it—most use that disgusting tobacco powder (snuff or chew) and don't brush their teeth before visiting us. Beneath them."

"And what of the *pochos* (roughly, Mexican Americans), Blanca?" I once asked. "Well, Davíd, I have a harder time advising the girls on them. Some are really sweet, raised over there (the States) and already acculturated to the 'other side.' Those simply want to try a girl from the "homeland" to see what it is like. They pay well, are respectful, and make good clients—but they never come back. No return business."

"And the others, Blanca?"

"Well, some call themselves either 'Chicanos' or 'Spanish (Gachupines)' and either don't speak Spanish at all or it is a very old style of the language. You've probably met some of these in New Mexico, Davíd. We get them from Santa Fe as tourists sometimes.

"They are very hard for me to comprehend—I used to believe I'd find one who'd marry me and take me to the other side—a girl's fantasy, you know! But they are too different from us. Of course, some are *malinchistas* (cultural turncoats) with disdain for Mexico, which makes it even harder. A lot of the girls resent the ones who think they are superior, more like the Texans, you know!"

Knowledge is power. Even in the Zona. And La Blanca was a storehouse of it. But I never managed to get her to talk about other girls or most dimensions of life there. Generally only the clients.

As I already told you, she owned property "off campus" but nearby. She rarely went downtown, when I'd sometimes take groups of the girls to el centro or the beach on a weekday afternoon. She was simply not a creature of the outside world.

But she was a master inside her own, eccentric world—and seemed fairly content. She didn't do drugs, went light on the alcohol, and smoked moderately. At first glance, she was quiet and reserved. And even after a lifetime of baroque institutional settings, she still had a kind streak.

She loved playing "mom" with the kids in Eva's complicated household. She'd have been a great mom herself, but, another of the girls once confided, she "couldn't have her own kids. *Tristemente, las pinches purgaciones dañaron sus tubos.* (Sadly, the frigging clap ruined her tubes.)"

117

On some Friday evenings during the year before I returned to baptize Olga, my life was ordinary. I didn't always go to the Zona with Canelo and Negro after closing the Rubi bar. Instead sometimes I went dancing, drinking Cokes and killing time at the Chapultepec dance pavilion—a huge raftlike affair right over the water, in front of the *malecón* (sea wall and promenade).

But on Saturdays, we nearly always went to the Zona after closing the bar. Mariquita danced at the Saturday midnight floor show—an event of import among the wayward males in the Guaymas area. Hell, it was an event even among those from afar! Mariquita regularly drew fans from as far north as Hermosillo (an hour and a half north) to Obregón (two hours south).

In 1970 she was still a relative newcomer, age about nineteen (she never clarified exactly how old she was—sometimes she was seventeen, other nights eighteen). She was a light-skinned, big-eyed beauty with a lovely face, honey blond hair, and a spectacular figure.

Her signature Catholic girls' school uniform always forced the crowd into an involuntary hush as the lights opened up on her center stage.

Her slow strips, open, unabashed, and surprisingly erotic love affair with the crowd, plus the recent sensation of a rich, local hotelier paying her ten thousand pesos salida, cash on the bar, plus whispers of a five-thousand-peso fee on top of that, had all quickly made her a force to reckon with among the stage girls.

But most importantly, her emerging power arose not from the sex she had sold, but the sex sold to the testosterone-crazed Saturday night male clientele—at double, even triple regular prices by the other viejas *after* her performance. Mariquita was a center-stage sensation.

The house needed her to jam-pack the place on Saturday nights, allowing them to double the basic cover charge when she danced, sell truckloads of booze (one hundred pesos front table— eight bucks in 1970—nearly two days' ordinary wages; fifty pesos back tables, about a day's wages), and reliably double the viejas' Saturday night take.

Once Mariquita came to town, more part-timers got a shot at fill-ins on Saturdays. Mariquita generated business. Made jobs. Her hard, erect nipples, rippled belly, and twenty-inch waist created the floor show equivalent of boom times.

By her second month, she actually had a performer's contract at the Río Rita, which, she confided, set her rent at five hundred pesos a month and paid her five hundred pesos weekly to perform for a maximum of thirty minutes onstage and a minimum of three hours weekly "on the floor."

Her actual stage time was usually about twenty-odd minutes, during which it rained "tip" money from hysterical spectators.

By the time she finished her dance, the small stage was nearly always oozing with banknotes, like clouds of New Year's Eve confetti. She could reliably count on two thousand pesos in "appreciation" money each Saturday night—the equivalent of three months of my hotel room rent at the Rubi or nearly six months rent on a modest studio apartment with bath.

On a big Saturday, Hermosillo businessmen and rich Obregón ranchers pushed that figure to between three and four thousand pesos, the pile of bills a fairly reliable sexual gauge of the frenzy with which her fans fantasized about "topping her off" with their own bodily fluids.

What most of her admirers never understood, of course, was that it was their *adoration* that got Mariquita off. She wasn't all that interested in the pleasures of sex itself. How big and hard they were didn't count for much. What aroused her was the size of the banknotes they threw at her.

When the pile of money at her feet was redolent with hundred-peso notes, she'd pinch her nipples and sigh, her pupils the size of dimes. When the pile was modest, she'd pout.

So Mariquita wisely only took one actual "client" on premises per week, leaving lots of business for the girls and taking little of the actual sex trade herself. After the payment of her ten-thousand-peso salida, she was no longer a commercial virgin, so her client price—one hour, like a shrink—no more, no less, was two thousand pesos.

She often also took a mid-week client for off-campus overnight dates to San Carlos, the nearby yacht basin. Salida at two thousand, the date at three thousand ($400 US in 1970—a fortune).

In short, Mariquita took in ten to fifteen thousand pesos a month during my time in Guaymas. Only businessmen, doctors and lawyers, and club owners made more locally.

She acquired power quickly, moving to the center at a surprisingly young age. Her power was exerted over details of the floor show set, costumes. The order of acts. The lighting. And of course no other blondes need apply.

She also had a mysterious "manager"—a woman she called "Camú." One of the oddest individuals I'd ever seen, Camú looked to be about sixty. Having neither hair nor eyebrows of her own, she was grotesquely wigged and painted. Camú had first brought Mariquita to the Río Rita, then reappeared, furtively for a night at most, about every two to three weeks.

Once when I visited Mariquita's private room, bringing her prescription from a downtown pharmacy late on a Monday evening, Camú was painting on her eyebrows, turbaned, her wig on the dresser. Mariquita shooed me out immediately but didn't shut her door completely.

Standing just outside, I got one clear glimpse of Mariquita and Camú in a quick embrace and lip-on-lip kiss. When I reentered, Camú, her suitcase, and the wig were all gone. Vanished, ghostlike, into the hot summer night.

There was only one door to Mariquita's room. What did the old woman do? Turn herself into a bat and fly out the window? Whoo! I'd seen some strange shit in my misspent youth, but this, like Mariquita, was a showstopper.

I asked Mariquita about her. But I got only a pouty, "She's my tía, Camú," nothing more. Right! Everyone has a bald aunt who they lip-kiss before she vanishes through a freaking window. No more prying. Subject closed.

What I do know is that Mariquita had an actual contract. Pulled in big money and split it between banks in Mexico and Tucson. I carried most of the Tucson money for her, bringing back the deposit slips. That is how I came to know her real name.

As powerful as she was in her floor show sphere, she never messed with the other girls' domains. She displayed open admiration, real or feigned, for Francisca, La Blanca, La Negra, and the other *veteranas* in residence, carefully using the formal and uncommon in the Zona *usted* form of address with them.

Mariquita never hustled her "colleagues'" clients, bad-mouthed them, or threw her weight around. The other girls became more prosperous on account of her, so she drifted quickly to the female core of the Río Rita's hierarchy.

She played her credulous, non-threatening role to perfection, gaining power through her ability to draw business and her exclusivity. Most around her, including me, initially thought her silly and immature. Wrong!

She was smart, spoke quite refined Spanish to me off campus. And often asked me to sneak books to her. She read Cervantes, Octavio Paz, Shakespeare in Spanish, translated Greek classics, and plays of all kinds. She was crazy about plays, if not obsessed with them!

In particular, she was gaga over Shakespeare's *Two Men from Verona* but thought he should have written plays where women were the main characters. Sometimes she'd act out key scenes, reciting both characters' parts flawlessly.

She talked to me a lot about other things as well. I was "different," she said. Like Lupita, she'd ask me about world history, my studies. As far as I could tell, in the Zona only she and Francisca actually understood what anthropology was. I took her to the beach at Primaverales on several occasions, until someone complained to the management there that I had brought a vieja to the "family" beach. I had history at Primaverales, so didn't push it.

Thereafter I'd take her, sometimes with others, to Las Playitas, opposite the old port, or to San Carlos. Nearly pure tourist community in those days, no one in San Carlos noticed, cared, or even made a connection to the Zona. In many respects Mariquita was bubbly, friendly, but emotionally detached, Camú a mysterious exception—unless there was a large crowd adoring her. She lived for that. Otherwise she did few favors and asked few for herself.

That's why it surprised me the afternoon I explained the dilemma of a certain Canadian girl in the Sanchez clinic downtown. Her fiancé had been killed in an auto crash on Route 15. She was seriously injured, one leg badly mangled. She was stuck in the maze of the Mexican medical and legal systems—procedural limbos with undertones of Kafka's *The Trial*.

It was going to take both money and leverage to get the young blond Canadian squared away fiscally, legally, and diplomatically before she was allowed out of the clinic and onto a plane from Hermosillo to her homeland.

Francisca and La Blanca were commenting on how much *palanca* (political leverage) this was going to take. In fact, a fair number of people in Guaymas were already aware of the young tourist's predicament. The American consul had thus far proved useless.

At least the Canadian one was energetic. But money and legalities intruded. The clinic bill had to be settled in cash before she was "released" from the clinic and an exit permit was granted.

Even though the young woman in question, Sharyn, still believes the Canadian consul and her mom, unaided, managed her extrication, it was Mariquita who applied the first pressure that began to tip the palanca in young Sharyn's favor.

Sharyn was caught in a classic catch-22 (ironically, the movie was filmed at Algodones Beach fewer than eight air miles from the clinic). Each additional day in the clinic increased the bill, but the bill could only be paid in cash. No checks. No Blue Cross reimbursement. No monthly installment plan. Just cash, at near American hospital prices. That was the law in Mexico to protect private clinics from foreign deadbeats.

Her family in Canada wasn't flush. Her mom was bewildered by Guaymas, the law, and, of course, the cops. Her only daughter had gotten banged up in a strange country where she couldn't even read the menus as she stood watch over her precious Sharyn day after day. She began coming into the Colmenar Restaurant for her meals since it was only a hundred feet from the clinic door. That's how I met her.

Mom was warm, gentle, determined. The Canadian consul persistent. The clock was ticking. Fees to send the deceased fiancé's body home. Fines for damage to federal property (the highway pavement)—a tack-on "criminal" charge you could count on in Mexico.

Then there was the missing luggage. Initial reports stated that the federales had first come across the bodies sprawled on Route 15 near Guaymas. Sharyn's assertion was that the first police there had stolen everything, walking away leaving her for dead, still moaning so softly that maybe, just maybe, they didn't hear her.

A later report said the local police found her. And by the time La Mariquita, sitting in the Río Rita sipping a limeade, "identified" with the petite, helpless *rubia* (blonde) in Sanchez clinic, those initial reports were already being altered.

123

Historians and researchers love to work in Mexico's archives, civil and church, in the steadfast belief that "they write everything down. Every detail." Silly rabbits! Mexican officialdom edits itself every bit as carefully as do Stateside agencies. They "lose" stuff when convenient. Deny stuff when convenient. Forget stuff when they are busy. And inadvertently screw up stuff, just like ordinary humans everywhere.

Later, after Sharyn was on Canadian soil, her government royally pissed, reports began to disappear. Nobody was responsible. "It is all an unfortunate misunderstanding, señora." Yeah, mierda!

Had whichever police forces were or were not involved (you choose) realized sooner that *la señorita rubia* (the blond girl) lying near death on Route 15 was Canadian and not a *pinche gringa*, things might have been much easier. Hatred and envy of prosperous, blond Stateside women runs deep in some circles.

There are those in Mexican officialdom who imagine them-selves "dissed" by the States. The more immediate reality was that they were also regularly, often nastily, "dissed" by the good-looking blond wives of Mexico's superelites. And there wasn't squat they could do about it.

Mexico's ruling class simply did not take kindly to the irri-tations of law and bureaucracy as imposed on more ordinary peo-ple or on gringos. So "the System" occasionally took out its frustration and rage on the only blondes it could shit on with rel-ative impunity—gringas.

Enter Mariquita, understanding the phenomenon completely. "It's racism!" She snorted indignantly. "It's because she's blonde and a foreigner!" Wanna bet that Mariquita never was forced to screw some local cops in Guadalajara or wherever she came from—mostly because she was blond and, incidentally, busted for stripping? Bad odds on that bet, given her visceral reaction.

She decided that she would "do something." Instinctively she focused on a certain hotel "manager" from San Carlos who had been pestering her for a particular kind of sex, rarely sold. Was he "prosperous enough and connected enough to begin to move things?" she asked of Francisca, who nodded yes.

Francisca asked, "So you're going to give him what he wants?"

"Yes, if he can freeze the clinic charges, lean on the mag-istrates."

"Shall I get him to come here?" Francisca queried. Mariquita nodded.

When Francisca was next visited by don Francisco, she recruited him to summon "Mendez" (not a real name) to the Río Rita to meet Mariquita. The ball was in motion. Unstoppable.

By Thursday of that week, Mariquita was lounging by the pool at the Posada de San Carlos, looking beyond spectacular in an imported and immodest new jet-black bikini and classy gafas (sunglasses). Chang and Francisca had "suggested" I have lunch out there and see that she was okay. Mendez wasn't old Guaymas, so he was an unknown—and neither the girls nor the house wanted anything to happen to her.

Within ninety-six hours of "I'm going to do something," Mendez was obligated to don Francisco for the invitation of his dreams, and Mariquita looked every bit as good as those dreams when I walked up to her poolside, asking if she was okay. She was fine, "thank you very much," commenting "Mendez" was busy with *procedural matters* at the moment.

I ate my sandwich, olive on a toothpick, with potato salad and a tall, icy limeade until Mendez reappeared, in suit and tie, looking at Mariquita, mesmerized, blissful, and smug. Just like the freshly laid and blown big-shot bachelor he was. Mariquita spent two full days at San Carlos gliding between the pool and bedroom.

By a Friday evening in August she was back on the floor of the Río Rita, declaring that she liked that lifestyle and had decided that's how she was going to live if she got the chance. La Blanca asked dryly, "And how are your knees, honey?"

125

"A bit chafed, but at least it wasn't my ass!" Mariquita grinned.

Thereafter Mariquita was a full member of the inner circle. She had "done something for somebody," which is what makes Mexico work. La Blanca gave her a little squeeze and moved on, chuckling.

Meanwhile the Canadian consul had magically started getting results. The legal system was lightening up, and a flight from Hermosillo, eighty miles north of Guaymas, had been booked for both mother and daughter—final destination, Toronto. On an August afternoon a young Canadian blonde went home for further treatment, a warm and loyal mom at her side.

The Canadian consul personally waited on the runway for mother and daughter's arrival from Guaymas, then ushered them, young, blond Sharyn cradled between two strong pairs of arms, onto the plane. The consul stayed right there and stood watch until the plane lifted off the tarmac, headed north. Lots of folks in the States make little jokes about Canada's government. I don't. Burro and I waited and watched their consul standing on the runway in August's 112-degree heat doing her job till the plane was out of sight.

Mendez became Mariquita's regular Wednesday-Thursday "off-campus" client. Her bank account grew bigger. So did her dreams. Don't scoff. Now and again, even in the Zona, a girl's dreams might come true.

La Negra (The Dark One) was also a part of the inner circle. Her special role focused on sorting out squabbles over the ownership of dress colors and "signature" outfits. The wardrobe mistress, as it were.

This was tense work for someone considerably less powerful than Francisca and Blanca, but it may have been delegated on the principles that familiarity breeds contempt and that maintaining power means not arguing over details. Backed by Francisca and Blanca, La Negra did a pretty good job of maintaining "peace in the valley."

The part-time girls who filled in on vacations, slow weekdays, and big Saturday nights, just like three-shift waitresses everywhere, simply lined up each night and were handed out old or nondescript frocks in pastel shades. Some looked smashing anyway—dark skin, jet-black hair and eyes set against a pastel lime background. Lighter skin against a soft pink.

Negra had other assets. Dark-skinned, from very humble central Mexican origins, she was a role model for the *"chunkas"* (generic name for Indian-looking) girls from the republic's narrow waist. Nowadays they are usually called "Oaxacas" or *"tejuanas"* for Tehauntepec, a small city famed for the beauty and graceful bearing of its Indian women. These girls were culturally very different from the lighter-skinned *norteñas* and big-city girls.

Most were Indian in every sense of the word. Quiet, and Spanish a second language for many. Raised in small villages of thatched roof houses with dirt floors, their fathers were small-time corn farmers or the equivalent of sharecroppers on one of the region's great haciendas, some still in the hands of the same aristocratic family for four hundred years.

Negra, a mestiza, or only part Indian, spoke some Mixtec, Zapotec, and enough of the Tehauntepeca dialect to break barriers and give orders in the first and therefore most authoritative language of squabbling girls. She understood who they were. She kept things orderly, particularly among those raised in the more ancient matriarchal enclaves of dying indigenous culture.

As a group I found these girls to be both the most beautiful and most mysterious. They talked with their eyes and hands. Some had faces that could have been lifted right off the great Mayan stelae. Others looked like Aztec princesses. They had rich mahogany skin, high cheekbones, brilliant dark eyes, and cascades of jet-black hair they scented with jasmine.

127

I wasn't the only one who found them exotic. A surprising number of fair-skinned, middle-class local men found them intoxicating. So did the genuine vaqueros and field hands out on a spree. The Stateside patrons I called "Tony Lama Texans" for their dandified lizard-skin boots and manicured fingernails were bull-shit, city-boy cartoon knockoffs of real cowboys and almost never paid any attention to the Indian girls.

In Mexico's culturally and economically stratified society, the Indian girls were on the C-list socially. But they made little trouble, demanded little of the house, mostly living in fragile extended families in the neighboring barrio, and brought in lots of onetime trade and a few regulars.

Negra dealt with any who made trouble or who were simply too countrified to make the transition to sleeping in beds instead of hammocks, eating two meals a day, and using indoor plumbing. Some even took Spanish lessons arranged by Negra. She loved her girls—there even being occasional but subtle speculation of Sapphic interest on her part. If so, she was deep in the closet, taking male clients regularly.

❧

chapter ten

AT THE SHRINE OF THE VIRGIN

La Indita was the only pure Indian girl "in residence," an extraordinarily beautiful woman of twenty-something from the Tehuantepec area. Coils of long braided hair wound around her head like the women on early-nineteenth-century coins.

She had high cheekbones and exquisitely turned lips, similar to those of a very beautiful Navajo woman. And she had unforgettable eyes—like huge limpid pools, which hid wondrous treasures just beneath their shimmering surfaces. If one's eyes really are windows to the soul, she had not only lived many past lives, but was in daily contact with the gods of her ancestors.

Could I have chosen any one woman I've ever met to be *the* Eve of that fabled garden in Eden, I would have chosen La Indita to be the mother of all humankind.

She had a quiet yet distant warmth that was mesmerizing. Usually guarded and watchful, those huge eyes recorded everything around her for use in her next life, like slow-moving nine-millimeter film. She opened up only after she became ill.

In the summer of 1970, several weeks after my initial fling with Francisca and before I took up with Marta, I had taken Negra, Mariquita, and several other girls downtown for a mid-week afternoon meal at El Pollito restaurant.

It was a lovely place, where the upper-middle-class "good" girls and their moms, aunts, etc., often congregated after a tough morning of tennis, beach, a swim. In short, the kind of place where headwaiters were sometimes asked to quietly remove the undesirables.

La Indita was in the backseat of my Rambler, where I got an occasional glimpse of her in the rearview mirror, watching me intently. Startling. She didn't even pretend to look away when I caught her. Yet she was totally expressionless, placid, serene, her face as still as a carved mask of dark brown jade.

But when I told the girls we were headed to El Pollito, La Indita whispered something in Negra's ear. Apparently Indita preferred a place with less tourism, "more typical." Fine by me.

So we drove on through town to a big open-air fish house right on the banks of the wide Rio Matapé estuary, adjoining Empalme. It was cheap, casual, not frequented by the prosperous set, and suited Indita perfectly.

In fact, she sat next to me, motionless and serene, watching me nearly the whole time. Never looking away or reacting when I glanced at her, smiling nervously to blow off my discomfort. Soul scanning, I assumed uneasily. And boy, did I ever have some naughty little secrets hidden down there!

As we finished and settled the bill (Dutch only—viejas' rules), La Indita switched places with Negra and sat up front. She pressed in next to me so close that I bumped her every time I shifted gears. Jade mask still unperturbed, her thigh snuggly pressed against mine in the three-across seating, she radiated sensual electricity. Still, she looked straight ahead, even more serene. Now paying no attention to me at all, her eyes were distant as if veiling secrets once revealed to her in Eden. It was if her body was in one place, yet her essence in another.

It was a *long* twenty-minute drive back to the Zona. Oddly, I was both terrified and aroused, my mind racing, imagination aflame. By the time we reached the Río Rita's porch, I was mentally lost in southern Oaxaca, walking through crumbling pyramids, turning over broken funerary urns, touching bright splashes of ancient painted mosaic. Carved faces like Indita's stared back at me from thousand-year-old stone friezes.

As the girls flung open the doors and started to pile out, Indita leaned to me. The mask moved, its lips parting for an instant, emitting but one word: "*¿Viste?* (Did you see?)" Jesus!

Involuntarily I nodded yes and looked toward her. But she turned quickly, scooted out, and ran up the steps, never looking back. Mariquita, who had hung back, stuck her head through the driver's window. "La Indita said she was going to read your future for us at lunch. We all wanted to hear it, but she must have changed her mind. Can we go out again soon?"

131

"Certainly…and does Indita often read fortunes?"

"Oh yes, and she's psychic—she can tell people where they are from just by looking at them. Thanks again for the paseo, Davíd. Will we see you Saturday night?"

"*Claro*, 'Quita. (Sure, Mariquita.)"

Before driving away, I reached for the pack of Pall Malls I kept in a little J. C. Whitney mail-order wire rack under the old Rambler's radio. Got to have necessities close at hand, you know.

I was so rattled that I had a hard time extracting *un cigarro*. On my second try I looked into the pack and withdrew a tightly folded bit of paper. No wonder! I lit a cigarette, inhaled deeply, and unfolded the paper wad—a short note in the careful, old-fashioned script lettering of a Mexican schoolgirl.

It read, *Sunday at one. Shrine of the Virgin.* Unsigned. The only one close enough to have put it there was Indita. Hmm?

Did that mean the shrine on the hill above the Zona? Probably, but there were more than a dozen small shrines to the Virgin of Guadalupe scattered about the Guaymas area. Well, I had a few days to think about it.

The Sunday after I found the folded note stuffed into my pack of Pall Malls, I couldn't help myself. I was dressed and headed for the Zona by eleven-thirty. The taxistas at the Rubi knew something was up since I rarely drove the Rambler anywhere early. They knew my routine. Lunch at the Colmenar about one forty-five, often Serdaneando, hitting the sitios and checking out the plaza.

I felt weird and furtive chugging along the dusty red road that bordered the west side of the Zona. I chose to take this route since the Río Rita was on the opposite side of the perimeter and my gray Rambler was instantly recognizable, even from a distance. This was the low-rent end of the Zona, run-down, hilly, and rocky. I actually had to pull the car into low gear for the climb.

Everything looked different from above. Fresh, warm midday air. No dust. No Zona noise. I could even get a glimpse of the sea—a narrow sliver of shimmering blue-green about a mile away. Everything seemed clean, clear, pristine.

Nopal cactus, saguaros, great brick-red boulders the size of small houses tumbled from the hills above. Gulls circled overhead. Yet below me sprawled the Zona, its huge square neatly outlined. The devil confined by the wide, dusty bars of his cage.

As I pulled up fifty yards below the shrine, I understood why this place had been chosen for the Virgin's statue—she reigned over and above the evil one. A girl could climb the hill, leaving her life, her persona, her sins behind her, pray and float in the pristine innocence of the Virgin's lap, even if only for an hour.

Dressed in pressed Wranglers, tan twill field shirt, Red Wings, and Panama hat, I would have attracted attention had anyone been there. But the shrine stood alone. No visitors. I climbed the narrow path anyway. No harm in a prayer. The hills were beautiful and peaceful. Timeless. The shrine inviting. Plastic flowers and a half dozen extinguished votive candles graced the statues' base. I sat, cross-legged like a kid, leaned forward, and closed my eyes, inhaling the distinctive scents of salt breeze and fragrant limes mixed with cold wax and burned wicks. I prayed silently. And lost track of time.

Sometime later the sharper scent of hot candle wax pulled me back into the present. Startled, I opened my eyes, a votive candle five feet from me flickering in the gentle updraft from the sea! I looked around without getting up. Saw no one. Then leaned back and twisted to check it out. No one behind me either. Weird. Unnerved, I stood and turned to leave but didn't get far.

There stood La Indita, not three feet from me. Blocking my exit. Lace head covering. Her deep eyes searching again. Face still masklike. I was rooted to the spot, trying to find words.

But she stunned me, speaking first. "You were born in a sea of gray. Only recently have you come into the sunlight. This gray place—I do not know it. Have never seen it before. Strange. I thought if you came here, I might be able to see beyond the gray."

"And could you, señorita?" I asked. "No, Davíd. But I could hear your prayer." She smiled. *Smiled!* The exquisitely turned corners of her mouth actually crinkling—the mask now alive. A human face after all.

Once the initial shock wore off, I quizzed her, a doubtful tone in my voice. "Is that the only reason you asked me to meet you? And could you really hear my prayer? I did not speak!" Her smile widened. "Meet me at the Plaza de las Tres Pistolas at seven this evening, and I will answer. Now I wish to be alone. *¡Hasta las siete!* (Until 7 p.m.!)"

Having dismissed me, she walked on past, silent as a ghost, and knelt at the feet of the Virgin. Conversation over. Mystery not. I walked down the narrow path, turned once to look at

133

her. Still motionless, she had entered that other world again. Remote, placid, still.

Of course I went to Las Pistolas, an older *plazuela* above the church. Roughly triangular in shape, its dense trees shaded the front of the once great town house owned by the late Cayetano Iñigo. It was little used, compared to the main plaza fronting the church. I sat on the raised, tiled sidewalk at Sr. Iñigo's house and waited. No Indita.

Twenty minutes later a taxi dropped her off at the plaza's far corner and parked. She walked into the trees—silent. Graceful. Carrying something large, she beckoned me over. No end to the mystery, she drew me to her like a moth to flame....

A picnic basket! I laughed; not so mysterious after all. "Are we going to eat?" "Yes, but not here." She motioned me toward the taxi—from a San Carlos sitio. Hmm! All of my own will in some odd state of suspension, I followed her to the taxi.

134

I should have been nervous, cautious. In control. That was the way I always approached unexpected situations. Instead I was calm, at peace, bemused. The taxi turned right—uphill at the next corner, climbing up to the high road (Route 15) overlooking the town. A left turn and we were headed north.

Finally I asked, "*¿A dónde vamos?* (Where are we going?)," pausing, surprised that I did not want to call her "Indita."

The enigmatic smile returned, the curved corners of her mouth rising a quarter inch, not more. "A small motel on the road to San Carlos. A balconied room with a view of the sea. *Reservado en tú apellido* (booked in your last name)."

So I asked . . . "and how is it that you know my family name?"

"A friend cleans rooms at the Hotel Rubi. I made inquiries since La Francisca refused to speak to me of you. She forbade me to see you . . . and you do not have to call me Indita . . . my name is Yasmín (Jasmine), but do not use it in public, please. Not in the Zona."

Palm-lined road to San Carlos. (Photo by Dan and Rachel Shaffer © 2004.)

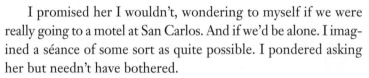

135

I promised her I wouldn't, wondering to myself if we were really going to a motel at San Carlos. And if we'd be alone. I imagined a séance of some sort as quite possible. I pondered asking her but needn't have bothered.

"Yes, to the motel, Davíd, and we shall watch the sunset alone. I will read your fortune when the moment is right." Eerie! And the first woman I'd ever met who didn't need you to explain yourself to her. Even talk to her. All you had to do was relax and follow. So I relaxed.

About twenty minutes later we pulled into a new motel on the left side of the road to San Carlos. The bay was but fifty yards away. I paid the taximan thirty pesos as she handed him a note. He nodded. She handed me the large basket and motioned me into the lobby while she stood outside, out of sight.

"Reservation for Señor Stuart?" I inquired. "Yes, señor. One hundred pesos, please—upstairs, left, facing the sea. Checkout

Teta Kawi hill at San Carlos. (Photo by Dan and Rachel Shaffer © 2004.)

136

tomorrow at eleven. Need anything?" Handing the deskman a hundred-peso note, I nodded. "Ice, please—a large bucket?" "We'll send it up in five minutes, señor. Good evening."

It was a lovely little room and the balcony offered a spectacular view of the sunset and water below. The room faced southeast, fronting the area where the Estero de Soldado meets San Carlos bay. Pelicans floated about. Gulls stood in the shallows; a local *panga* (small flat-bottomed boat) floated past into the estuary, a lantern hanging from the bow. Someone in San Carlos would have very fresh mullet in the morning.

The ice came, then we were alone. La Indita set two places on the little patio table, digging into the large basket. Either she had done subtle but remarkable research on my tastes or was truly as psychic as she appeared. Several bottles of Orange Crush. Potato salad with onion, cilantro, peas, and a touch of lime. Tortas

Cerro Bacochibampo from Miramar. (Photo by Dan and
Rachel Shaffer © 2004.)

of *jamón y queso con aguacate* (ham and cheese with avocado).
Fruit—mango, papaya, small, sweet oranges. Two bottles of
Bohemia beer. All Güero favorites!

She pulled the chairs together facing the water, pushing my
plate to me, the mask warmer, gentler, softer than I'd ever seen
it. She ate a little, not much.

Afterward she leaned back, began breathing to the rhythm
of the surf, soaking up the last glimmer of sunlight. She sighed
occasionally but did not speak. I slipped into the same rhythm.
At peace.

A small mountain, Cerro Bacochibampo, rose nearly a thousand feet from the shimmering water, hiding our view of
Miramar beach. Once the orange, pink, and peach colors of
sunset faded, the sky turned its Guaymas blue. Still silent, she
pulled the two bottles of Bohemia from the ice bucket as the

sky changed again from blue to indigo and the stars came out. They glittered like sequins, vibrating in the warm air that swirled up from the surrounding hills, an offering from the sun to the gods of the night.

She touched me on the shoulder, motioning me inside. The bed already turned down. A candle lit next to the bed. Mistress of silences. She wore a thin silk robe, a soft moss green, her hair down, cascading nearly to her waist. Dark swirls remembering the twist of her braids. She touched my face, tracing my mouth, then whispered, "Anything you wish. Anything! But you must ask it out loud. I do not wish to guess."

Anything? Anything! But at that moment all I wanted was to hold her, feel her close to me. Put my lips to the warm pulse beating in her neck. Smell her hair. Touch the recurved bow of her lips, so I voiced it: "May I hold you?"

She folded herself into my arms, hanging softly to every curve of my body as I held her and squeezed her. Gently I ran my hand over those elegant lips, slowly exploring the exotic curves of her face with my fingertips. Just like stone, she was cool and dry. Yet the stone yielded. Soft like a woman. Her face was moist as I ran my lips across her cheek. A tear? I started to form a question, but her fingers sealed my lips.

It was a long while before I realized that the robe had vanished. Even longer before I discovered the small green jade bead mounted on a gold ring piercing her right nipple, already nearly as hard as the stone. I pressed my tongue to the stone. She sighed.

I saw pyramids rising from great knots of strangler figs. Torches floating in the forest. Smelled copal, the traditional incense that summoned ancient gods. A great dance ground unfolded in front of me. Deep-toned drums beat a slow cadence.

Then two long ranks of plumed warriors separated, an Indian princess emerging from their protective formation. Regal, remote, dressed in the purest white. I drifted into the air and flew to her. The warriors looked up. Amazed. She moved toward me. Lips curving, her limpid eyes glistened, softening the stylized lines of her mask. Moaning as if in pain, she reached out and touched my face. The dancers disappeared.

Then she told me my fortune. "You will be loved, just as you will finally be able to love. But there are to be tragedies. Your life will be a contest between the gray veil and the sunlight. That veil is not a place, as I first thought; it is the door into your soul and has not yet fully opened. As a child you flew, as did I."

Nothing more said, and exhausted, I drifted off to sleep. She awakened me gently about twenty to one in the morning, everything except my clothes ready for exit.

"The taxi will soon be here; I must be back to the club before Francisca returns from a short trip this *madrugada* (early, a.m.)." I touched her face again. She grabbed my hand and held it against her lips. The wondrous curves of her mouth soft to my touch.

139

As we headed out the door, cued by one quick, discreet toot of a taxi, she squeezed my arm. "Thank you for holding me. It was my wish . . . that and to have a real date, if only once."

I started to speak, but she silenced me again, shaking her head. As we entered the taxi, her mask hardened and she retreated once again to the ancient places where she dwelt.

On the drive back she touched my hand, softly caressing my palm, but said nothing. The taxi deposited me at the Avenida Diez and the Serdan, then turned downhill toward the Zona. Discretion, I assumed.

As I walked downhill toward the Almita, I tried to sort out our "date." How did she know I had flying "dreams" as a kid? Sailing over the rooftops of my neighborhood, free and excited by the view from aloft but sometimes afraid I couldn't find my way home!

I told my mom, but no one ever believed me. Not even when I knew my dad had patched our roof one spring with four red

Statue to fisherman, looking toward Rubi. (Photo by Dan and Rachel Shaffer © 2004.)

140

shingles that didn't match the rest. I'd long forgotten those childhood flights, which had once seemed so real and so haunting.

When I reached the Almita, the bright lights and boisterous truck drivers were too much for me. This wasn't a night for parrot jokes. So I walked down to the corner of the malecón and sat on the sea wall by the statue to the fisherman.

Overcome and surprised by a profound loneliness, I wanted to see pyramids again, smell the jasmine in Indita's hair and hold her. Trace her lips with my fingertips and breathe slowly to the rhythm of the surf...

I was grappling with the surreal. As if I'd been in a semi-hypnotic state the entire day, floating in an existential realm where religion, mysticism, and the erotic were magically real—if only one could really let go and neither speak nor demand control. So unlike me.

Back on guard again, I slipped into the Rubi's lobby, but still under her spell, I dreamed of gray veils, an exquisite jade mask, ancient rituals, and the mother of all humankind. Sometime in the night I handed her our firstborn. She nursed the child and smiled at me, her huge eyes moist and full of warmth. I was at peace.

I saw La Indita again the next Wednesday at the Río Rita and several times thereafter. I stared at her often, imagining that the curled corner of her mouth softened and turned up ever so slightly as I sneaked looks at her. I yearned for her, but the girls, I was convinced, actively worked at keeping us apart. Why? I didn't understand.

Once when Francisca and Blanca were gone, I started toward her, but she shook her head no, then smiled openly. Damn! I wanted her. Hungry for both her warmth and those amazing visions, I was disappointed.

141

So I didn't actually "talk" to her again until one evening a few weeks later when Francisca leaned to me and asked a favor. La Indita was ill and needed medicine from the *farmacia* Santa Rita downtown on the Serdan. Could I go get it for her? Quickly! *Arreglado con el farmacéutico* (already arranged with the pharmacist). "No problem, Francisca!"

At the pharmacy they were waiting for the Rambler at the brightly lit all-night window fronting the Serdan, bag in hand. A ten-second stop. Easy. Not like the States. As the Rambler pulled up toward the Río Rita, La Negra was waiting at the steps— motioning me down the street to the residencia. My U-turn put the headlights on Francisca, standing in front of a room below.

I pulled up, driver's window down. She leaned in quickly, snatched the bag, and instructed me to park behind the room block, where I jacklighted another of the Indian girls waiting for me.

Indita's room was small, tidy. Half a dozen votive candles flickered in front of a modest plaster statue of Guadalupe, the Virgin. Originally protectress of Indian Mexico, by later colonial times she had taken on the whole country.

Indita lay on the bed, one of my own Kmart fans from Tucson blowing over her, her usually placid face twisted in agony. Francisca was readying her medicine. She swallowed the pills, gasping. Sweat poured from the brown jade, cascading onto the sheets like a tropical rain. She gasped and shuddered. Stunned, I blurted out a question. "What medicine is this? What is wrong with her?"

Francisca answered, "A compound with codeine that the *dentistas* use, but it is not strong enough." Then she pulled me aside, La Negra and the other Indian girl taking over. "Davíd, she needs morphine. She is dying of cancer. It is eating her ovaries, the doctor thinks. For months now. There have been a few better periods, but the pain is now beyond control. We need morphine. That is why you are here."

142

Oh no! I thought, and stood there—stunned. Sick inside. Francisca shook my shoulder, panic in her eyes. "*¡Davíd!*"

"Do they not have morphine at the Santa Rita, Francisca?"

"*¡No! Ya se acabó.* (No, it's used up just now.)"

"What can I do, Francisca?"

"Go to Nogales, Davíd. *Está arreglada una cantidad suficiente, e hipodérmicos también.* (A quantity of morphine and hypodermics has been arranged.) *¿Regresas pronto a la frontera a comprar cosas?* (Are you going to the border to purchase items again?)" Apparently everyone knew about my "import" activities.

"I have no plans to, but there is business waiting. I could go. Give me the instructions."

"We need it pronto, Davíd."

"I'll go tomorrow, Francisca, but why me?"

"I trust you, and don Francisco said you were experienced at such missions, and my Francisco ought to know."

"Okay, but why is La Indita not in the hospital, under treatment, Francisca?"

"Money, Davíd. The cancer was already advanced, so she was determined to conserve her life savings. We are to send her money home to Oaxaca when she is gone." The knot in my belly tightened till it hurt.

Late the next night I delivered the morphine and needles. When I made my late-night delivery to the residencia, Francisca administered the drugs. The other girls quietly surrounding Indita, caring for her. Adjusting the fan. Replacing her candles. Later they sent me downtown for new cotton diapers. Tampax.

No matter how often she soiled herself, she was clean within ten minutes. I brought chicken soup to her from the Almita on a number of occasions, but she gagged on it. If Chang knew anything, he gave no indication of it. Then came the phone call at the Rubi one Tuesday morning in August. "Come now!" ordered Francisca. "*¡La residencia!*" Her voice was urgent. I dressed quickly and went.

Indita had become thin. Hollow-cheeked, her eyes very cloudy, as if the light within them had faded. Those who had cared for her gathered, somber, in the little room. The small statue of the Virgin nestled under one arm like a teddy bear. "She has something to tell you." Francisca shrugged, one eyebrow raised like a question mark. I leaned down to the arc of her lips as she whispered, "Thank you for coming to the *ermita* (shrine)." She sighed deeply and drifted back to sleep for a few minutes.

When she awoke, she motioned Negra to her and spoke in the strongest voice that she could muster, smiling. "I have been so happy these last weeks. Such fortune to have been treated so well. So much love!" Exhausted, she fell asleep.

I wanted to hold her once more, but Francisca and Negra shooed the rest of us out, sniffling. She never woke again, yet La Negra insisted that when she died that afternoon, a smile was still on her lips—happy and as innocent as a child taking her nap.

That evening the girls quietly gathered up a collection. Four thousand pesos on top of the twelve thousand and change she had saved in the bank account Francisca had opened for her.

Brigido "took a short vacation" and accompanied her casket on the Pacífico train to Guadalajara. Her transport and funeral paid for by "The House." Packed in dry ice from the shrimp-packing plant, her coffin reached Oaxaca late on the third day.

According to secondhand accounts, the local padre met Brigido, who delivered the bank draft of her savings drawn in the priest's name. He had educated her and half a dozen of the other local orphan girls in his spare time. Indita's dream had been to build a village school for the girls so they "could raise themselves up and have better lives."

According to Brigido, she was buried there, her small statue of the Virgin still nestled under one arm.

144

In 1975, when I visited a noted Mesoamericanist and former professor, the late John Paddock, at his home in Oaxaca City, we took a side trip at my request. Ruins. Little known but magnificent sites like Maquilxochitl (Five Flower, in the Aztec language), where he had excavated.

Late in the day we reached Indita's village. I saw her grave and recognized it since she had given me her first name. The graveyard's statue of Guadalupe was only forty yards away. I lit a candle there for her. John, who had lived an eccentric, expatriate life himself, asked no questions.

By then there was a newish but small two-room school next to the tiny orphanage for Indian girls. She was buried there, among the great forest trees that crept into the poor end of the graveyard. Rest in peace, princess. Rest in peace, mother of all humankind.

chapter eleven

AT THE EDGE

While some girls in the Zona understood the difference between illusion and reality, others clearly did not. Many of the veterans, even some in the residences, lived in a world where drunk and sober, sane and insane, happy and miserable, in control or spiraling helplessly into one or another vortex were moment-by-moment dramas.

Generalities don't capture the starker realities, but I am tempted into several by observations that any fool could have made. Alcohol was a problem. A big problem. A number of the girls, especially the Indian ones, self-medicated on alcohol to dull the realities of the path they had taken.

They had all started out as little girls, with little-girl dreams. Some of those dreams shaped by the endless flattery of hopeful local men around them as they became señoritas. Unfortunately for a number of them, they had been sexually abused long before puberty. Pain. Anger. Self-hatred. The burden of "secrets" had crushed many Zona flowers even before they opened. Hence the common question to me, "Wife, children, girlfriend, *sisters*?"

Actually, with that question, many were assessing my odds of being a pedophile. In the States one asks, "What do you do professionally?" when folks meet. Among the girls in the Zona, its equivalent was, "*Who* have you done?"

They divided men, with a fair degree of accuracy, into, "Definitely—but he pays well, the bastard"; "No, I don't think so, but perhaps"; and finally, "Not likely. Might actually be human."

Nonetheless, these instinctive judgments, coupled with the inevitable group discussions of new clients on clinic day (more about which later), guided decisions for a surprisingly small percentage of girls on the floor.

It was common for a girl like Beatriz, a dark, very young-looking mestiza of about twenty from Guadalajara (she claimed) to take older clients who did things like ask her to call them "daddy," then openly role-played her as a little girl, asking her to wear kneesocks and a plaid skirt, her hair in pigtails.

She did it over and over, making big fees for low-grade kink, then spent most of her money getting shit-faced on booze that the taxi drivers would bring her or that she'd snuck in on clinic days. She was usually only "with it" on late Sundays and Mondays. Smashed again by Tuesday, asking some fifty-year-old creep if he'd like to "do" her while she played with her *peluche* (stuffed animal).

She had an uncanny knack for identifying these guys instantly from across the room, drawn to them by some twisted, magical force. She'd pop the peluche question and disappear. Only to emerge forty-five minutes later, looking dejected, the client quickly scuttling off into the night.

Then she'd spend her entire fee on the booze and wake up the next day with a raging hangover. Endure her regular scolding from Francisca or La Negra. Then do it all again the very next night.

On a quiet Thursday there might only be thirty guys in the place, but if even one of them was into little girls and teddy bears, she was on him like a kid on an ice cream cone. Uncanny. She was civil with me but otherwise paid me little attention. Later I discovered that was a good thing.

And she wasn't the only vieja in Mexico to work the teddy bear routine. Once another archaeologist and I visited a club in Chihuahua City. A colonial-style town home with interior courtyard, its tiled courtyard had been turned into the bar and dance floor. Two stories of patioed rooms surrounded it in a big U. It was a grand old place with lots of atmosphere. Several of the guys at the bar belonged in a Clint Eastwood movie.

My friend engaged a cute hooker upstairs. I waited down at the bar, nursing a Corona and ignoring the "*pinche gringo*" taunts in low tones to see if I'd react. Nope. I'm not that stupid. All was right with the world until piercing screams erupted from above, creating a huge racket on the upstairs balcony. Result: total pandemonium.

The chick had donned her kneesocks and pulled out her teddy bear, rubbing it over my colleague in all the wrong places. He had once played football for Vanderbilt and was simply not the teddy bear type. Full of tequila, embarrassed, vastly irritable, perhaps even a touch hysterical, he came out to the balcony stark naked to throw the bear over the railing, claiming he'd paid for tail, not a toy.

The little hooker protested, grabbing frantically for her teddy. He merely snatched it back, humped the stuffing out of it while the girl shrieked, then disappeared into her room, dressed, and returned to the bar as if nothing unusual at all had happened. Meanwhile it had gotten very quiet—a bad sign.

Several of the locals may have had momentary visions of carving smiling jack-o'-lanterns on a couple of gringo asses. But my bro simply whipped out the biggest mahogany-handled Buck lock-back folder they'd ever seen and proceeded to trim his fingernails with it.

He casually ordered another beer with a shot of tequila and grinned at the assembled, declaring the bear wasn't very "tight" (*apretada*). Definitely not worth a hundred pesos! The crowd roared in laughter, one sinister-looking guy proclaiming in Spanish, "This *pinche gringote* (big frigging gringo) is crazy! Loco, hombres! Loco!"

In spite of the renewed sense of mirth, it was time to leave—*quickly*, before the laughter died down. The waiters rushed about, frantic to replace all the beers tainted by the incongruous cascade of snowy *peluche* stuffing from the balcony above, now floating in the foam. The round of beers on us, of course!

Playing eight years old was a dangerous game. But Beatriz at the Río Rita played it anyway. No winners in this little pantomime. Just self-hatred and tragic self-medication. Chang sent her away within the month as she spiraled downward. Not on his watch! He gave her a bus ticket and food money to go home. Rumor had it she spent it on booze and was drunk somewhere in Empalme, turning tricks at the railroad yard.

148

The Río Rita actually discouraged heavy drinking. Drunken girls were trouble. Some merely went comatose, not even fully aware they had taken clients. Then not even certain what they might have done during the encounter. Blackouts, you know. Only Stateside fraternity boys seemed to enjoy sex with a blotto "date." Mexican clients complained.

Other viejas threw hissy fits after a few drinks. Bitchy, their anger rising to the surface. Not good for business either—it destroyed the gay, lighthearted pantomime on which everyone's livelihood depended.

In economic terms, the drunks were bad business all around. Hell, serving them a real drink instead of tea water also ate into the house's profit margin on booze. That's why Francisca had to demand a "real drink" after a certain don Francisco incident in 1970, the subject of Chang's first oblique lesson to me on local pride.

But it wasn't drinking fake highballs that gave the real boozers away. They ordered beer, which couldn't be faked since fake, or watered, beer pours flat, no bubbles. No foam. Those chicks also sipped from their date's real drinks when the guys got up to pee.

The other, fortunately rarer, self -medication problem among the girls was cocaine. Not snorted, but highly cut gift cocaine in minute cellophane packets from the occasional drug handlers who floated through the Zona on "business trips" from Sinaloa to the border. A few of the girls rubbed it on their clits and got a rush from it.

Cocaine was a new and baffling problem in the early '70s. But some girls with repeat customers driving clean Sinaloa trucks became addicted enough to steal an extra fifty- or hundred-peso note from a resting client's billfold now and again. That kind of thing was totally forbidden at the Río Rita.

Worse yet, some who played around with the drug gifts later spent their money on other, more widely available painkillers, mostly codeine-based compounds. Most of these girls eventually wound up blank, broke, and zombified as their intake increased.

Another group on the edge were the lesbians, "*tortilleras*" in local parlance. While the house made few moral judgments on them, the lesbians, playacting at being heterosexual, made money. These viejas engaged in the most flagrant pantomime of all, pretending to enjoy sex with men—a version of the Zona's illusion that would have deeply troubled most of their clients.

Mexico was flat hung up on heterosexual sex. Anything else, forbidden. Creating fear and revulsion. Not in the natural order of things. Not feminine.

Even more troubling, some among the gay viejas were very aggressive. Especially so when obsessively trying to seduce the cutest, youngest, and most credulous girls among the recent arrivals. Occasionally one succeeded. If word got out, all hell broke loose in the "central committee."

It was Francisca, La Blanca, La Negra, later Mariquita who were the day-to-day "sex cops." We don't do *that* here! Nothing perverted is for sale in the Río Rita! Chang's orders!

We are *professionals* here! This is not *la frontera*. Nothing *degenerada*! *¿Comprenden?* (Do you get it?) *No somos cochinas aquí* (we are not pigs here); we are professionals! *De categoría.* (High class.)

Most did understand. But in a world where many had arrived at the Río Rita's doorstep, their lives already torn asunder by men who had abused, abandoned, or exiled them, the temptations of love and comfort from another woman were likely significant.

I reckoned that the house's level of fear and denial closely matched the level of actual temptation. So the tortilleras were tolerated so long as they "stayed in the closet," Pop open that door and there was tension.

La Blanca once confided that on a "disturbing" night several years before (late '60s), a possessive young "*lesbiana*" had actually gone after her tortillera's client with a broken beer bottle. Passion-driven rage. The bottle wielder was sent away that same night, Brigido himself putting her on a bus for Nogales, where that sort of thing allegedly went on.

And falling in love was the hope/fear of at least half the girls in the Zona. Like medical examiners and pathologists, they required emotional distance to do their work.

When you "fell in love" with either another girl, a member of the male staff, but especially a client, the situation was fraught with risk. Someone was going to get hurt. The girls' fragile illusions often rippled bravely in the night breeze—until the canyon winds of "feelings" rose, gathered force, and the fabric tore. Shredded illusions. Ruptured compartments. Souls exposed—big trouble in paradise.

Girls in love also perturbed the Zona's business model. The viejas' corporate culture required that a girl never give favors to a man. No free sex. No meals, gifts, treats, love notes. *¡Nunca!* Nonetheless, these proscriptions were often violated.

The girls did silly stuff when they fell in love. They didn't charge, having to come up with room rents, tips, etc., from earnings with other clients. They lingered in the working rooms too long, enjoying themselves, while the other girls waited in the halls, getting hot as their waiting clients cooled down and walked away.

Girls in love also violated other norms. Some delivered oral sex. Others even gave the forbidden *culeadas* (anal sex) or actually lent money to "their" client. Such girls believed in the existence of a "Prince Charming"—someone totally unlike all the men who had put them there in the first place.

Elsa, la Chuleta (Pork Chop), was a case in point. She was a veteran, gorgeous and "in residence," but floated just out of the center of power because she was in love. Then in her mid-twenties, she had a spectacular figure. An ass so fine she'd have automatically been Brazil's premier light-skinned samba queen. And she was proud of it. Had a huge following of clients but was in love with one of the local fellows and didn't know what to do about it.

151

She had been at the Río Rita about seven years, she told me during one of our weekday excursions downtown. She had a little money in the bank. A fairly light-skinned mestiza, she wanted "a house, a man, a family. Respectable, you know." Someplace far away from Guaymas and its Zona. Therein lay one huge rub.

The gent she was crazy about was Guaymense. Many generations. A stable, decent working-class family that lived in a pleasant, multigenerational adobe and tile-roofed house compound on a hill above el centro.

Her gentleman friend was legally divorced. And he loved her. But he was rooted in Guaymas. Not going anywhere. Born there, like his father and grandfather, his rosary would be recited at San Fernando when his time came. Just as he had been baptized there and presented to the crowd at the plaza some thirty-five years before.

She gave him free sex. But she had to take on even more clients to compensate. The wider her circle of clients, the greater her need to start a new life somewhere else. Respectable, "*¿Sabes?*" Yes, I knew.

But it was tragic. At times her friend would show up at the club when she was "*occupada*" (working). Hard on him. He was gentle, warm, reliable, a hard worker, neat and clean, and a family man at heart. Very hard on him.

Then, sensing the tension, Elsa tried to reel him in just as she'd been trained since childhood in Mexico's ritualized sex roles. Make him jealous. He'll give in. "We'll go away and everything will be perfect," she told me. But just when did she think the images of her walking past him into a working room would fade? As she intrigued, those images had been burned into his brain as if by a soldering iron. This had "Greek tragedy" written all over it.

Then she began to seduce some of his closer friends into a client relationship. If a little jealousy didn't work, she'd throw more clients on the fire and raise the heat. She went through clients like Kleenex. Frenzied.

In one case she took one of his drunken "friends" to a working room, refused any money, and simply cried for twenty minutes before emerging. That strategy gave her "boyfriend" absolutely zero reinforcement. He assumed his friend had balled her. It came off as contempt. Humiliating.

She began drinking more, then had to take even more clients to support her habit. She was no longer invited to Sunday brunches and avoided the downtown excursions.

By the time I returned in the summer of '71 to baptize little Olga, this "relationship" had faded away. He, hurt and sad. She, convinced that it was just an illusion—like so many of the young viejas who still dreamed of being rescued. He was an ordinary cabrón after all!

But it was the pinche pantomime that had ruined her chances. The love had been real. Not an illusion. The evil one rattled the wide, dusty bars of his cage and roared in victory. La Chuleta was his! And that ass of hers would be in high demand where he reigned.

153

chapter twelve

DECISIONS

A s I sat on the porch of the Río
Rita again (1971), talking to Francisca and La Blanca, trying to
decide if/when I'd go back to the Club Guaymas for one last try
at talking to Marta, a dejected Chuleta sat inside, drinking alone.

Sad. But who was I to judge? The woman I'd once slept with
and then had insisted we were "only friends," nothing more, was
doing the same damn thing a block and a half away.

Marta had reminded me again and again that I was merely
the ambiente's equivalent of what would now be coarsely referred
to in the States as a "fuck buddy." No "love" went with the deal.
Then she wrote that she "loved" me after I left Guaymas in 1970.
Now that I was back, she was piling on the guilt and humiliation.

What did make these girls tick? What separated them from
ordinary housewives or cute, single shopgirls? Why did some
seem in control while others appeared to be totally out of it?
Sexual abuse? Self-esteem? Heck, I didn't know, but Mexico
had a ready-made national answer. "They have no choice, the
pobrecítas." Pregnant or desperate, fate had driven them to this.

They had no choice. "Destiny. Beyond ordinary will." In Mexico fatalism runs deep.

I'd heard it dozens of times since my days as a twenty-year-old student in Mexico City. The first time it came from a local college friend explaining the existence of the famous, flamboyant Barba Azul (Blue Beard) club down in the old Calle Honduras district, less than a mile from the Zócalo, the nation's plaza.

At the Barba there were *three* floors of "pobrecítas" ensconced in a huge old *vecinidad* (housing complex), a live band on the ground floor, jukeboxes blared on floors one (our second floor) and two (third).

On the front steps of the club, an armed detachment of Mexico City police handed out numbered "tickets" for twenty pesos ($1.60 US) each. "What are these for?" I asked my friend. "Protection—a service fee. If we do not come out by morning, they will go in and call your number. Safety. Not a high-class club."

"Okay," I responded. Wow! They sure didn't have anything like this in West Virginia, so we entered. A cultural experience, I rationalized.

It was surreal. Three floors packed with good-looking, mostly dark-skinned girls, twentyish on average. Couples slow dancing, hips grinding away. The street-floor band was loud enough to make your nose bleed, so we grabbed cheap Corona beers from the bar and headed upstairs. Elbow room only. *Well*, I thought, *At least I can get lost in the crowd and watch the scene.* Not!

Two minutes later a gorgeous young thing in a tight gray party dress popped out of the crowd, grinning. "*¡Qué güerito bonito!* (What a cute little white guy!)" "*¿Baila, chulo?*" Yeah, why not! As I took her hand, my friend briefed me, "A single dance is twenty pesos." Okay by me, so I nodded and went out on the packed dance floor. She was warm, smelled good, and clung to me like I'd given her my high school class ring to hang around her neck.

Five minutes later she popped the question, "*¿Vamos a coger? Doscientos, un ratito?*" I was still learning Spanish, so I drug her over to my friend for a translation. The tone in her voice made the question seem urgent, even though all I understood was, "Let's go...."

He explained laughing. "*Coger* is 'screw,' you *fresa* (strawberry— a rube)." Perfectly at ease, he negotiated for me. "I told her two hundred is too much. She'll screw you for a hundred fifty ($12 US). I have rubbers. Use one. Do you want her? She's good-looking for a *morena* (dark-skinned girl)."

"Thanks, but I'll pass—just taking in the scene."

Truth was, I'd still never been with a woman and didn't feel like beginning this way. It seemed so... unromantic, impersonal. But my friend interpreted my refusal through his own cultural filters. "Another night I'll take you to a very classy place near the American embassy. The girls are much higher class. Fair-skinned, just like you are used to!"

157

"Great!" I said. Relieved at both the easy out and the assumption that I was, uh... "experienced."

As we headed out the door, turning in our numbers, I asked why so many hookers and so young. "Fate," he said. "Misfortune drives them to this."

A week later we went to the "classy" place in the Zona Rosa, just off the Reforma, Mexico City's main boulevard. Jacket and tie. Piano. Big leather chairs. Small but excellent jazz band. Beers at forty pesos ($3.20 US) in 1965! Dances were free. The girls' drinks were not.

Sweet Jesus! Every blonde in El Distrito Federal (Mexico City) not already married to a member of the ruling elite must have been in that large, elegant salon.

Green eyes, hazel eyes. Light blonde, dark blonde. Expensive jet-black party dresses. Some emerald greens. One silver, sequined, clinging "mini" nearly pulled my eyes straight out of their sockets. This must be what it was like to be at a Hollywood cocktail party with hopeful starlets. I danced with an emerald dress. Green eyes, dark blond hair, lighter highlights. She spoke English, Spanish, French. Perhaps even Russian and Italian. Nice mouth, a long neck like Audrey Hepburn's... and legs far too nice to describe genteelly.

My pulse was at one-sixty, headed for two hundred, when she quoted her price. "An hour with me, perhaps, *joven*? Three thousand pesos...?" Three thousand pesos! My testosterone levels and heart rate were literally screaming, "Yes, yes. Do it!" But three thousand pesos was two hundred forty US dollars!—in 1965! Almost five months of my rent, including fourteen meals a week, for a big room with bath in the very classy Polanco district just eight blocks away. I shook my head no, my testosterone screaming, "You can walk home to West Virginia next summer if you have to.... Do *it*!"

But I shook my head again, explained I was there only as a university companion to my friend, who had already disappeared with the silver-sequinned dress. She smiled, brushed my cheek with her pouty lips, and whispered in English, "If you change your mind, invite me to another dance." *Not fair, baby!* I thought, but merely smiled lamely. The working girls in this place were clearly not used to guys on a student's budget.

I returned to our little table, nursed my Bohemia (no Coronas here), and tried to keep from either fainting or losing it in my pants as she sat across the room making eyes and slooowly inching her dress ever higher while she crossed and recrossed her legs. Ah, jeez! Emerald green panties to match her dress and eyes. I was not enjoying this.

Now I knew how the bulls that fought on Sundays at the Plaza México felt. They tease them with cows in season but never let them have sex. They arrive in the plaza as virgins. Seriously pissed off. Only to wind up with barbed flags stuck in their backs, a sword through their hearts, then cut into little pieces and sent off to orphanages for the evening stew. Still cherry. I could relate. Poor bastards!

My friend returned, looking sleek, satisfied, and smug. "Four thousand pesos—pricey but worth every peso! Did you not find anyone to your liking?"

"Yes—the girl in the emerald dress—green eyes. We danced. But I couldn't afford her. Beyond my *cartera* (wallet) right now. Tuition."

"You pay your own *matriculación!*"

"Yep, I'm on my own down here. On a budget." He had, like nearly all the wealthy set's eldest sons, a very hard time processing that reality. But he was nothing if not *culto* (cultured, polished) and I was nothing if not still a pinche virgin.

But that one visit to the high end of Mexico's ambiente really made me wonder just how much "fate drove the girls to it." Any girls as beautiful and as educated as those at the salon must have had other options in life.

At least some among them must have actually preferred the ambiente to the life of a highly decorative "corporate secretary" that the big companies in the Mexico City area regularly hired by the dozens. Still, a definitive answer to my wonderment didn't come for years. But when it did, it made an indelible impression.

It began early one Sunday a.m. in August of 1970 as we left the Río Rita. Canelo, one of the older waiters, Felipe L., and Chang had taken to free late-night rides into town courtesy of my '62 Rambler. Hey, twenty pesos saved was twenty pesos! We had exited late, after 4 a.m. It would be light in less than an hour.

As we piled into the Rambler, headed for the Almita, one of the men noticed a girl standing in the middle of the dusty street in front of the B-47 club. Her cheap cardboard suitcase in the dirt beside her, she alternated between reading a note and staring at the door to the 47. Canelo went over to investigate.

A poor girl, perhaps seventeen or eighteen, a "girlfriend" had, according to her story, given her this address after she confided that she was pregnant. After toughing it out at home in a single-Pemex-station town south of Obrégon, she had finally taken the bus to Guaymas. She had come to this place as suggested but was "afraid."

We watched her for a few minutes, discussing the situation. Too young, Chang decided. Canelo agreed. "*No sabe lo que hace.* (She doesn't know what she is doing.)" Chang got out abruptly and went inside. He took up a small collection from the waiters still cleaning up. A little money from the house, then he returned, asking Canelo to "go talk to her." We put in twenty pesos each.

Canelo went over to her with several hundred pesos and the address Chang gave him of a Catholic home that took in pregnant teens in Hermosillo. A cheap trip—only a third-class ticket, thirty-five-peso (less than three dollars) bus ride away. She took the money, thanked him, then walked away, the wadded bills still clutched in her fist.

Dawn was breaking. Jeez! The poor thing was at least six to seven months gone. Belly protruding, she was already waddling, one hand easing the soreness in her back.

Relieved, we watch her walk down the street to the corner where the city bus stopped. Mission accomplished! We congratulated ourselves.

I cranked up the Rambler and started to pull out. Chang was the first to spot her about-face. Shit! Banknotes still wadded in one hand, the suitcase in the other, she had gone only forty yards before turning back. I killed the ignition, the pregnant teenager now again facing the 47's huge front door.

We discussed this one more time. "No place for a baby to be born!" declared Chang. "*¡Sacan las bolsas!* (Pull out your money bags!)" He went inside again, came out with nearly five hundred additional pesos from the girls. We kicked in another two hundred. Several of the Río Rita's "in-club" residents came to the door, bleary-eyed, watching discreetly. Now shareholders in the mission.

Canelo went for round three, Chang with him. They talked four or five minutes, arms waving, then palms up in supplication. When they returned to the Rambler, it was with a sense of wary confidence, mixed with concern.

"*Esperamos un rato* (We'll wait a bit)," announced Chang. We smoked, except for Chang, who had no vices save Coca-Colas. Once again the pobrecíta walked halfway down the block, then returned again! Just standing in the desolate street and staring at the door.

It was an odd scene. Dawn had turned to sunrise and all was radiant for a few minutes, the poor pregnant child bathed in the long, soft rays of early morning sunlight. But there was no radiance in the Rambler—only silence. A hush on the porch of the Río Rita. It was as if the cosmos held its breath while the child decided her fate. For ten minutes nothing moved. Stone silence overtook the Zona.

Several times more, the waddling teenager turned away from the door, walked twenty yards, then changed her mind to return and stare at the 47 again. Back and forth. Back and forth. Mesmerized, we sat it out in utter silence. She had been given a thousand pesos—more than three months' food and rent in a modest pensión. Dammit! She *had* a choice.

About five-thirty, she picked up the suitcase again. That drew a sigh of relief in the car and furtive movement on the Río Rita's porch above us. But instead of walking away, she made a beeline for the 47's front door. The huge iron-studded door opened quickly to her knock and she disappeared within.

The drama over, I backed the Rambler away from the porch, now vacant, and turned downhill. The clear morning sunlight faded abruptly; a sharp breeze carrying the scent of salt air swallowed the car—and it rained. Huge, ice-cold drops created miniature bomb craters in the dusty red soil.

Each drop hit the Rambler's roof, echoing like the rattle of bird shot off the sides of a metal grain silo. The first rain of the season, it added to the sense of pathos. In Guaymas it almost never rains in the morning.

I drove on down the wide clay perimeter of the Zona. Apart from the angry pinging of the rain, it was a long, unbroken period of silence. Finally Canelo pulled out his comb, restoring the James Dean to perfection, noting softly in his deep voice, "*¡Dios mismo Llora!* (God himself cries!)" Someone murmured, "Yes!" from the backseat. I commented, "*Con razón* (With good cause)." No breakfast. No more talk that morning. It was nearly 6 a.m. when I dropped off Canelo in the old San Vincente district and drove back to the Rubi to sleep.

At least I had an answer to the question I'd formed as a twenty-year-old in one of Mexico's highest-class "clubs." The pregnant teenager who had walked into the maelstrom of the 47 had a choice—not an easy one, mind you, but a choice nonetheless. An Hermosillo phone number in her pocket along with a thousand pesos, she had a choice . . . and chose poorly.

I bet myself that the beauty with emerald eyes, dress, and panties who I'd danced with so long ago had also made a choice. As a nation, Mexico was in denial, I reckoned as I tried to slip into sleep.

Choosing to go into the sex trade violated the ideal gender roles and behaviors Mexico wanted its young women to follow. So "Fate" became the conventional culprit, allowing those who had made bad decisions some psychological cover. Just as it did for the men who paid them for their services.

But many other girls at the Río Rita didn't have the luxury of a "choice," I discovered as I got to know the viejas better. Some talked wistfully of La Indita once she was dead and "*reposando en su tierra* (resting in her homeland)." She had come to Guaymas simply because another girl from her village had arrived before her and sent her a letter. In Mexico it's not only "the economy, stupid!" it's also "the network, stupid!"

Her girlfriend had come two years before her, found a modest job, then a guy, and was already long gone somewhere else by the time Indita got off the bus at about age nineteen, twenty pesos ($1.60) to her name. That didn't last long. She looked for work. Hotel maid. Got minimum wage (about $3 a day) and one daily meal. But she was beautiful, so everyone tried to get her into the sack. The waiters, the guests, then the management. Yet she was a virgin. Said no! Got fired and blackballed, according to the viejas.

When she came to the Zona on a local bus with another down-and-out Indian girl she'd meet in el centro, she was hungry and frightened. Negra took her in, got her a dress, fed her. Taught her how to be a hostess.

"She never made lots of money, but she was happy. Then she got this crazy dream—a school for girls like her. Some god-awful village near Tehuantepec—you know—where they eat iguanas and poop in the forest," according to La Blanca.

"For a while she told fortunes for clients and the other girls, gaining a reputation. But that was only ten pesos here, ten pesos there. She just had to build that pinche school," sniffled La Negra afterward. "She'd been raised by the nuns and had never even had a date when she took her first client.

"It changed her so. It was terrible to see. She had been lively, smiled a lot, but then she took a client, put the money in the bank, and retreated within herself. Never came out again."

La Blanca butted in. "And she could actually read and write, just like a white girl!"

"Had she not been Indian, she would never have been here," Negra went on. "So beautiful—yet so 'Indian.' No one is going to hire one of her kind in an office. But she could have done that work easily. Later she thought of telling fortunes as a business at one point, leaving the Zona. But the gypsies own that here in Sonora. No way."

Indita had a dream and only one way to achieve it in Mexico of the late 1960s. Whore? Lost child? Wrong time at the wrong place? Wrong race? You decide. I still consider her the mother of all humankind. A real-life personification of the human condition. She gave of herself to make one village better for others.

And there are so many more like her in Mexico. The dreams vary, often more modest—a kitchen for my mom so she can cook inside, a *dormitorio* for the children so they do not have to sleep in hammocks under a *ramada* (a branch lean-to) in the rainy season, a set of false teeth for my abuelo.

"An operation for my littlest before he dies. The doctors say he has only a few months now." If one was born indigenous in the 1960s, the needs were immense, but the choices were few.

And so it was at the Río Rita. Eventually I came to understand that some had chosen to walk through the front door, their eyes open. Francisca. Perhaps Mariquita. Others were driven by the fortune, or misfortune, of their births. La Indita and others like her.

Some were drawn to the sad pantomime of acting out their own sexual abuse again and again so that they might magically purge themselves of it, like La Eva (at the Rubi). Others never made or never even had a "choice" at all. Like La Blanca, born at the Club del Bosque in Torreón and raised in the maelstrom of el ambiente from birth.

Little Lupita, my mandadera, abandoned by her mom on the street at age five. Dead at age eleven or twelve—who really knew?

164

La Indita—dead at twenty-something—and like Lupita, no last name on her grave. These lives and thousands more were the wreckage of el ambiente. But only Marta, my former lover, still had any real semblance of *decisions, choices* that she could make. And even hers, by any reasonable standard, were quite limited. Still, whatever her pain, she should not have abandoned her son!

Of the girls I knew well at the Río Rita, only Francisca and Mariquita, both light-skinned, educated, smart, and with money in the bank, probably had enough financial and social capital to recast their own fate. Perhaps that's why they wound up on the "central committee" in the first place.

Later I decided, in fairness to Mexico, that the nation was only in half denial over "Fate drives them to it, pobrecítas." In baseball .500 is a great average. In real life it sucks. There's the rub.

chapter thirteen

SUNDAYS IN THE ZONA

Though the incident of the pregnant teenager was never again mentioned among the men, it deeply depressed those involved. The tragedy had multiple dimensions. Many layers of comfort were violated when the 47's immense iron-studded doors opened to receive the mother-to-be that Sunday morning. First, it shattered Mexico's national, Catholic, yet surprisingly Calvinistic myth of fatalistic destiny.

Second, mixing the role of mother-to-be, sacred in Mexico, with puta-to-be stunningly violated several archetypal behavioral domains that were ordained to remain separate. None involved had ever before experienced anything quite its equal.

The tragedy of it was enhanced by the fact that the young woman actually had a choice. A *choice*—that rarest of treasures among Mexico's down-and-outs. After the "collection" she had enough cash in her pocket, most of it earned the hard way, to better her situation. Some of the girls in the Zona would have given almost anything to have magically traded places with her.

As a consequence, the B-47 club lost its veneer of professionalism due to the incident. The Río Rita did not, repeat not, take in pregnant country girls. Principle—Chang's. And also good business practice.

Turning frightened, pregnant kids loose "on the floor" not only looked déclassé, it announced that a club was desperate. Had no standards. Even worse, it was the cultural equivalent of giving the finger to the Mexican social icon of "the mother."

And not even the Zona could ignore the fundamental dictates of Mexican society. Indeed, the nation's Zonas existed only so long as they respected those dictates and behaved like good citizens within the unfortunate social compartment to which Mexico had assigned them.

The Zona's citizens may have been de facto outcasts from "polite" society—but they too had a right to dignity in their own realm if they earned it. Their secrets were as sacred as anyone else's so long as they played by the rules and understood the full meaning of those four wide clay streets that defined them.

And turning a scared teenager into a hooker late in her pregnancy was simply not in the official rule book. Too "border." Too "Tijuana." Too *desmadre* (literally, "unmotherly").

Worse yet, it had happened on a Sunday morning. The hooker's sacred day. Turning out a pregnant teenager on Sunday wasn't merely "desmadre," it was outright blasphemous. La Francisca explained the gravity of it to the girls helping her prepare for brunch on the following Sunday. "Sunday is our private day. How dare those cabrones next door recruit on the Virgin's day!"

True, it was hard to define just when Saturday night transformed into Sunday. And business did intrude upon traditional, clock-driven distinctions. Still, an "all-night" assignation on Saturday evening ended by 3:30 a.m. or so—not "first sunrise" as on other nights of the week. I thought of it, irreverently, as the Zona's "vampire rule."

When the sun first threw open its Sunday morning curtains, its unfettered radiance cleansed. As if in rhythmic response to each Sabbath dawn, the black flower had already resignedly folded its protective petals. Go to bed a hooker. Wake up a normal girl.

And Sunday's theme was "normal." Virtually none of the girls had a clue as to what that actually meant in the outside world, but it mattered not. On Sundays all of the male staff exited the Río Rita by dawn. The girls were on their own. Waiters went home to their families. Clients went home to their wives. Some hookers went home to the neighboring barrios, and guys like me wandered back to el centro, alone.

That's another reason the B-47 incident rankled. It broke the rhythm. Rhythms of daily life in Mexico were few, but ancient, *de costumbre* (customary)—therefore sacrosanct. Most things in Mexico trickled like water from a garden hose—flowing unexpectedly here and there, taking odd paths to the next clump of flowers. Forming unexpected pools, creating eddies and confusing back currents.

But at precisely 3 p.m. every Sunday—for centuries—the bullfights had begun in the Plaza México. Floor shows began exactly at midnight, and for centuries, when the sun's rays first lit up the nation's Zonas, the "evil one" was cast out of his cage for a weekly cleansing. De costumbre. No exceptions.

So the B-47 incident had required the cancellation that afternoon of the hookers' Sunday brunch, which began at precisely 2:30 p.m., de costumbre. A day of mourning at the Río Rita. Another poor girl, like so many of those who had donated pesos to give her a choice, fallen into a life so easy to enter and so pinche hard to exit. *Triste.* (Sad.)

La Blanca, also irritated, got in her two cents' worth. "...And she wasn't even pretty, poor thing! Knock-kneed and fat, face like a horse—what is she going to have to do for clients to make a living? She'll get a few clients among those obsessed with pregnant women. Then what? It's too ugly to imagine!" Francisca ended the conversation. "It will ruin our Sunday to go on. Let's get ready for our guests."

The Río Rita's Sunday brunches were a closely held institution, organized by the veterans at the center. Francisca, *la doyena*, reviewed all potential invitations. No clients! Few men, and those who were invited came with the tacit understanding that they were beyond the boundaries of el ambiente.

A few of the girls had favorite gay guys who sometimes did skits, hair, or wardrobe around the Zona. They were amusing, usually great talkers, not judgmental, and definitely not clients. The really flaming queens weren't invited in my time. Simply too upsetting for any straight males there.

Ten to twenty would gather for lunch, 80 percent of them the viejas in residence or part-timers with no family. The Sunday brunch was, first and foremost, a mimicry of "family." Perhaps an eccentric family, but family nonetheless.

When I was first invited, I quietly consulted Chang. He was surprised. "It's an honor, Davíd. I would not have expected it given your early history here (the Francisca incident)."

I asked him to explain further. "They do not invite clients. But that is clearly now in your past . . . and you have gained palanca with some of them because you take them places in el centro. *Cojonudo* (ballsy), Davíd. They have taken a liking to you—especially after the fiasco at the Miramar *baile*. They knew you defended your prometida's honor. Such things are noticed. It's an honor; accept their invitation."

I accepted Francisca's invitation, but Chang had few details since he only knew of the proceedings secondhand. So I asked Francisca outright, "Guide me, I must know what is customary—how am I expected to comport myself." She smiled. "Two-thirty sharp. Dress as you do for un baile. Be yourself. Relax and I will sit next to you. Guide you. We make conversation.

You are educated. It will be of benefit to the girls. We take turns guiding the topic of conversation. Sometimes we discuss a book or a movie. It is healthy for us to eat as a family. No business. Just family."

"Shall I bring anything?"

"Just yourself. But it is always considered gracious to bring something modest. A pack of cigarettes. A large bottle of Coca-Cola, *algo así* (something like that)." I nodded. Sounded interesting.

When I arrived that first Sunday in 1970, promptly at two-thirty, I was in black dress pants, pressed white shirt, freshly done Red Wings, hair and mustache trimmed just the afternoon before at the Rubi barbershop.

This first invitation had come long before the 47 incident, so I still didn't know most of the viejas very well. As I mounted the steps to the Río Rita's porch, one of the girls ushered me to a hidden side patio near the older residential rooms. They had set up tables and chairs, with fancy tablecloths for coverings. About sixteen places had been set.

171

I stood and chatted with Francisca and La Blanca as some of the more junior girls finished the table and the last of the guests arrived. Several women from nearby clubs, a "gentleman" from Hermosillo named Rodrigo, one of the male hairdressers, a veterana from the Club Marlin, someone's *prima* (cousin), plus the core of the Río Rita's resident veterans.

Francisca at the head of the table, La Blanca at the foot, they nodded for us to be seated once the initial introductions and hand shaking, so important in Mexico, were out of the way.

Seated on Francisca's right, my left hand free not to bump anyone (nice touch! I'm a lefty), I seated her, just as a gentleman does anywhere. The *maricón* (gay) hairdresser seated La Blanca. Rank has its perks everywhere. But nowhere is it more appreciated than where life is fragile, fate is harsh, and fortunes are changeable. Mexico is such a land.

Now that we were seated, hot tea came first, lime water at each place—no booze! And cucumber sandwiches on white bread, crusts trimmed. In Sonora? I wondered who had been watching old British movies!

Everyone sipped daintily and passed the sugar and cream as Francisca initiated the conversation. Topic: the culture of central Mexico and contrasts with *El Norte*. Nice. She had been educated in Mexico City, her original hometown. This allowed me to both participate and learn something. Most there had never been to Mexico City. But pictures of it appeared in every schoolbook in the republic.

She described the old city's center, built on the Aztec's capital, and its main districts, commenting on the great muraled library at the National University. The sheer size and splendor of it. Then she invited me to comment on the "prehistory," telling others I had actually studied there, worked as a student in the New Museum of Anthropology at Chapultepec.

I gave a quick sketch of the old pre-Columbian city states, now suburbs of modern Mexico—told them what most of the old place names meant in the Nahuatl language of the Aztecs. One of the rather Indian-looking girls there (not Indita) seemed pleased. Raised in Toluca, west of the city, she had heard Nahuatl daily as a girl. From the looks of her, some of it might have even crossed her girlhood dinner table.

I noticed that the body language of the table was quite different on Sunday. The girls touched one another gently and often. Several were even holding hands, just like teenagers of the day with their school chums. But the men there, unlike during the rest of the week, did *not* touch the girls.

Sorting out the "*tú*" (familiar address) and "*usted*" (formal address) was tough. The girls all used "usted" for the males, except for the senior ones who had invited that male. Those who had issued the invitation used "tú" with their own male invitee. Usted with the others. And all of the junior girls used usted with Francisca, La Blanca, and La Negra. Divided on Mariquita, who was still establishing her *puesto* (place, position).

At one point, using "usted," I started to answer a question about the ancient Mexico City suburb of Xochimilco posed by one of the younger girls. Francisca guided me, as she had promised. "*Es propio tutearlas más joven, Davíd—y mas fácil grammaticamente.* (It's proper to use tú with the younger girls and easier grammatically.)" And it was easier for me.

Then the conversation turned to customs and politics. *Norteños* were viewed as far more politically conservative, independent, more business-minded. Less formal in dress, but more organizationally efficient. Those from El Districto viewed as more formal, more socialistic. Their class distinctions far more exaggerated and defined by birth, skin color, accent, property than those in the north, where "one could still make their own destiny."

173

That led to discussions of the "fountains of culture" in Mexico. The influences of just whose culture played the strongest part in the *desarrollo* (evolution) of "modern" Mexico. Nearly everyone commented obliquely so as not to offend but laughingly making their points.

Conclusion—central Mexico had a lock on the great artists, poets, writers. Worthy. But the north had a lock on progress and equality. After all, the convulsive revolution of the early 1900s had been engineered and driven by troops, generals, and supplies from the north.

At one point I commented on having once briefly met the legendary Octavio Paz, author of *Labyrinth of Solitude*, in an upscale coffee shop in Mexico City. He was between or on leave from diplomatic assignments (ambassador to India, I think). I wasn't sure which.

That raised several pairs of eyebrows. When some among the viejas know of your work, you have clearly had an impact on your nation. Mariquita got my signed copy of *Solitude* several weeks later. A token for her behind-the-scenes role in the Canadian girl's saga. She was ecstatic. Well, not quite ecstatic enough to give me a freebie, so let's modify her reaction to merely "pleased."

At about 3 p.m., the main courses were set out. Bowls of mashed black beans sprinkled with white goat cheese and sprigs of cilantro. A large bowl of chilled garlic–steamed shrimp with limes. Sopa seca de arroz. Both flour and corn tortillas—the norteñas generally ate flour. The others corn.

Everyone chattered and laughed during the main course. Lots of girl talk. A few inside jokes. Some clever double entendres. The gay hairdresser doing excellent impressions of several of the girls. He had Francisca down cold. The slow, stately walk and casual swing of her hips were perfect.

It was pleasant, and the girls not only seemed different but looked different. Demure printed summer dresses. Flats. Subdued makeup. Some surprisingly fresh young faces once stripped of their working makeup and costumes.

Then came coffee. Dessert. I broke out the two packs of filter tip Raleigh 903s I'd brought wrapped in tissue paper. Someone got a glass bowl, filled it with the cigarettes, and set it at the center of the table. Folks helped themselves. Most of the girls smoked. Hooking is stressful.

At this juncture La Negra and Francisca excused themselves. Indita was sick but still alive. I asked softly if I could join them. Francisca nodded. I stroked her wrists. She smiled. It was sad. About twenty minutes later we returned and rejoined the conversation. It was almost 5 p.m., the hottest time of Guaymas's brutal summer days. Finally Francisca formally excused herself.

The guests then began Mexico's elaborate "shake hands and compliment everyone" by-your-leave ritual. The handshake instinct was so powerful I'd even seen clients shake their viejas' hands après sex. At first it struck me as incongruous, a "thank you, miss. You are *preciosa*." "Why, *muchas grácias, señor, muy amable*. We must meet again sometime." Certainly not how a man Stateside takes leave of a woman he just met in the biblical sense.

Only later did I understand these rituals in deeper context. The pantomimed "intimacy" of sex in the privacy of the working room was actually counteracted by the more formal public ritual of thanks and handshakes—especially since the handshake wasn't a pantomime. Each had it own compartment in Mexican society, and the gentleman who troubled to shake hands publicly was also conveying respect to the vieja. Dignity restored. Frankly, it was culto.

The girls appreciated it when it happened. So did Chang and the house—this was the kind of clientele the house most encouraged. The sort of gesture that was actually more real, more enduring, and of greater social value than the sex itself. Emotionally, client sex meant little to the girls. But the handshakes meant a lot.

Such clients, much like men wearing a tie in the States, got preferred tables, their drinks poured generously. The girls didn't hurry them if they became return guests. In Mexico when you give respect, you are almost always repaid in kind.

And Sunday was about respect in the Zona. To an outsider the viejas' ritual Sunday tea and brunch might seem surrealistic—a Mad Hatter's tea party borrowed directly from *Alice in Wonderland*.

But this was when the real girls appeared at the table. Just young women who still dreamed of being normal. Having a real life someday—of starting over again once the cash was in hand for a dowry: two hectares of farmland in Sinaloa, a new motor for dad's *panga* (fishing boat), a bedroom, a bathroom, technical school for a beloved younger brother, "an operation for my sister/mom/aunt, abuelo . . ."

The ones already lost in the illusions, addicted or alcoholic, were rarely invited. Sunday brunch was reserved only for those who could still see beyond the evil one's cage, whose souls were not yet lost. And its goals were respect, normalcy, and *mejorandose* (improving one's self).

I liked the girls best on Sunday. They were natural. No sexual tension. No "business." No makeup. No bullshit. Their stage personas left behind, most were pleasant. Easy to be around. Curious. Many times they asked me about the States. Had I been to Las Vegas (yes), seen Hollywood (no); did I know New York (yes, shot pool there in my glory days before a horse in Ecuador screwed up my stroking shoulder), Washington, D.C. (yes).

But mostly they asked about the mysteries of Stateside culture. Like Mariquita. "Do guys really marry in church girls who aren't virgins?"

"Yes, often."

"Do the girls wear white anyway?"

"Yes, unless they are divorced and it's a second marriage."

"Is it true that men don't keep *casas chicas* (little houses for their mistress)?"

"If they do," I answered, "it is guys who are so rich that no one ordinary knows them."

"Really, Davíd—not even someone like the mayor (*presidente*, in northern Mexico) of the town you are from?"

"No! Especially not a man like that, Mariquita. The voters would not approve."

"And there are powerful women," Francisca had butted in animatedly, "a woman actually owns one of the important newspapers. Don Francisco reads it to me sometimes (yes—the *Washington Post*). There are even women *médicos* and *profesoras* in the universities. Imagine, power based on education instead of sex! I used to wish I'd been born in the States, but a prima lives in Los Angeles and writes me that it is comfortable but very lonely."

La Negra took her turn. "...And here if one is not born well, it is one long *battalla* (battle). Too dark-skinned—no power. Poor parents, no way up unless you are beautiful and become some rich cabrón's mistress. Perhaps someone in film, *un actriz*, could be an exception. But here we have only '*la cama*' (the bed—meaning 'sex'—not a word actually used on Sunday) and *la Virgin* (patron saint, Guadalupe) from which to gain earthly and celestial power for our battallas."

Thus on Sundays after brunch and perhaps a nap, some of the girls, like La Blanca, slipped off to the nearby barrio for family evening. Sometimes the braver and darker Indian girls actually mingled with the crowd at a small chapel in el centro favored by Guaymas's Indian people (Yaqui, Mayo, Pima Baja, and a few Apache, Tarahumara, or Seri mixed bloods).

Many of the remaining girls went en masse to the tiny shrine of the Virgin on the hill above the Zona about 7 p.m. One of the gay guys had, I'm told, been an altar boy in his youth. He often presided over a makeshift version of Low Mass. There the girls floated in the strength and purity of the clean air and their faith.

Some, I would guess, prayed to be magically delivered into a "normal" world. A man, a baby or two. A neat, tiny house. Family nearby. A life where the pantomime was unnecessary.

Others may have simply prayed for no nasty surprises on clinic day—no cops, no *purgaciones* (clap), none of those frightening "Xs" on your blood report (syphilis—the number of Xs denoting the stage of it).

But most of all the girls wanted no hassles with the "*gente del centro.*" No humiliations. No nasty scenes. Downtown unnerved many of the girls. It was there where they too often had to face the fact that, though they were integral to Mexican

Typical downtown street scene. (Photo by Dan and Rachel Shaffer © 2004.)

society, they were still outcasts from major parts of it. Their "place" lay in the Zona, not on the plaza.

Their concerns about going downtown, or simply leaving the Zona, were the mirror image of the male's behavior on entering it—both defiant and exhilarating. But as in many dimensions of life, it was much more difficult for a woman to cross behavioral and social boundaries than for a man. A young man "sowing his wild oats" was simply not viewed as judgmentally as the woman receiving those oats. And at that time in Mexico the judgment "gap" was huge.

The girls going downtown risked much more than the guys coming from downtown. Rejection, nasty scenes, ejection from "family places," and the whispers were all bad enough. But *the* worst was being passed on the street by a regular client you'd laid more times than his wife, only to be *desconocida*—ignored. Denied. You didn't even exist!

This was the hardest part of a working girl's life. Most had been raised on flattery and male attention, Mexican social art forms of the time. The prettier they were, the more they got. The cold shoulder, the "sorry, have we met before?" on the street if they dared even nod or wink in passing was like an arrow through most girls' hearts. An emotional flogging.

The irony of it was that the taxistas could figure out just which businessman was screwing just which vieja by the fact that he so studiously ignored her on the street. The average guy with nothing to hide winked or smiled.

The working-class guys and bachelors weren't even subtle. They gaped, turned, made comments—even stopped in their tracks, lit cigarettes, and watched as firm young asses disappeared into the distance. Like tourists gaping at the *Mona Lisa* in the Louvre.

These risks gave me a role that I stepped into pretty much by accident. One Monday, I saw Mariquita downtown with several of the other girls post-clinic, pleading with Brigido to take the minibus down the malecón so they could "enjoy the sea." Not on Brigido's route. "Not wise. Too forward." The clinic the girls used was a modest one near the bus station—not the toniest part of town, and folks were always coming and going. Discreet.

I'd been at the bus station having a bowl of *menudo* (tripe soup) before I ran into them. Listening to the pleading, I asked Brigido if I could take several of the girls along the malecón in my Rambler. Once the offer was made, he had no choice. Squealing girls all over him, he relented so long as I promised to "bring them all back before five—and *no* group *paseos en el centro.*"

I agreed, asking if a walk in the sand around the peninsula near Las Playitas (The Beach) was okay. He nodded—"No one there during the week. *A las cinco*, Güero, or..."

Malecón south to Las Playitas. (Photo by Dan and Rachel Shaffer © 2004.)

Much preferring my arms in their sockets, I needed no further explanation. Mariquita and three friends piled into the car and I drove straight to the old part of the malecón, turned right, avoiding the Serdan and plaza, *rumbo a* (bound for) Las Playitas. In the process I passed the sitio at the bus station.

It probably only took about an hour for the news to make it to every sitio in greater Guaymas. El Güero—in his gray Rambler, headed for Las Playitas with four, count 'em, FOUR viejas including the luscious Mariquita. *¡Hijo de tú tal madre!* (Son of a gun!) Four viejas to the deserted beach! My stock skyrocketed as their imaginations ran free in the fields of lurid fantasy. Heck, I was just twenty-five—it didn't bother me at all.

At the narrow beach, treeless but shaded by a half dozen small *palapas* (palm-thatched lean-tos), the viejas flew out of the car, squealing, dashing headlong to the water and sand. Sandals

Shrimp boats near Monarch dry dock. (Photo by Dan and
Rachel Shaffer © 2004.)

tossed off, they waded in up to their knees, splashing, playing,
giggling, and throwing water on one another. Just girls, free for
an hour from social compartments, the Zona, even their dou-
bled-edged sexuality.

They collected shells, threw rocks into the water, and hunted
for sand crabs while I lounged alone under a palapa, smoked cigarettes, and studied the Guaymas skyline from across the bay.

Great rocky hills rose above the malecón. Pastel buildings,
dominated by the dome of city hall on the left and the whitewashed
towers of San Fernando in front, stood out in brilliant relief—
the usually harsh sunlight softened by the high row of hills to the
left, which separated downtown from the Zona and Miramar.

Guaymas. So gorgeous! The harbor dotted with large clus-
ters of their great shrimpers, high pilot-house windows glittering in the slanted rays of the afternoon sun. A half dozen

of the huge tub-shaped hulls were up on the long pontoons of the Astillero Monarca (the Monarch dry dock), their rust red and black hulls being repaired, rewelded, sleek and round like immense fat seals.

The whole scene was punctuated by the great buttes and jagged reddish cliffs that rose above the town, just five or six blocks from the water. Cerro Antiguo, Cerro Malakof, El Vigía.

So high was the ridge of El Vigía that the town once posted lookouts on its peak in the days of the great sailing barques. A signal fire told the town when sails were sighted. Dories rowed out to the small islands and sand spit guarding the outer harbor to pilot the great ships in.

Fresh water, oranges, and limes. Charcoal for the ship's galley. Ballast cut from Punta Lastre (Ballast Point) in front of the Hotel Rubi's far end once replaced part of the cargo as the ships left for places like San Diego, Acapulco, San Francisco, even Manila and Hong Kong.

Every now and again one of the fast norteamericano clippers from Salem, New York, New Bedford, or Boston was blown into the Sea of Cortez after rounding the Horn, bound for San Francisco. So timber, pitch, a dry dock, shipwrights, and blacksmiths were all available in Guaymas during the glory days of sailing.

Food, rope, fresh water, hand-forged nails, gunpowder, canvas, spare spruce yards . . . and, as always, beautiful women could be found in Guaymas. The vast majority were nice, gentle Catholic girls, so there had long been a Zona.

For generations men came to Guaymas from strange places, seeking supplies. Many found unexpected beauty, sometimes true love and a wife. And some stayed, adding to Guaymas in subtle but important ways.

I lounged under the palapa, savoring a Pall Mall, lost in such reveries until Mariquita approached me. She had gotten several Danskins from someplace—none of the girls knew where, but they speculated endlessly. Priceless among the viejas and considered the sexiest tops on the planet, they were virtually unobtainable.

Hers, a formfitting jet black, showed off her spectacular waist, hard butt, and rippled belly. Okay, for a moment I *was* still hopeful, but it was my "choices" she wanted to ask about. "Davíd, is it true that you are seeing a girl they call 'La Flaca'?"

"Yes, Mariquita—but it is still quite casual." She wasn't buying.

"Francisca says she is worried for you. She says you need to date someone smart and interesting."

"And why does Francisca worry about me so much?"

"Well, Davíd, I do not know that answer, but she speaks of you often. Your living on the beach drove her crazy." She paused, wanting to say something more, so I helped. "And La Flaca?"

She smiled. "She says that you are in love with her legs, not her." To soften the blow of a direct hit, Mariquita kissed me on the forehead. Her full lips lingering just a bit longer than necessary, she brushed my cheek with her hand, whispering, "Francisca has better legs than this Flaca."

183

Mariquita's message was simple. In translation it meant, "Don't take up with a vieja, *pendejo* (dumb ass)—but if you do, why not one of us?" Though a few of the girls in Francisca's inner circle might have been able to score a bull's-eye on my motives, assisted by "La Pancha," resident nurse and clinical psychologist— it was actually Francisca they didn't fully understand.

Francisca herself never came downtown, not even to the clinic. When she slipped away on Sunday evenings after brunch, it was always in one of those taxis from an Hermosillo sitio. Expensive. Discreet. Just like the big shots.

She likely went to the clinic in Hermosillo, if she went at all. Sometimes she'd be gone from Sunday before 7 p.m., when the girls went to the Shrine of the Virgin, through the evening hours of Wednesday, just making it back for the mid-week floor show at midnight after rushing in from an Hermosillo taxi to change. The girls speculated that don Francisco kept a small love nest in Hermosillo. But I knew something they didn't.

The big Aeromex jet from Hermosillo to Mexico City left Sunday evenings about 9 p.m., returning Wednesday evenings about the same time. Just as Francisca fancied that she understood me, I fancied that I understood her.

Those trips, I reckoned, were about money and power. Her political connections. Her bank account. Perhaps even a lover in government. A real big shot, a national league *cabeza grande*. She had the looks and education for it. Francisca, I believe, really may have had a passing crush on me—but I had neither the money nor the power she needed every bit as badly as a junkie needs heroin.

Since fate and her own addictions to *plata* (silver/money) *y palanca* (political juice) had precluded a relationship with me, I guessed, she intended that none of the other girls should get me either. Every time Mariquita or others, like Indita, showed interest, even curiosity, she warned them off. No matter; she was one hell of a woman. Beautiful, classy, sophisticated, funny, and oh so complicated.

But many of the other girls were surprising too. Appearing to be hard-core viejas on Saturday nights, when they were all "*Vogue'd* out"—their sex-machine, man-killer roles honed to a wicked edge. Then on Sundays and Mondays, a surprising percentage restored themselves weekly, if only temporarily, into the ordinary twenty-something girls they were at heart.

The devil only got those unfortunates who were stuck in their character roles, rather like young ingenues in Hollywood.

I was still glowing—in the manly, erotic sense of it—from Mariquita's lips when the other girls gathered to ask the time. Four thirty-five. Brigido! Five o'clock! "Oh, God, gather everything up and take us back to the Zona. Pronto, Davíd!"

I grabbed one last look at the exquisite harbor as they threw shells, starfish, sandals, handbags, everything back into the Rambler, acting like Stateside college freshmen sweating curfew.

We made the porch of the Río Rita just about one minute after five. In Mexico, this is on time. The girls piled out, dashed up the steps, still giggling and laughing.

Brigido waited at the door, like the Grim Reaper. They darted past him, scattering sand, shells, and smiles, their huge handbags bouncing. Very un-Brigido–like, he stepped out on the porch and actually grinned at me, closing his thumb and index finger in the "okay" sign. For Brigido, the grin and "okay" were equivalent to a major breakthrough in psychotherapy.

This was the first of many trips. Some of which had seriously pissed off both Lupita and Marta at the time. But I enjoyed them. I'd have never known about "Dad's outboard motor," "my little brother's *técnico* (technical school), "my mom's kitchen" without these paseos. And I'd never have met Indita, the epitome of a girl who didn't belong there . . .

And I'd never have understood that some of the girls were still whole, cute, largely normal, while others were already swirling endlessly into the cone of the vortex, slowly being sucked ever deeper to its narrow bottom—a primordial portal to oblivion. The dark, silent sleeping quarters of endless nothingness. That horrifying domain of all things hollow and empty.

No wonder so many of the girls, like Indita, made the weekly climb to the Shrine of the Virgin. Perhaps that's why they also harped endlessly on the theme of "Davíd, marry a nice girl!"

chapter fourteen

QUINCEAÑERA

And I did have one real, but fleeting chance at a "nice" girl in Guaymas. It was unexpected and came late in the summer of 1970, only a few days before I returned to the States on short notice to continue my graduate studies.

I was killing time at the Río Rita after Lupita's death. A quiet evening alone. Lost in my shock and grief, I suppose. Chang picked up on my funk immediately. "Davíd, what you need is a party. That is what you need. Sunday a compadre and I are hosting a fiesta, a *Quinceañera* (a traditional coming-out party at age fifteen) for several of the girls in our family. Would you come, please, as my guest?"

So compartmentalized was Guaymas that I still knew nothing of Chang's family. Though I gave him rides from the Zona several times a week, I didn't even know his home address. When I dropped him off, it was always at the Almita or on a corner several blocks away.

This was typical of Mexico and of Guaymas, where life on the street was one discrete domain and life at home another. Public versus private social compartments. I was flattered at the invitation and intrigued, so I accepted.

That Sunday afternoon in early September of 1970 I met Chang, his wife, a son, and a daughter at their home in the old San Vicente neighborhood not far from the downtown. On a wide street just past the terminus of a never-finished pavement project only four blocks south of the Serdan, his house was in the middle of the block.

They were waiting at the door for me, about three in the afternoon, so I only saw the front room. It was pleasant but ordinary. Tile floor, the big couch. Dining table at one end of the room. Pale yellow walls, black-and-white-tile floor. High ceilings, typical of the older houses. Everything neat and spotlessly clean.

Though hot as blazes in August, I was attired in my dress outfit—dark slacks, white guayabera, my blue handkerchief rolled under its collar. I had a fresh haircut, trimmed mustache, and polished black dress shoes, inherited from my dad, then dead three years.

A Quinceañera is a big deal in Mexico: a lot of dancing, some drinking, a lot of food—always a good time. After formal introductions and handshakes (his wife, son, and daughter), we walked to the party from Chang's house.

Strolling down the forty-foot-wide street, we passed rows of brightly painted houses, mostly greens and yellows, both poor man's colors. The more prosperous homes included creams, pinks, and even salmon. Those colors cost more than green and yellow at the local hardware stores. Many of the houses were multicolored: green on the bottom, cream on top—turquoise on the bottom, cream on top.

Most of the houses in this district were massive thick-walled adobe and stucco, domed windows with bars and shutters, flat roofs, and fitted with huge wooden doors to the streets, which were seldom open. Most had interior courtyards. Some of the

Typical neighborhood in old downtown area. Note mix of architectural styles. (Photo by Dan and Rachel Shaffer © 2004.)

large, older houses had been broken up into small bakeries (*panaderías*), tailor shops, and *tintorerías* (laundry shops). There were many neatly hand-painted signs on these houses, where front rooms had been converted into family businesses while the rear rooms and courtyards were still used as living quarters.

It was interesting and lively. A blazing hot day in September, the afternoon shadows were already lengthening as fall approached. Still, there was a rippling, hazy glow to the air, and Guaymas was temporarily dry again after having survived part of the hurricane season, with more to come. The unpaved side streets were dusty but already heavily rutted from recent rains.

As we strolled along, Chang chattering as was normal, I wondered if his family actually knew where he worked and what he did. The Río Rita was a very famous nightclub, and even though in the Zona, I simply could not make myself fully believe

Typical café built into an older residential district. (Photo by Dan and Rachel Shaffer © 2004.)

that its veil of secrecy was opaque enough to hide "Dad's" occupation from the family.

Chang had asked me to help him and his son carry cases of rum. I was soaked in sweat after only ten minutes. His daughter, Barbara, reached over and mopped my brow. Nice! She was quite pretty, dressed up in a very splashy, bright party dress. A dark-skinned girl and slender but surprisingly tall, she looked much more Mexican than did Chang himself. Still, those diluted Oriental genes had added hints of the exotic to her face. She was about eighteen, I guessed, sweet and bubbly like her dad.

We made our way down the street four or five blocks through the barrio, laughing and sweating. Folks stared. The gringo tourists almost never made it down into this district. I had no trouble at all telling when we were arriving at the house where the fiesta was in the final planning stages.

The organizers overflowed into the street. First Chang introduced me to his compadre, who managed a bar of his own—like taxistas, the club men stuck together. He had an immense, old-fashioned house that, like Gorda's, had probably been built by a prosperous merchant at the end of the 1800s. It was no longer elegant, but as the barrio went, it was a very impressive edifice. One entered through a tall pair of heavy, wooden-domed Spanish-style doors, a long step up from the street.

The sidewalk in front of the house ran along only one side of the block. Raised up about two feet out of the street, it appeared to be nonregulation—a handmade brick-and-concrete walkway, it had likely been built as a project by the householders on that block, using their own labor and local materials. This is how many of the things got done in Guaymas's older neighborhoods during the 1960s and 1970s. A number of '50s vintage cars were parked along the street, taxis coming and going. This was the gathering hour for the fiesta.

Loud ranchero music was already pulsing out into the street, several pairs of teenyboppers dancing among the taxis, lost in their own self-centered world. Free music. "¡Qué honda! (Cool vibes!)"

Obviously the traditional live mariachi band had not yet arrived. That would come later in the evening after food, introductions, handshakes by the hundreds, and short, formal speeches introducing each fifteen-year-old girl being presented, along with her family and padrinos. For the moment all was still casual, breezy, a bit chaotic. Typical. So typical.

As we entered the front room and ditched the rum, we passed along an impromptu "food bar" formed by a long row of tables, lined up for the day. A half dozen women were already frantically setting out huge, steaming pots of tamales and immense *ollas* (large serving jars) of beans and Spanish rice.

Stacks of tortillas were arriving in towel-covered baskets, still fresh and hot, from a small, neighborhood tortilla "factory" just several blocks away. Every neighborhood had its own local *tor-tillería* in those days. Most are now long gone, now replaced by *supermercados*—some actually owned by subsidiaries of Wal-Mart and Kmart. Old family businesses now destroyed by the internationals, just like contemporary main streets all over the States.

The first room we passed through was perhaps eighteen feet wide and twenty-five feet long. This was the great, high-ceilinged "*sala grande*" (the traditional public room) equivalent to a Victorian parlor. Impressive towers of soda pop were stacked high against one wall in their old-fashioned wooden cases. All of the sala's ordinary furniture had apparently been moved out for the occasion.

Past the temporary row of serving tables a wide, glass-paned door on the far wall opened into a large interior courtyard. Next to the courtyard door a pair of tables held the plates and utensils one needed before moving to the food line. For fiesta day, the old formal sala grande had become the reception hall and serving area.

A courtyard fanatic, I asked if I could duck outside and take a look. "*Está en su casa, señor.* (Make yourself at home.)" It was lovely, porticoed all around. Several large trees shaded it—a lime, an orange, a mango, plus several smallish palms. Cascades of pink buganvilla framed a small, tiled fountain/well (long dry). Large pots of bright flowers and herbs were scattered everywhere along the portico.

In one shadowed corner I spotted a large stack of folding burlap cots. Families fortunate enough to own an entire colonial-style house, including the courtyard, slept there during Sonora's sizzling hot summer months. At night poorer folks simply pulled their cots outside onto the sidewalks.

When I stepped inside again, the owner asked if the courtyard was to my liking. It was, I commented, adding that I dreamed of owning a house such as his one day. Pleased, he gave me a tour!

192

Adjacent to the sala there was an impressively long room that fronted the street as it rambled down the block. It was no wider but was at least forty feet in length and probably created from two or three smaller rooms, the inner walls long since removed.

As with the front room, all its regular furniture had been stripped from it except several of the huge old armoires (*roperos*) that functioned as closets and consumed three of its corners. The remaining wall space had been lined with chairs. Some were wooden folding chairs much like ones used in Stateside churches fifty years ago.

I assumed that some of these had been rented or borrowed. In older Mexican neighborhoods, a local association, or "*cofradía*," often owned communal furniture for use at such occasions. If you were a member, you paid a small monthly subscription over the years. If not, you rented from them.

Beyond that room was a third one, the premium one, at the very corner of the block. It had a huge window, a lovely rounded glass transom above it, which faced the side street and another facing the front (south). Both windows were seven or eight feet tall and barred.

The immense iron-barred windows flung wide open for the fiesta, floor fans drove a warm, steady breeze down the long row of rooms. I guessed correctly that this was the owner's own suite. It was like Gorda's, only larger, lovelier, and meticulously maintained. No makeshift kitchen area, of course, but one huge ropero remained.

Tour over, the private rear rooms along the courtyard not visited, we returned to the front room, where the crowd was already both swelling and sweltering. More fans arrived minutes later, driven by electricity carried from the house next door by long, spindly extension cords.

There was a remarkable assortment of people. Very prosperous-looking folks mixed with others of more ordinary means, judging by both dress and skin complexion. There were even a few other mixed Orientals, both Chinese and Japanese, I assumed.

But only two of Chang's "working" acquaintances from the red-light district were present. Old Felipe L., the most senior waiter, a dignified old gent, and the sedate *corbata* (tie)-wearing accountant who labored on the books on Mondays when the girls were at clinic. Both, I guessed, from the style of greetings, were actually compadres of someone or another in Chang's extended family.

So few familiar faces was an important clue, in my mind, that Chang's private life was much removed from his professional one. Still, there were two or three hundred people at the gathering by 4 p.m. or so. Even if Chang's professional "colleagues" were a bit exotic, it certainly hadn't put a dent in his immense public network of family and *socios* (colleagues, friends).

There was an obvious compartmentalization of people by age grade. The first room, where the women were serving food, was heavily dominated by the older matrons and widows, the ones you called *doña*. Lined up in chairs along the patio-side wall, they surveyed everything, keeping an eye on everyone. A stoic, formidable black-clad phalanx of chaperones, they served as enforcers of "the code." Looking suspiciously like crows lined up on a Kansas fence row, several even cawed if a passing *chica's* (girl's) skirt was too tight or too short.

Frankly, they scared the bejeebers out of nearly every single guy in the place, me included. Apparently they enjoyed both their power and the frisson of fear they created when cawing.

The largest, center room was where the dancing got going. The younger folks were drawn to it like a magnet. With music and no row of crowlike chaperones, many dresses underwent quick, furtive shortening after safely passing the phalanx.

The "girls" (ages thirteen to twenty-three) were primarily on the street side, the "boys" (eighteen to twenty-eight) primarily seated in the row of chairs on the courtyard side. There were some

194

young engaged or married couples, but singles ruled. The children were everywhere, uncontainable and running free from room to room in dresses or dark pants—like frenetic adults in miniature.

The posh rear corner room at the end of the house was where the older men gathered, talking, smoking, swearing, and drinking *"fuerte"* (real booze). Clearly the phalanx of widows scared them too.

Most of the liquor was served in the form of Cuba Libras, rum and Coke with lime—ubiquitous, traditional, and heavy on the Coke. There was also a pineapple *ponche* (punch), lightly spiked, probably with a quarter-liter bottle of cane alcohol (*aguardiente*) in a mix of about five gallons. Probably about 3 or 4 percent alcohol, it had about the same kick as West Virginia 3.2 beer. It was served in an immense, ornate, beautiful blue Talavera bowl positioned in the front room right under the watchful eyes of the black-clad matrons. This punch was considered appropriate for the mature women and younger, unmarried males.

195

There were also *"refrescos,"* now called *jugos* (juices), of two kinds. Mango, blended to create a homemade fruit drink, filled huge, lidded glass jugs that looked like immense pickle jars. Long metal dippers inserted in the jars, the matrons carefully dipped out paper cupfuls for the kids, who nearly always tried to fish out the surviving chunks of mango with their fingers! It was sweet, gooey, and made a huge mess—everything kids love!

After one punch I switched to the mango. The "crows" kept a mental tally, talking cattily about just who had drunk *cinco* (five) ponches at someone's spring Quinceañera. One had the impression that they remembered each overimbiber's tally forever. Forever undoubtedly meant at least twenty years after the overindulgent were already dead.

The other refresco's featured flavor was strawberry. Huge quantities of ice and lumpy fruit juice kept the jars full. In the background a blender (*One of the ones Lupita and I had brought to town before she died?* I wondered.) whirred full-time, trying to keep up with the crowd's thirst. By about 5 p.m. every kid in the place was happily and indelibly splotched with the orange-yellow stains from mango or shocking pink strawberry.

One large sideboard in the front room was beautifully decorated with a local floral centerpiece. Though flowers were cheap in Guaymas, the centerpiece would have been considered Waldorf-Astoria quality Stateside. The fresh lace tablecloths under the massive centerpiece were likely gifts from the various and sundry compadres in the Quinceañera courts.

The "court" of padrinos and madrinas (usually two or three pairs) each girl had chosen were obligated to make gifts and share in the fiesta's cost—gowns, the band, food, punch.

Those obligations would later be repaid at another Quinceañera months or even years hence. Others, usually friends of the parents, donated or brought the stacked cases of soda pop. Others had chipped into bring a few cases of beer for the men. As noted, Chang brought rum, Oso Negro (Black Bear) brand.

Most of the Tecate brand beer was in the back room, where the older, early arrivals among the men were drinking beers and Cuba Libras. Though laid out for display, food was not yet actually being served in the front room when we arrived.

At approximately five o'clock in the afternoon, after we'd already been there a while and the last, frantic preparations had come together, the formal ritual of the Quinceañera began.

First Chang's compadre, who was hosting the event, made a short introductory welcome. Then Chang spoke, thanking important compadres and padrinos of the event, including close neighbors. Several slightly younger men followed, compadres of the girls who were coming out, (there were three of them), who announced that this was in honor of señorita so-and-so who, at fifteen, was now a woman and therefore being presented to Guaymas and Colonia San Vicente.

Chang's compadre then reemphasized that people were to make themselves at home, that there would be the presentation of the young women, the formal dance, then dinner and casual dancing later on.

Then the young women were brought in one by one, their father on one arm—their *nino* (padrino) on the other. If a father or padrino were deceased, other male relatives, uncles, older brothers, even older cousins, vied for the honor. Like raising aloft a freshly baptized child to the crowd on the steps of San Fernando, this was a once-in-a-lifetime ritual. A milestone never to be forgotten. Such roles were coveted.

Girls raised in extended family networks powerful enough to put on Quinceañeras, even if the financial obligations had to be spread among twenty married couples, fully apprehended their good fortune. In the crowd that day were dozens of poorer girls who would have only a cake, a small family dinner, and perhaps a locket or new shoes as gifts when they came of age. A big Quinceañera drew suitors, announcing that the young lady had family, possibilities, and horsepower to offer.

197

The girls paraded out into the center of the large "dance" room, each accompanied by father, godfather, and their "court" of four (two male, two females) padrinos, chosen for the occasion. The three girls were lovely but not ostentatious in matching white gowns. That made sense if one assumed these would become bridesmaids' gowns in the next several years.

Chang was godfather to one of the señoritas, his compadre godfather to another, and there was a third godfather, also a member of the extended Chang clan. The three girls were very cute but just fifteen. They seemed like babies to me.

But perhaps my sense of contrast was enhanced by too much time ill-spent in the Zona. And these señoritas were so excited! Understandable. This was the first time in their lives when they were openly allowed to socialize and accept the attention of boyfriends, go on "dates." Imagine—"I can now meet a friend on the plaza Sunday afternoon. Have coffee!" Big-girl stuff.

In Mexico, girls dream about these parties and plan for them years in advance. They are a big deal. In old Mexican society, especially before the 1960s, girls were considered marriageable at this age. From age fifteen on, it was open season in Mexico's elaborate mating rituals. Subsequently the age of marriage has tended to creep up.

Most girls now get married when they are between eighteen and twenty-two or twenty-three. Still, many in Mexico marry not long after their Quinceañera. Early marriage in Guaymas is most common among the girls from the poorest families. Then and now.

The introductions were elaborate—everyone's full names were formally announced: girls, parents, and padrinos. The hired announcer, microphone in hand, speaker box on the floor, managed the rhythm as the groups circled the room and names were announced.

All of the girls had their hair done similarly, matching white flowers woven into their lush, dark French rolls. All three of them sported new gold jewelry. Traditionally the different godparents give each a piece of jewelry. Usually the jewelry was on the order of a gold necklace with pearl or a chaste old-fashioned cross, even a pendant fashioned from a family heirloom coin, often an old gold peso passed down through two or three generations.

Then the girls danced. As in many parts of the world, the first dance was with Dad, then Godfather, and finally the younger male "padrinos del corte." The dancing partners were announced again—everyone having two last names. One last name for Dad (in my case Stuart, the other for Mom—in my case her maiden name, Densmore).

The ritual dance completed, all of the older participating couples danced one round, a waltz in those days. Then the host and announcer invited guests to eat. That created pandemonium as the lines slowly worked past the rice, beans, tamales, tostadas, and tortillas.

The men dressed typically in dark slacks, black or brown polished shoes, dark socks, white shirt open at the neck or a guayabera, ubiquitous blue handkerchiefs folded under their collars. Several of the really old abuelos wore wide ties, vests, and gold watches, marking their rank as deans of the colonia.

Men in their sixties and seventies gloried in their survival, which made them men of distinction in working-class San Vicente. Men in their eighties, the true *ancianos*, were outright legends. Even the black-clad widows paid them elaborate respect. Those gold watches, inherited from fathers and grandfathers, connected them to Mexico's past—the revolution. The Indian wars. Their ancestors, now in the municipal graveyard, not gone but merely *reposando* (resting) until the family visited them again on the next Day of the Dead.

One old boy wore his Croix de Guerre as the fob to an immense gold watch. Unorthodox, but he had actually fought with the French in the Great War. His ancestry was mixed French and Mexican. Another old geezer wore insignia from Pancho Villa's Division del Norte, which had taken Mexico City in the winter of 1917 during Mexico's revolution. Heroes right in front of me at a Quinceañera in San Vicente!

There were also guys in Guaymas who had fought in World War II in U.S. units, their families still divided by the border. Over the years in Guaymas, I saw Bronze Stars and Purple Hearts won at places like Guadalcanal and Anzio. Growing up in the States, I'd never heard about any of this, so it fascinated me.

This being San Vicente, the large and more ordinary crowd tended toward dark-skinned and working class. There were few upper-class blondes or brunettes. And girls were dressed in every color imaginable—shocking electric blues, pinks, lavenders, purples, yellows, and limes. Most of the single "women" there ranged in age from fifteen to twenty-two or twenty-three. I found it colorful and lively. A temporary antidote to losing Lupita and the depression that followed.

I lined up with the others wedged into the line as I passed the long serving tables staffed by the mature women. I was handed a very pretty pink china plate, real bone china and probably someone's prized possession. A foreign guest, you know! So I was very careful of that dish as I ate. The little kids got paper plates. Not cheap. But replaceable.

The pork tamales were simply wonderful! Cooked in corn husks fresh from the big steam canisters, they were stuffed with pork in an amazing red chile sauce made exotic by hints of spices I couldn't even describe. I also went for the mashed black beans sprinkled with a white goat cheese and sopa seca de arroz.

There were also trays of tacos and enchiladas. It was quite a feed. Once through the line, I stuffed myself, then circulated a bit, hand out for the shake ritual. I said *"hola"* or *"buenas tardes"* to all kinds of people I'd never even met before. So pleasant. So lively and *so* gracious. I almost felt like my old self again.

As everyone ate, the single men eyed the single women and vice versa. The mating ritual and dance to come was on many young minds. Heck, that ritual is the essence of a Quinceañera.

I was "with" Chang's daughter, Barbara, who was tall, gangly, and a little shy. To my surprise, Chang didn't seem to mind. Perhaps that was because I'd already accepted a Sunday brunch with the viejas and could no longer buy a piece of tail in the Zona, no matter how hard I might try.

Barbara wasn't a formal date, but she stuck to me like glue. She wore a splashy blue dress and had nice eyes and a big, gentle smile. She also had long, skinny legs, the kind that they call *popotes* (straws) in Mexico. She was a sweet kid. And compared to the girls in Dad's "club," she *was* still a kid—in the midst of that dreamy, clumsy, slightly goofy transformation that plagues girls as they become women.

After an hour or so of eating, talking, and visiting with the folks Chang or Barbara introduced me to, I noticed that a number of people stared at me, especially the kids. Gringos weren't common in Guaymas's working-class neighborhoods and they were certainly rare at a party like this. I spoke halfway decent Spanish and was appropriately attired but obviously a gringo. Though tanned, I was still the lightest-skinned man in the place, though darker than the lightest-skinned woman.

I saw a number of people that I thought I recognized from the street in Guaymas. But most were uncertain who I might be, especially since I wasn't wearing the signature Red Wing boots and tan field shirt. I had likely seen many of these people simply while going about my business because I used to walk all over town.

Noticing, Chang saw to it that I was formally introduced to a number of the more important guests by my correct name, Señor Davíd Stuart. Chang was careful to introduce me as a North American and a fellow with his master's degree, "*maestro en la antropología*." At a guess, I reckoned that nearly everyone to whom he announced that profession had no clear idea at all what anthropology was. But they did understand that I had a master's degree from a North American university, which was a big deal in that era.

Virtually everyone in Guaymas was familiar with the University of Arizona, and all were proud of their own state university in Hermosillo. Most in that crowd might never have been on either campus, but some hoped one of their sons might get there one day.

I didn't yet have my doctorate, but a master's degree from a university in the States was considered the real thing. The real McCoy. That wasn't the context in which most people in town knew me, but on this, a very formal occasion, all such formalities were adhered to. I discovered that some there were also university educated, the title *licenciado* denoting that.

About six-thirty a norteño band showed up, done up in modified mariachi style, and the dinner line ebbed. The fancy china was taken out to the courtyard to be washed and put away before the liquor flowed too freely. Again the owner of the house, a good-looking fiftyish gent with streaked silver hair, and Chang, both rotund and resplendent in his best embroidered guayabera, stopped the action for another brief round of public introductions before the party flowed on, taking its own direction.

The girls were reintroduced with the explicit wish that they be well received into Guaymas society, etc. The compadres and the comadres took another bow. This second round of introductions over, a round of applause erupted from the several hundred packed into the house. The band introduced itself while photographs of the girls, family, and "courts" were taken.

Since the Quinceañera was nearly as important as a wedding, a photographer had been brought in. He worked a vintage, large-format portrait camera, the kind where the photographer ducks under a hood. It was an ancient, modified Linhof. Now probably worth a fortune, it used old-fashioned glass plates. Those monsters took spectacular pictures.

The small photographic shops in Guaymas often used seventy-year-old equipment but did stunning work. Your average tradesmen and craftsmen in Mexico were not to be sneered at. Their level of technical competence and skill was amazing. I saw photographs of this event a year later, prints from those glass plates done in sepia tones, probably with a hand-mixed chemical process handed down in the family. All done in some back room only a few blocks away.

Photos taken, the band hit it. Party time! A fast *paso doble* to get things moving. And palpable suspense as each señorita chose the first partner of her womanhood. Critical choices, weeks in the making, this was the first time in their lives they were allowed to choose.

And such a choice, if the fellow was interested, could lead to a date on the plaza, other dances, someday even a child raised to the crowd on the steps of San Fernando. The only unspoken rule was that the guy couldn't already be known to be "attached." No stealing a friend's declared beau!

The old women in black crowded the wide doorway, anticipating outcomes. Cawing among themselves and over the possibilities, their visions of grandchildren or great-grandchildren to accompany them to Mass already forming.

Each of the three young señoritas chose her partner and started to dance. Some "oohs" and "aahs" rippled through that threatening gaggle of black dresses and stout shoes. Young men on the single guys' side of the room reacted too. Some were happy for their best buddy who had so badly wanted to be asked. Several others slipped out, grim-faced and rejected but officially unnoticed. The humiliation thing.

Soon nearly everyone under thirty was dancing, the mating ritual in full motion. Now a few of the older men joined the old women draped in black, all staring intently at the dancing pairs crammed wall to wall. Some are just born to be chaperones. I danced with Barbara. A good dancer. As gangly and as awkward as she seemed off the dance floor, she was smooth and graceful on it. I had a good time.

After several more tunes, the music livened up for the younger folks. Got to make certain they head home dead tired, you know. The live band mixed loud paso dobles with *cumbias*.

The cumbias were my favorite thing at the time and young Barbara loved their beat. Her captivating smile never vanished for the next hour and a half. Now nearing dusk, the character of the fiesta began to change.

The live band packed up about eight-thirty, replaced by a record player and speaker box. The announcer took over again as stacks of records came out. Many of the young married couples and some of the old men and widows took this opportunity to shake hands, thank the hosts, and give formal goodbyes. Designated nieces and granddaughters staffed the street door waving goodbye, even walking several of the old ladies home, half a block away.

A new round of food was set out, the ponche stiffened with extra aguardiente, and the record player's volume doubled. Take off the ties, fellas! Time to do some real drinking, dancing, and get outrageous.

Etiquette dictated that if a woman was alone, which meant merely seated or standing by herself—no babe in arms—it was perfectly legitimate to ask her for one dance. The dance over, you then escorted her back to the chair or the place where you met her. You were almost never refused one dance. A refusal might humiliate. Not done!

If by chance you stumbled onto a young woman unattended but whose husband/fiancé had just stepped into the back room for a Cuba Libre—you were never turned down unkindly. The response would be something like, "Oh, I'm honored, señor, but my husband said he would be right back to dance. Forgive me!" Gracious. No Stateside-style cold shoulder crap in working-class Mexico.

Barbara even handed me off several times to her curious girlfriends. I was likely a novelty of sorts, just as I was to the viejas. It also sent a clear but oblique message to the assembled that the two of us were not an "item." I had a good time, forgetting about little Lupita for a few hours.

After dancing myself tired, I floated back to the front room to smoke and chat with some of the adults. Partly because Chang was there, I chatted casually with quite a variety of guests. A number asked where I was from, what I was doing in Guaymas. People were friendly, outgoing, having a good time and courteously curious.

That's when I first focused on a girl who seemed to be working hard at catching my eye. The viejas had hounded me endlessly to establish a "proper" relationship with a marriageable young woman. They didn't reinforce my eccentric, on-again, off-again relationship with Marta. She simply did not meet their minimum standards for the rehab project they had designed for me.

By the time of this Quinceañera my sexual relationship with Marta had gone south—well, "soft" (*gacho*, in local parlance), to be more direct. That happened after Lupita died.

I had dated "nice" girls in Mexico over the years. But those relationships either didn't blossom or wound up in dead ends. In short, everything was normal—I was lonely again. Acutely so, with Lupita gone.

Now this young woman was making herself obvious. For at least an hour she had been everywhere I was in the big dance room.

I didn't know her name and didn't ask. But as I stood and talked with Chang and the married folks in the front room about ten feet from the doorway to the dance area, she was constantly in my view, even if she had to dance alone. Not common. Quite obvious.

A striking girl, perhaps twenty, she had very unusual light, pearly skin, which glowed as if it were opal. She also had the most remarkable chestnut brown hair with reddish highlights that I'd ever seen. That luxurious chestnut mane cascaded halfway to her tiny waist. It glistened with sienna highlights—perfectly matching the irregular, reddish flecks of color in her irises. She had huge, medium brown eyes. A long, delicate face punctuated by stunning eyes, she was slender and graceful. Everything about her struck me as intensely alive.

And I so needed to quit thinking about death—little Lupita stiff and clammy, her fingers still curled as they had nailed shut her handmade coffin. The images of her death so fresh. So sur-real. Such a contrast to this pearly-skinned young woman.

I was disconcerted. Part of me badly wanted someone nice. A woman I could laugh with, dance with, be with—for the long haul. The other part of me simply wanted Lupita back. Kid or not, Lupita had shown me the best time I'd ever had.

Cautious, I watched the mystery girl furtively. She didn't wear jewelry, and her clothes were modest. It didn't matter. She was naturally luminous, emitting a jewel-like radiance. I wanted to ask her to dance. But I didn't. Only a week before, I'd left all my inner courage, splattered like mud, on Lupita's sodden grave.

As the party rolled on, the chestnut hair and opal skin came and went a number of times. But I didn't even have the balls to ask anyone who she was. Then came the moment that is frozen in time. As clear now as when it happened, I had turned to fol-low Barbara, who beckoned me to come dance another cumbia....

As I crossed the threshold onto the dance floor, the girl with opal skin came straight toward the wide doorway and stopped—right in front of me! She actually blocked my path, as had Indita. I held my breath and watched her move toward *me*. Bold. Deliberate. Brazen. And I was helpless—absolutely riveted to the spot, as if everything had gone into slow motion.

Was everyone in the place watching? Perhaps. A momentary hush surrounded us as she looked straight up into my eyes and smiled. She was so close! Just eighteen inches away. For thirty seconds we looked into each other's eyes. And for that time we were utterly alone together. The flecks of red fire in her eyes seemed to reach out, offering me my secret dream. Her pupils dilated, like obsidian discs. She *wanted* me.

Even compared to Indita's soul scanning, this was the most intense look I'd ever experienced. In my most secret dreams a woman I could never quite picture looked at me just like this, her eyes glit-tering until we became one and I awakened, full of yearning.

I was lonely. I should have asked her to dance, but I did nothing. Said nothing. I was speechless. Frozen. Is this what death is like? Passion? If passion, it was far more powerful than I had ever imagined....

I sensed that I could have simply smiled, asked her to have my child and run away with me. Then. There. Had I done so, I believe she would have taken my arm and walked me out the door in front of everyone, never looking back.

Motionless except for the fire dancing in her eyes, she stood waiting. The stuff of dreams. A scene straight from Shakespeare—the kind of intensity that one reads about in literature, wondering if it could be real. My one chance, I feared. Was this the "you will be loved" that Indita, God rest her kind soul, had foretold just several months before?

I should have done something. Said anything. Even a wiseass, "Señorita, how shall we name our first child?" could have worked. Instead I merely flinched and looked down at my shoes. Like an ass-kicked puppy. Her smile faded. Still, she continued to stare. It was my last chance. Now was the moment. Or never—

Throughout history men have thrown away their lives, their marriages, gone to war, even murdered friends for one such moment, and this might be mine.

Raw, elemental electric passion...and I stood on the very threshold of it. I had but to step forward into the crackling current of her desire and bask in its voltage.

Instead speechless, I merely stood there, riveted to the spot. Once again the lonely kid in an empty school yard. The child once locked away in a dark basement. Unable to do anything right.

I both hoped and feared with equal desperation! Equal and opposing forces. My soul in the middle—motionless, like my body. It was as if basic physics also applied to countervailing forces of the human condition, thus nothing moved.

Within a minute it no longer mattered. She disappeared into the crowd, then—according to Chang—slipped out the door and into the night as I continued to stand there, still in a trance.

To retrieve the situation, Barbara called me in to dance. I went but was distracted, still mesmerized by those flecks of red fire in an unknown lover's eyes.

We stayed, dancing for about another half an hour. Then Barbara asked me to escort her home. We walked back to Chang's house, one of the family kids chaperoning. Appearances, you know. Chang stayed on. Obligations as cohost. About quarter to ten at night I deposited Barbara at her door, shook her hand, and thanked her for her company. Then walked all the way back to the Hotel Rubi. Alone. Alone.

It was a long night. I rocked on the upstairs balcony, turning a big wooden rocker to face the malecón, and watched the shrimp boats bob on the harbor's undulating, light-streaked water. I looked over at the roof of the shrimp-packing plant, inhaling its distinctive smells mixed with the smell of salt air, and took long pulls on a bottle of tequila.

Lupita dead but still quite alive in the private part of me that was in denial, I asked her opinion of the girl with chestnut hair and the glowing red coals in her eyes. Though only another illusion, Lupita leaned against the balcony railing. Wiggled her toes, her rubber flip-flops tossed casually onto the concrete floor.

She spoke to me often after she died but could not hear my responses. That night in September of 1970 was no different. "Güero, you must overcome your fear of love—you did not even ask her name!"

"Can you get it for me, Lupita?" No response.

Then, after shrugging casually, she continued, "I'd rather share you with this one than La Marta—I still do not care for 'La Flaca.' Too angry. Marta needs you, Davíd, but does not love you.... Did you ask the new one if you and I could still be together? Will she accept me? I am still your employee, you know. We have business! It's time to go to la frontera again."

"You are dead, Lupita—why would I ask the one with chestnut hair about you now?" No response, but she shot me one of her dreamy grins. "La Flaca will be *bien molestada* (pissed off)—sitting downstairs on a Sunday night while you are up here *chupando tequila conmigo* (chugging tequila with me)." Lupita faded away, still grinning, as I rushed downstairs to see if Marta was waiting.

Marta usually came about 11 p.m. and it was already midnight when I stepped into my room. There was a note under the door. A chaotic message in mangled Spanish, it was hard to read. Judging from the empty half liter bottle of Castillo rum on my nightstand and the sprawling script, she'd been drinking heavily again.

But the message itself was clear enough. "Did you enjoy the fiesta, cabrón?"

Well, at least she wasn't actually in my room, swaying back and forth, cursing me, the jug of rum gripped tight in one angry fist. The tragedy was that she had let her guard down, trying to comfort me after Lupita's funeral. That's when I truly saw her as she was, unraveling the relationship.

I didn't sleep well that night. Turbulent dream fragments. I wanted Lupita. No, I wanted the girl with chestnut hair! I missed Indita. Shit, at one point I even missed my grandfather, John, dead fifteen years. The only threads that wove these together were the deep sense of loss and my inability to speak. Each vision spoke to me. But I was a mute. Isolated by my own silence. Lonely. Remote. Imprisoned behind the gray veil again...

A few days later I left Guaymas, but before going, I stopped by the Río Rita to say goodbye. It was afternoon, the place nearly empty. Chang, bubbly as ever, offered me one last Coca-Cola on the house. "Chino," I said, "I have decided to go back to the other side."

He wasn't surprised. "I thought perhaps so. I had heard from Canelo that you were thinking of returning to Albuquerque, at least for a time." I nodded. "Yes, I'm going to finish my doctorate and see what comes of it." That's when he asked, "Did you enjoy the fiesta?"

I responded, "I had a wonderful time. I was so pleased to have been invited and included. I enjoyed dancing with Barbara. She is a treasure. It was very kind of you to take me with your family. Very gracious. Please tell your daughter I thought her very charming."

I went on, commenting that it was one of the most memorable events of my stay in Guaymas. He grinned. "Oh yes, I should think so. There was a young woman there who, oh, how she wanted you! *¡Como quiso ella*, Davíd!"

Hesitant, I fished, "Did anyone notice?"

Chang laughed, his Buddha-like belly jiggling. "Not at all! Only two hundred people noticed!" Well, at least *he* was enjoying himself.

"But why?" I asked. "Nothing really happened."

He was animated. "Nothing happened! How can you say that nothing happened? The two of you looked at each other!"

Defensive, I asserted, "But nothing was said! Why is this such an incident?"

"Ah," he said, "you are sensitive about it. For you it was the road not taken. Still, you do not understand yourself, do you?"

"No, Chang, perhaps not," I admitted. He stuck the fork in. "And yet even now you do not ask me her name."

I said, "No, it does not matter now, but perhaps I wish you had told me a week ago how interested she was."

"Oh, but Davíd, you knew! I did not have to tell you such a thing."

I conceded, "Yes, I suppose that is so. Are you really certain that people noticed?"

"Oh yes! The old women are still talking."

Now really curious, I pressed, "Is that so unusual?"

He grinned, his hands spread in supplication. "A look like that? Oh yes! Old Antonia Marina (the black-clad queen of the block) said, 'Ah, if only someone had passed a match between their eyes, it would have burst into flame. Such intensity!'" Elaborating, he confided, "Doña Marina said, 'I hope they never meet again, those two.'"

I asked, "Why would she say such a thing, Chino?"

"Passion like that destroys, Davíd. Like a fire, it consumes its own substance—now go see Francisca. She is waiting for you...."

As I walked out the door, Chang shouted a name. "María Sonora Corral!" *Now he fuckin' tells me!* I thought, pissed off—mostly at myself.

I didn't know it then, but it hadn't been my once-in-a-life chance. Within several days of my visit to the Río Rita, I returned to the States, me still gacho and Marta still angry. I mourned Lupita, having promised to return the next May and baptize a yet unborn child. And unexpectedly, I'd meet the woman I was to marry.

These memories of the Quinceañera and of Lupita's imaginary rejoinder to let go of my "fear of love" churned in my head as I waited for Marta on the porch of the Río Rita nearly a year later....

chapter fifteen

MARTA, 1971

Baptism over, the week was passing quickly. My memories of 1970 were now history, and Marta had still not come out. In spite of the early warnings from Negro, Francisca, Mariquita, and La Eva as our "relationship" first got going in 1970, I don't think I realized just how little I understood Marta until after Lupita died. That's when her thumb sucking in my bed at the Rubi had hit me like a lightning bolt, decisively ending the sexual part of our relationship.

We continued to see each other, taking walks and slurping ice creams on hot Sunday evenings. I gave her a going-away gift before I left... and had gotten her full baptized name "so that God could find her" if she died. She did not want to have a little white cross like my mandadera's, only a first name stenciled on it. She even told me where she was from. All privileged information on the streets.

But as the overt sex vanished from our relationship, she became more volatile. Drank more. Already hysterical over the relationships she imagined I had with Lupita, then the Canadian "blonde" and the girls from the Zona I had taken on Monday and Tuesday "outings," she had no frame of reference for our relationship once the sex no longer defined it. The Quinceañera hadn't helped, either.

Marta simply did not seem to understand the concept of "friend." In that sense she wasn't fully socialized. At least not in the Mexican meaning of it. Later I was to discover that she didn't even have a friend in Guaymas. But she had once understood "mom," keeping her cute, dark-haired son, then somewhere between six and eight, well away from her half life in and out of the ambiente at downtown hotels. He was the only human on earth to whom she was consistently kind.

As I sat again on the porch of the Río Rita, already knowing that the girl from the 47 club next door had made her inquiries, the biggest mystery to me was why Marta had come to the Zona when I returned to the States—leaving her son. It seemed both ominous and incomprehensible. And where the heck was her fragmented little family now? They had simply "moved away" from the house in the San Vicente neighborhood. No one seemed to know anything. Not even the taxistas. Spooky.

The taxistas could find almost anyone, knew everything. In fact, I'd taken a couple of "locate and advise jobs" through a guy in El Paso, connected somehow to the J. J. Arms Detective Agency in '69 and '70. Though I never met Arms himself, he had a quite reputation in northern Mexico. Allegedly brilliant and exotic, he had lost both forearms as a kid.

Later fitted with "claw" prostheses for both arms—single-shot Magnum pistols supposedly hidden in each—"J. J." specialized in international kidnap cases, wealthy—and wanted—Stateside millionaires who had disappeared behind the Tortilla Curtain. Or the occasional, vanished trust-fund daughter, usually found near a swimming pool with a guy not on the family's social A-list.

Through the taxistas, I'd collected several finders' fees over the years. Blue-eyed blondes with expensive tastes, big wallets, and tiny black bikinis weren't hard to find in those days. Whether lounging on the porch of the lovely Los Arcos Hotel in La Paz or nearby at San Carlos, the Guaymas taxistas all had brothers, cousins, compadres who worked as waiters, bartenders, taximen. Any place in Mexico where a visitor requires services is not a hideaway.

But Marta's family had simply vanished. Her son, aunt, and the aunt's boyfriend gone. No trace remained in '71. A huge blank. Though I'd tipped heavily, made inquiries through trusted friends, *nada*. Dead ends. Poor families, of course, require few services. Everyone knew where Marta was, but her family was another story. Had it not been for the son she doted on, I'd never even have needed Chang's warning about "burned coffee."

215

Her son had been my evidence that somewhere hidden beneath her sexuality lived a richer human being. Multidimensional. Capable of warmth, of bonding. She loved the kid—wore the blue dress I'd bought her *only* when she was with him. I'd seen her with the boy two or three times only and by accident.

Once at the Copa de Leche she was up on the roof terrace with him, spooning ice cream into his mouth, staring dreamily at him, oblivious to everything else around her. I'd watched her from below on the Serdan. Touching.

That's the Marta I wanted to be with. And I'd actually had fleeting moments with that same woman on Sunday nights when I held her. Forty minutes of hurricane-force sex, followed by forty seconds of warmth and tenderness, then retreat into her shell. It took me a long time to realize that I'd actually gotten more of both emotions from just one paid assignation with Francisca.

But even Francisca, warm and direct as she was, felt like a pale shadow of my one surrealistic "date" with Indita. Indita had actually shared her soul, her inner self—and flown with me. The emotions unleashed were everything—the sex, what little I remembered of it, incidental. That I should have been her one "real date" in this life affected me powerfully. As I discovered that she intended only that one date and nothing more, I became frustrated and sad.

So I had drifted further into the relationship with Marta, hoping to release the hidden life force within her. In reality, I had already begun foundering in my own illusions, quite like the girls in the Zona.

Later, when I discovered that Indita was mortally ill, I felt inexpressibly sad for her and at the same time responded to Marta with a sexual frenzy that bordered on insane. It was as if the most primitive part of my brain processed "sex" and "life force" as one and the same.

Marta certainly wasn't complaining, but my lust neither drew a warm, gentle Marta to the surface nor generated enough primitive life force to save Indita. And it was the contrast with Indita that eventually forced me to accept that in my ongoing relationship with Marta, sex was everything but the emotions incidental.

Indita's one date had meant more to me than all the dates with Marta combined. She had loved me, I told myself, even if only for a few hours. Yet Lupita, just a big-eyed kid—no sex involved to cloud my twenty-five-year-old brain—had meant more to me in real life than *all* of the others combined. It was she, as wounded and wary as one would expect for a kid abandoned on the street at age five, who had begun to emerge from her protective turtlelike shell. That gave me intense pleasure.

Lupita vibrated when she "felt things." And every time she vibrated on the outside, I quietly vibrated on the inside, responding to the harmonics of her emergence from a neglected orphan's protective shell. As I vibrated in response, my own shell became thinner, more lucent. I had actually begun to believe that the cycle of recurring emotional losses in my own life might be over. In mid-summer of 1970 I was happy. Amazing and addictive.

But by the end of summer 1970, both Indita and Lupita were in their graves. Horrifying! The same old pattern. And I was left with only Marta. A cipher. Just one compartment of my life in Guaymas. And not even the most important one. She sensed that, poor thing, and complained about it when she wrote to me in the States, claiming that she "loved" me.

I was still trying to sort out the various meanings of "love"— my feelings for Marta, Indita, and Lupita had been different, yet all were "love." Or were they? Lupita was love, but had Indita only been "hope" or "fantasy"? Had Marta been about "passion" and nothing more...?

I didn't know, but that one word—*love*—had brought me to find her in the Zona and square things up, if possible. Did she mean it? Did she even have a clue what "love" might be? Her behavior suggested no, but the son argued yes. And now she'd abandoned him.

"Sitting on the Río Rita's porch will *not* get you more answers," Francisca reminded me gently as she touched my shoulder from behind. Damned viejas—were they all mind readers? But Francisca wasn't through. "It was unfair of her to use the word *love* in her letter. *Es una trampa* (it's a trick), even if she does not yet realize it. Why do you half believe it?"

"Her son, Francisca. *Su hijito* (her little son)."

"*Bueno*, Davíd—we have asked ourselves the very same question. But she abandoned him and came to the Zona. And your relationship with her was finished even before you left Guaymas last year! There is no love left inside her, only anger and need. I have seen this many times. Elena from the 47 carried your message. But Marta will not come out tonight. She is in her room, "*repistiada*" (totally smashed). Go downtown to your comadre and the others. Please! I will call you at the Rubi tomorrow if there is news."

Just then Burro pulled up in his old Chevy. "Got your call from La Francisca, 'mano. They are waiting for us at your comadre's. Afterward you and I can go eat, have a beer." I was being sent downtown to attend to my real obligations and walk away from my dangerous, lingering illusions. The hooker's version of "study hall."

I got in. Burro, as effusive as ever, tried one more time to convince me to stay in Guaymas "just for the summer, *Güero*. Fall weddings are *de moda* (in style)." I laughed and blew it off, but he went on, "*Mira*, some of us miss you—and your movidas— here. The chingadazos you invented for the boleadores to give La Companía (the CIA) were masterful—and everyone made good money. They cannot say so, but certain officials *en el palacio municipal* (town hall) miss you as well." My spirits soared. We had pulled some cool moves in '70.

Burro was referring to my plot to earn money for Lupita and the shoe-shine boys while paying back the CIA recruits who constantly drifted through town, rifling through my dad's army footlocker at the Rubi. When they found nothing, they invariably chatted me up in the Rubi bar, variously asking me if I knew where to "score grass, drugs, man," or, "I need a hundred Colt Armalites for a client. Can you put me in touch with the right people?"

This bullshit invariably came from a twenty-three-year-old greenhorn sporting a knit Rooster tie, tan khakis, and the fragmentary but very formal Spanish that strongly suggested they had been straight C students since the day they decamped from Daddy's country club and went to college.

I had first attracted their unwanted attention in Guatemala, closed to Americans for a while in the spring of '66. Of course I went.

These idiots thought they blended right in with the University of Arizona kids who sometimes floated through Guaymas on road trips. What no one had told them at Princeton, Yale, Rutgers, or wherever was that the last U of A student to wear a tie in Mexico was long dead. About 1956, I'd guess.

Did these characters or their bosses really not know that every male of their generation except them was already (a) in Vietnam or long dead from the experience, (b) in Canada, (c) in the Peace Corps, (d) in graduate school, praying to beat the lottery, or (e) hiding in a commune like New Buffalo up in Taos County, New Mexico, dressed liked a movie extra right out of *The Good, the Bad and the Ugly*?

Well, perhaps I thought of them too harshly. There were also some guys like me—between worlds. The shadowy and "dangerous" expatriates who sold fans and blenders, wrote poetry on a beach, a copy of *Tropic of Cancer* in their back pocket, or the ones who haunted the high country east of Guaymas looking for Don Juan, his muse, and peyote. This last crew were usually escapees from places like New Buffalo but "dangerous" nonetheless.

219

The two big embarrassments of my time in Mexico had been the fake, flashy "Tony Lama Texans" (one of the girls at the Río Rita summed them up with memorable clarity: "I'd rather screw a snake. Serpents are better lovers—and far more considerate") and "The Compania Boys."

These Boy Scouts gone horribly wrong were both a ludicrous embarrassment to the United States and a pain in the ass. I could do nothing about the self-styled, cartoon "Texans"— you'd have to shoot one to get his attention. And I simply was not into violence.

But the CIA Boy Scouts presented a more manageable target. They almost always came to town in clean, new rental cars engaged in Tucson or Nogales. And their bosses apparently had enough contempt for Mexico that they rarely "registered as foreign agents upon entry," required by both international and Mexican law. In this oversight, I had seen opportunity.

Early on, I trained Lupita and Juanito to spot these guys. First, check out the car! No fishing gear? Keep an eye on it. You're looking for white guys (yes, whiter than me!). Twenty-two to twenty-eight years old. Knit tie, polished loafers like Canelo's (they nodded—got it!). Khaki pants. Short-sleeved shirts, *gafas* (sunglasses)...and if they smoked, the clincher—usually filter tips like Winstons with *no stateside tax stamp*!

I showed them the little yellow tax diamond on my Pall Mall Reds, bought in Tucson. These CIA clowns were too cheap to buy their cigarettes on the street and so got them by the truck-load from Stateside military base PXs.

Yep, the kids got it! And *so* easy to spot from a shoe-shine boy's perch as the big gringo hanging over you, one telltale penny loafer on your box, lights up. If the ID looks good—go steal the plate off the car and take it to city hall for a "reward."

While I arranged fines in '70 to spring one "Mr. Smith" from the Guaymas jail, I had whined casually about the CIA guys going through my gear at the Rubi. To my delight, the local authorities were interested. "Finders' fees" were not out of the question: "It would be a *service* to the nation. Our sovereignty is not respected." Nice! I'd hit a big, juicy hot-button issue—one pregnant with opportunity.

Lupita and Juanito trained the other kids for a cut. Within weeks every Stateside rental car in the Guaymas area got the twice over from a bunch of tatty six- to ten-year-old urchins that most folks ignore. Knowledge is power. Power means plata. Plata means beans and tacos. Beans and tacos means, loafers, khakis, knit tie, and no tax stamp on the pinche gringo's *pitillos* (street slang for cigarettes).

I'm told, secondhand, that city hall really squeezed those who were "outed." The kids got fifty to a hundred pesos per bust—

big money on their level in the Serdan's food chain . . . and Güero's room at the Hotel Rubi became more tranquil. By the end of summer '70, Rooster ties and gafas had become somewhat scarce in Guaymas. The Boy Scouts began drifting over to La Paz. Rumors of a secret submarine base on Cedros Island drew them like maggots to dead meat.

Burro really had me laughing and in an up mood by the time he dropped me off at Mercedes' house near the plaza. I didn't know till then that he even knew of it—but Juanito had spilled the beans during the fall after I went back to the "other side," asking Burro if it was still *propio* (appropriate) for them to bust "la compania" once I was gone.

The street kids assumed (wrongly) that I skimmed cream from the top of the milk before it trickled down to them. Not true. Though my motives were muddy and highly influenced by a seriously unpleasant reintroduction to the CIA in Veracruz, long before Guaymas, my hands were clean.

Burro dropped me off at my comadre's as Francisca had instructed. Mercedes was waiting—her tiled front room near the plaza, bright, clean, and cheerful. Little Martha Aurora watched me drink café con leche again and didn't hide this time.

I held baby Olga, rocking her till she figured out I was a stranger. That sent her into scream-and-squirm mode again. Mercedes took her back, grinning as always.

Simply being near Mercedes and her children grounded me. Her home was modest, but love flowed through it—profound as the smell of her freshly ground coffee. She showed me photographs of her family. Natural, now that I was her compadre and part of it. She had three sisters and a brother in the Guaymas area. Her mom and dad still lived down south on a *ranchito* (little farm) in Sinaloa. A sister who lived nearby dropped in for a few minutes, chatting with me before stepping out under the gun-metal blue evening sky.

When I said my goodbyes and walked back toward the Rubi, little Martha stood framed in Mercedes' doorway, watching me go. Still the wary, intense wolf pup, we had not yet established full contact. She acted much like Lupita when I'd first seen her in the passageway to the Colmenar a year before—watching from a safe distance. Martha Aurora even looked a bit like Lupita—shaggy mop of dark hair, slightly freckled. Wary but curious.

As I passed Lupita's streetlight on the Serdan, I stopped to caress it again. The cast iron still warm from the early June sun, it reminded me of how remarkably warm to the touch Lupita had always been. The kid was a miniature disposal unit who could easily have outeaten a biblical swarm of locusts.

Olga, Mercedes, and little Martha Aurora were real, full of life. But oddly, both Lupita and big Marta were now ghosts. I had dealt partially with Lupita's death but not Marta's spiral into desperation.

Until I returned, I hadn't realized that Marta, "La Flaca," once my lover, had already begun to abandon the world of the living and embrace the world of the night. It's eerie to realize that some-one physically alive may already have started to take that long walk toward the dark side. Seeking cold nothingness, her soul already on its sad journey.

Oh, Lord! Where *was* Marta's little son? Who was holding him tonight? How could he ever understand why his mom had "gone away"? Even worse, like Lupita, had he figured it out—his mom, a puta? Why are so many kids left as wreckage in the follies of life? And just what was I going to say to Marta if I saw her? Confused again, I hit the Rubi bar. Burro was out on a run. Back soon, they said.

I talked to wise old Mateo for a few minutes. Then he too had a fare. Enrique, doing his "cigarette dance" and on break from

Doney's sandwich shop, where Burro and I sat at the counter behind closed metal grills. The second story is new. (Photo by Dan and Rachel Shaffer © 2004.)

the Rubi's bar, invited me to have beers with him on the beach at Miramar after the bar closed for the night. We made a date for about 11 p.m. As Enrique headed inside, Burro pulled up, honking. "Get in, Güero. *¡A comer!* (Let's eat!)" My mood lifted. My plaid-shirted bro was an "up" kind of guy.

Burro passed Lupita's streetlight, chugging slowly along the Serdan, then pulled quickly into an open space right in front of Doney's sandwich shop near the plaza. Situated right on one of the best corners in town and still busy at 9:30 p.m. Parking karma.

Burro cut through the crowd, maneuvering for two stools facing the Serdan through the tiled, open-front-seating counter. Premium people-watching posts.

The huge grill where Doney's charcoaled their *carne asada* and bundles of sweet onions for *tacos al carbón* was only fifteen feet to the right. Doney's was a sensual feast—bright lights, heavenly smells, huge condiment trays of every possible version of salsa—with avocado, without, jalapeño, *serrano*, *pico de gallo*, *chiltepín*, even *Salsa Yaqui*.

The latter concoction, a commercial brand for the true chile aficionado, its afterglow was good for a least an hour. Strong enough, in my view, to dechrome an auto's bumper, this was the very same sauce that, in the summer of '70, had been used by one of the viejas in the Río Rita to put an obnoxious tourist in his place.

He had demanded "a red-hot blow job." Pissed off, she sent one of the cleaning women for a bottle of the Salsa Yaqui. When it arrived she stepped into the hallway, took a huge mouthful of the salsa, ducked back inside and went down on him.

It was a very brief assignation. He moaned and twitched all the way to the Rio Rita's front porch, walking quite oddly. Alarmed, Chang immediately sent Brigido for an explanation. He returned, laughing so hard he could barely talk. That event—and the young hooker—became an instant Zona legend.

Remembering it, Burro grinned and punched my shoulder when our platters arrived and I reached for the Salsa Yaqui. The tacos, as always, were spectacular. Better yet, the black-and-white-tiled counter gave us a front seat "in the action" view of the late-evening crowd on the Serdan.

Burro carefully appraised every young woman to pass by, commenting on each. "Nice legs, *bien formadita!*," even emitting a few of those involuntary gurgling sounds that single males sometimes make. Clear evidence they aren't getting laid. More "Americanized" again from my winter on the "other side," I settled for checking out every other cutie and omitted commentary.

I did have to concede, when Burro loudly raised the issue, that the Guaymas women were the loveliest on the planet. And very few of them ever made their way to the Zona. Too nicely raised. Too secure in their large, old, solidly rooted extended families. I personally only knew one vieja with Guaymas origins. Virtually all the rest were outsiders.

It might have been more culto for Burro to initiate such a conversation quietly. Guy talk between just the two of us. But he apparently thought it an appropriate topic for the assembled patrons as well. Several of the teenage girls giggled.

Two well-dressed matrons preened a bit, and nearly everyone appreciated the thought, particularly since Burro was stereotyping the local women much as a sculptor might have: "regal," with nice posture, almost like the famed women of Tehuantepec. Strong, intelligent, *"bien formadita"* (Nicely put together—a touch edgy, but not crude).

This running commentary produced both giggles and some appreciative nods. Finally the coup de grace: *"Tan bien educadas y fieles* (so well raised and faithful)." Burro was trolling again.

Applause! Short and subdued but applause nonetheless. Working-class Guaymas attitudes right out in front. In essence, "We may not be rich, but we've got a lock on the best-looking, most decent women anywhere." And they had—one reason the outsiders in the Zona prospered.

What a stunning contrast to my university environment in the States, where any ordinary male sexuality was loathed! Feared. Derided. Even "looking" at a woman on campus was formally defined as "ogling," an unethical and professionally castratible offense. They even had committees to deal with offenders. The testosterone police.

Yet at Doney's, Burro's conversation drew not only a polite round of applause, but an inquiry from a handsome thirtyish woman seated alone at one of the rear tables.

"And you, señor, are you married to a Guaymense?" "No, *señorita* (Burro, you shameless flatterer!), but it is my highest priority so be so favored one day soon. I am looking!"

More laugher and giggles, but ten minutes later, when "thir-tyish" had finished her meal and stepped outside, she slowly strolled past us at the counter, smiling. Then stopped dead at Burro's taxi to flamboyantly read its sitio and number. Finished, she smiled again at Burro, then walked on down the Serdan. Slow, regal, and sensuous. Burro gurgled.

Several days later, just before I returned to the States, Burro reported, "La Irma (a fake name) from Doney's met me for cof-fee between *turnos* (shifts) on Sunday. Divorced but never mar-ried in church, only the civil. Two children—boy and girl.

"She has a small house in the new neighborhood they call Gil Samaniaga. Works for a lawyer here on the Serdan. Went to *prepa* (similar to an older U.S. high school's vocational programs). What do you think, Güero?"

"Do you like her, Burro?"

"Yes, she was fun. La Irma has a sense of humor. But she's four years older... and the kids."

"*¡Ayy!* Why ask me, Burro—consider my history with women. What do I know?"

Burro laughed. "You—you did a *chingo* of *padroteando* with the *viejas* last summer (a heap of screwing them for free—the deli-cious rumor legacy of my downtown trips with the Río Rita's finest). You were an artist and the pinche Zona your canvass. What was it like 'painting' La Mariquita?"

"Burro, they were merely friends! Truly!"

"*Como tú dices* (whatever), Davíd!" he shot back, rolling his eyes and leering. "But I still need advice."

"Then go to La Eva at the Rubi bar—give her a free ride home. Talk. She knows more about such things than anyone else I know."

"Can't, Davíd, we, ah..."

"Really? Now there's a woman for you, Burro! She likes you."

"I know, but it became a bit like you and La Flaca—she won't give up the ambiente. I hinted at marriage, but she

226

insisted our relationship stay at a certain emotional distance.
I can't bear it that way."

"I'm sorry, Burro. And yes, I do understand." Marta.
"Dammit! Why did you go to the Zona?" I asked myself again, pat-
ting Burro on the shoulder. I'd still not seen Marta or actually
talked to her... so had no answers. I didn't know it then, but I
would never get any.

Enrique and I sat on the beach near the old Miramar Hotel after
tacos with El Burro at Doney's. He had bought an eight pack
of icy Bohemias in town. I drove and provided the cigarettes.
He wanted to talk. We assessed the idea of marriage. He was
preparing to pop the formal question—in Mexico you dressed
in your Sunday best and made a family appointment after the
girl agreed privately to the formal engagement. "Dad" gathered
the family. Made speeches. Asked you questions. Then gave or
withheld formal permission.

If you agreed with Dad's stipulations—usually along the lines
of, "Comport yourselves modestly until married in church! Be
kind and faithful to my daughter. Accept that we shall be family. Take your obligations seriously," etc., you responded with,
"Yo cumplo. (I will fulfill/comply.)" Handshakes, some booze,
and a light dinner usually followed.

You were then *prometidos* (promised) and had entered into a
very formal *compromiso* (mutual agreement). From that moment
forth, no backing out and no sampling the merchandise until the
padre smiled at you. Enrique was about to take that huge step.
He knew I'd once been formally engaged in Mexico City, "where
they do these things de costumbre." He bounced his little speech
off me. I liked it. So Enrique. So decent. Thoughtful. Simpático.

The beach at Miramar was gorgeous. Under the starlit sky,
faint shimmers of iridescence undulated across Bacochibampo

Bay from the lights of San Carlos about four miles away. Cerro Bacochibampo rose up to our right like a huge black paper cutout. Flat as a stage prop against the inky sky, it cast its shadow across Playas Primaverales, where I had once lived on the beach and met the fiancée who had brought me back to Guaymas from South America the year before.

Bacochibampo Hill also hid the Estero de Soldado and the small motel where La Indita, dead nearly a year, had once "told my fortune." I missed her still . . . and needed her advice. She could see the future. Knew answers to the mysteries of life.

Indita had exercised the few, tragic choices ever presented her with an iron will, actually managing to snatch some permanent goodness from the cage of the evil one. She had sucked the money for her little schoolroom right from Satan's gizzard. Cheated him of both her soul and her destiny. She would have known how to handle the Marta situation.

That night I dreamed of Indita, the ferrocarrilero's daughter, and Marta. Marta was distant, fragmented. Like women everywhere, the others merely watched, waiting to see what the defective half of the species would do next. Well, at least Lupita didn't make a guest appearance, tossing in her two *centavos'* worth of advice.

The next day Francisca didn't call the Rubi with "news" as she had promised at the Río Rita the night before. I was on my own. But I had a plan. While walking the Serdan, I had hit upon it when one of the taxistas at the Centenario commented that it was Friday, a big night in the Zona. Hmm!

Plotting, I worked my way up the Serdan to the Sitio Medrano on the corner of Avenida 19. My head was clear. I passed out cigarettes, telling everyone how beautiful my little goddaughter Olga was. Identifying the members of my new family. One guy ragged me, commenting on the transformation from "*padrote*" (in this context an "old man"; i.e., doing the viejas for free). Everyone laughed.

I paid them back, saying that "La Mariquita sent her regards and had suggested the Medrano raffle one of its taxis, then draw lots to see who got to visit her." More laughter as the Oriental taxista known as "Japón" commented that it was an interesting proposition "but would leave one family out of work."

"Yes," I responded, "La Mariquita had considered that carefully but imagined that whoever laid her could claim 5 percent of the fares from the other twenty merely to describe the experience to the rest. Something that they could ponder at night as they waited for fares."

They laughed again, teasing me like schoolboys. So I cranked up the volume. "Besides, she said she'd throw in *la vendida de una buena mamada* (the bonus of a good blow job) to the lucky one if he swore in church to name his next daughter after her."

That shut 'em up. From the startled looks on several of the younger ones' faces, they were already calculating the odds of selling off one of the older taxis. My bullshit would get around, I figured, so I thought it wise to brief Mariquita that evening before the taxistas began bringing fares to the Zona. I could do that before I went to Club Guaymas to see Marta.

My lunch at the Colmenar was excellent. Fresh triggerfish, pan-fried *papas* (potatoes), and sopa seca de arroz. Lots of lime and a big mug of café con leche. Mercedes, radiant as usual, asked me to make some time for her and her family early Sunday evening before I returned to the States. *Propio!*

After lunch, I walked along the malecón. Watched the ferry leave for Santa Rosalia in Baja, then enjoyed my quiet time on the Rubi's roof terrace. An Orange Crush in the Rubi's bar, some dice, and an agreement to meet Canelo and Negro later at the Río Rita and I was off to the Zona.

It was nearly 8 p.m. Still early. The Río Rita was still not yet ready for the evening, so I had to go down to the residencias for

Mariquita. I explained my retort to the taxistas that afternoon, apologizing. In Mexico apologies are very powerful

Fortunately, she wasn't all that insulted. I'd taken her lots of places downtown the year before, once snarling at a restaurant maitre d' that she was no vieja, but my "cousin from Los Angeles." The girls had gotten a major hoot out of that—and a nice lunch. So she merely laughed, scolding me that I was naughty to have implied such a "*vendida*" for only one taxi!

Then I asked a favor—"Who is the manager of Club Guaymas? I need the name!" She understood, nodding. "I'll see Francisca right now. Stay here." Mariquita returned several minutes later, a name neatly lettered on a small piece of scented stationery. A gift from don Francisco, perhaps? I wrote my note at Mariquita's dressing table, said good-bye to her, and went down the hill.

Twenty yards below, someone shouted after me from the Río Rita's porch. I turned. Chang! "Davíd—wait. I'll be right there!" Chang puffed his way to me. "Are you certain?"

"Yes, I must talk to her!"

"Okay, Davíd, but let Brigido deliver your note. More dignified. The manager will get it himself and privately." I accepted. Sometimes a little help from your friends is a good thing.

Chang left, replaced by Brigido, who nodded. Saying nothing, he disappeared down the hill, those laundry-fresh white high-tops a stunning contrast to his dark, catlike presence. He appeared again about five minutes later, motioning me down to the club.

I stood across the dirt street in front of the Club Guaymas, lit a smoke, and waited. It was nearly dark when Marta came out—a lone, shadowy figure making her way toward me. I knew her from the tilt of her head, the sway of her hips.

As she stepped into the light of the small open-front store behind me, I got my first real look. She had changed. Eyes downcast, arms folded tight across her breasts, all of the old, smooth facade had eroded. She had lost lots of weight. Almost anorexic. Her once pretty hair was now shaggy and lifeless.

Eyes hollow and haunted, she shivered in the hot June night as if she were cold. Her once sleek black skirt now frayed and faded. A nondescript top, the same black flats on her feet, scuffed and coming apart at the seams. It made me very sad. Even that high-voltage aura of sexuality, which had once surrounded her every-where she went, had dimmed like a guttering candle. Used up.

I said, "Hello," and asked her how she had been. I paused, hoping for a response, but got none. She didn't even look up. At a loss, I told her gently that I had not meant to hurt her. She sniffled a bit and shivered again, but still said nothing. I offered her a cigarette. She took it. I lit it for her. Finally she made eye contact, tossed her head back, and inhaled deeply.

"Take me away from here. Now! Marry me!"

"Oh, Marta." I sighed. "You told me last year that you could never marry. That you had married in church and never divorced. You should be with your family." Big mistake! She sobbed until her anger, mingled with desperation, erupted in a raspy, tortured moan. "Then go away, cabrón!"

I reached out to touch her. "Marta." But the tone in my voice obviously made it even worse. "I don't want pity from a pinche gringo!" she snarled at the top of her lungs, then slapped me hard. Not yet unburdened, she spat on my Red Wings, hiss-ing, "Go away, gringo, leave me alone!"

I didn't move. Indeed, I could not. She turned, shivering again. Then ran into the Club Guaymas, sobbing as she went. Several of the girls at the door cursed me loudly as she rushed past them. "*¡Puto!* (Faggot!)" "*¡Gacho!* (Limp dick!)" "*¡Pinche gabacho!*" (Roughly, "frigging white trash!")

I watched her go, still frozen in the same spot. Several clus-ters of passersby had stopped, taking in the entire scene. I don't know how long I stood there. It must have been quite a while. Part of me wanted to go after her. Another part of me felt as if her icy wind had just blown through me, taking all my body's warmth with it. Empty. Weird . . . the temperature was still about ninety degrees Fahrenheit.

Someone touched my shoulder, startling me. La Negra, from the Río Rita. "Davíd, your friends are waiting for you at the club. I have come for you! *¡Vámonos! ¿Listo?* (Let's go! Are you ready?)"

I followed. She steered me gently. Partway up the hill she confided, "I heard everything. Saw it all. I am so sorry."

"Sorry? Are you not angry too?"

"No, Davíd. But many saw the scene. There will be talk."

I nodded. "*Yo sé.* (I know.)"

Just before we mounted the steps of the Río Rita she squeezed me and confided, "Indita asked me to give you something when you returned. A keepsake. I'll bring it to the table when you leave tonight."

Inside, a table waited. Negro Jacinto, Chang, and Francisca. Front row. The band was in tight rhythm. Dancing, laughing, girls giggling, the constant squeak of the huge chalkboard over the bar racking up the drink tallies, an irritating counterpoint to all the warm, human sounds.

Chang and Negro were bubbly, nonchalant. Only Francisca seemed nervous, squeezing my hand as I sat down. "Dance, Davíd?" Not waiting for me to respond, she dragged me out to the floor. Privacy in numbers. "You okay, Davíd?" English? I'd never heard her speak it. I commented; she grinned. "You didn't answer my question."

"I don't know the answer. *Me siento un poco vacio* (I feel sort of empty)," slipping back into Spanish.

"I hear your boots took a beating, Davíd.

"News travels quickly. Negra warned me." Conversation over, we slow-danced for another five minutes.

Back at the table, Chang asked when I was to return to the other side. "Monday evening." Negro, now a bit more nervous, finally leaned to me and asked "*¿Estás bien?* (Are you okay?)"

"Yes, Negro, but as Chang suggested, the coffee below was bitter."

"But you swallowed it," Chang butted in. "It is done. Forgotten."

Francisca at my side, this was tantamount to an order. Chang's rule of silence was in motion again. She nodded, excused herself, and disappeared for a few minutes. The girls' central committee already enforcing Chang's gag order by the time she returned. Dignity. Important stuff.

At midnight, the floor show began. Still lots of tourists in town. Canelo was late, so I said my goodbyes and departed. La Negra caught me at the door, pressing a small, tissue-wrapped package into my hand.

233

Once outside, I hailed a taxi directing the *chofer* (driver) to Playas Primaverales, where I lay on the beach, staring up at the stars. Saddened by Marta...and feeling guilty, too. The image of her running back into the club, wailing, was unbearable. I prayed for her. But Indita was long dead, and she had been my only proof that a prayer could actually be heard. So I suppose no one heard mine for Marta.

Indita's neatly wrapped box in my pocket, I walked up to the Miramar Hotel about 3 a.m., catching a taxi into town from the hotel's sitio. By 4 a.m., unable to sleep, I'd taken yet another taxi to the Zona. It might be over as far as Chang was concerned. But I was far too troubled to let it go. At the least I intended to shove some money into Marta's fist and again urge her to rejoin her son. Futile or not, it was worth another try.

We pulled up to the Club Guaymas, its front door already closed. Without its gaudy streamers of flashing Christmas tree lights to distract attention from its reality, the club seemed shabby, dirty, and sad. The taxista waited while I banged on the door. Tired and irritated, the same manager to whom my note had been addressed opened the door a crack, "La Marta?" I asked.

"*Se fué! Recogió sus cosas y salió a las tres con una maleta.* (She's gone! Gathered her things and left with a suitcase about 3 a.m.)"

"*¿Verdad?* (Honestly?)" I asked. The suspicious tone in my voice apparently pissed him off, royally.

"*Se fué. ¡Ya!* (She's gone. Enough!)," he growled, slamming the door savagely. The sharp metallic sound of its bolt echoed into the night like a gunshot.

Gone or not gone corporeally, as the taxistas subsequently insisted, it really didn't matter. She and her once glittering sexuality had simply faded away, ghostlike.

For several years I took comfort in the notion that she really had left, as the manager of Club Guaymas insisted. I told myself that she wised up and rejoined her family.... The latter proved to have been cheap comfort. I never saw her again.

234

chapter sixteen

TO THE "OTHER SIDE"

It was already Saturday afternoon and I had only another forty-eight hours in Guaymas. Time had become precious. Soon I would have to tear myself a second time from the one place on earth where I truly belonged, return to my homeland, and marry.

Friday night's horrifying images of Marta were balanced by the hope that she had really left the ambiente to rejoin her family. Denial, perhaps. But I was determined to put those images aside and make the most of my day. Burro wasn't driving that shift, so I asked old Mateo to drive me around, merely sightseeing. Not a problem. Not even expensive.

First we headed south to Empalme. Taking the high road, I gorged on the beautiful glimpses of Guaymas spread out below. San Fernando's white church steeples beckoned, and the outer harbor shimmered beneath the steep, narrow streets that cascaded straight down to the water from Cerro Cabezón. Terraced garden walls spilled thick streamers of buganvilla into the tangle of pastel-shaded streetscapes.

A partial view of Guaymas from above. (Photo by Dan and Rachel Shaffer © 2004.)

236

As we drove on, broken Coke bottles cemented onto the tops of courtyard walls both glittered in the sun and announced the more prosperous households. Then the Cabezón's great sandstone prominence temporarily hid the town from view. We emerged, still heading south, rewarded by an iffy vista of the town's electric generators, tangled wires, and a glimpse of the south harbor. A Mexican gunboat moored alongside the flat, man-made peninsula guarded the area where huge quantities of Sonoran farm goods, copper, guano, and timber were exported.

As we descended the steep grade fronting the Bay of Guaymas, we passed the old Pleamar Club on the right. Then closed by the government, it had staged the first floor show I saw with Canelo and Negro—'69, I think. Spread in front of us was Puente Douglas, which arched upward, then down again to deliver us to Empalme.

Vista of outer harbor. (Photo by Cynthia M. Stuart © 2003.)

We stopped in Empalme, buying cold sodas, ice, and tortas, then headed south to Cochorit beach. Almost deserted on Saturday, the locals would be swarming all over it in less than twenty-four hours. Sunday was reserved for church and family outings.

The taxi provided the only shade available. We made do and ate our lunch. On this clear but hot day, I could barely make out the fuzzy gray line at the horizon created by Baja. The sodas gone, we drove back through Empalme, stopping at the chapel where I was to have been married in 1970. Iliana, my former fiancé, had been young, lovely, and pregnant by another man. She had gone away to have her baby. I'd no idea where she was.

It seemed odd that Guaymas itself could be so solid, permanent, and grounded, yet I kept losing people I cared for. Pregnant. Dead. Whereabouts unknown—or just faded away. And why always women?

Vista of Las Esmeraldas Bay at San Carlos. (Photo by Cynthia M. Stuart © 2003.)

238

One of those lost to me was Iliana's little sister, Lisa. She would have been about eleven. So adorable. So sweet. So happy and easy to please. I'd brought a Kmart box of Hershey bars with almonds from the States for her but hadn't yet worked up the balls to visit the family house in Empalme.

Old Mateo drove past slowly, the narrow lane and white picket fence at once so familiar and so dreamlike. My heart raced as we pulled up to the gate, close enough to the passenger window that I could have reached out and opened it. Mateo saw me shaking, smiled, and extended his hand for the tissue-wrapped box. "Dulces," I said. "Please don't leave it in the sun!" Lisa's name on it, he left it in the shade of the front porch.

Back at the wheel, he smiled—"You'll soon have babies of your own. Meanwhile the little one inside is watching you as we speak. But her brother is there. Good thing you didn't go in. That one is strange and cannot accept the fact that his sister played *la chiva* (cheated) with you. Pride."

At the end of the lane Mateo startled me, braking hard and turning the taxi abruptly to retrace our path. "As we pass, I'll sound the horn. Wave your sombrero over the roof. The *cabrón* will see only me at the wheel. The kid will know your hat."

We sailed past, tooting, my Panama waving animatedly over the roof line. "She got the candy, Davíd—I saw her running toward the mangos with it as she waved. Her brother is loco. Mean. No one likes him," declared Mateo, pumping his near arm inward toward his body, fist balled up, Mexican sign language for "you just got screwed, hombre."

I laughed as we exited the alley. Mateo was the most effusive I'd ever seen him. Usually calm, wise, and serious, he had enjoyed this! "*¡Casí un chingadazo!* (Almost a big-time screwing over!) Don't you think?"

"Yes." I laughed. "You put the chingas on Chuey. He'll have a *pinche parado* (a hard-on, and not the happy kind) for a month at least."

"Beer," croaked Mateo, laughing. "You owe me a beer." We drove back through Guaymas, stopping at Playas Primaverales for a cerveza at the bar. Mateo was still enjoying himself. "This is great work, Davíd. Beach. Tortas, beer, a chingadazo to remember... and a hundred-peso fare. We must do this again."

He then reminded me that I had not yet visited Mendez, the poor fishmonger who lived on the hill above the High Road and had always been gracious to me at the Rubi bar. I conceded that but asked for one more stop first.

On to San Carlos. I left Mateo under a huge palapa bar at the left of the road, another cold beer to keep him company, and walked about a hundred yards beyond to the little motel where Indita had engineered the one and only "date" of her sad life. No one in the office. I went out back and hustled up the steps to the

239

balcony where Indita and I had once relaxed, breathed in harmony, and watched the sunset. No one there. So I took a few minutes to remember her and drink in the view. Before going, I said goodbye to her, touching the little table where we once sat silently and picnicked.

As I walked back toward the palapa, already in a sweat, Mateo pulled up. "*¿A Guaymas?* (Back to Guaymas?)" I nodded. We took the high route again, branching left at the entrance to the Serdan, marked by its miniature triangular park and "1854" obelisk that Lupita always insisted was a "statue." It had defined the limits of her world until she met me.

As my *mandadera*, she had traveled with me to "exotic" places like San Carlos, Hermosillo, Kino Bay, Nogales, and Tucson. The child of the street had become a woman of the world in a few short months. A force both in local commerce and in my heart. I sighed at the memories, then put them out of my mind. . . .

Once into the jumble of buses, pedestrians, and roadside businesses all squeezed together in the high road's narrow, dynamite-blasted passage above Guaymas, the going was slow. Turning left up a rutted road at the first break in six o'clock traffic, we climbed to Sr. Mendez's rustic domain.

His house jutted out from the rocky hillside, perched uneasily, as if it would tumble any minute. Old mattress coils locked together in a circle formed a small corral for milk goats. Chickens ran everywhere. A tiny garden at the side of the house was fragrant with mint and herbs.

Mendez usually stopped into the Rubi bar about noon—had one soda (a luxury), and chatted. He sold fresh fish to the small restaurants, nearby homeowners, and occasionally the Rubi dining room, eking out a living along the Serdan from days that began about 4 a.m. and ended about 4 p.m. Every day of his life, except Sunday.

Fairly far down in Guaymas's commercial food chain, his profits were small, but his dreams were as solid as he was. Built like a block of concrete and about five feet two, he was dark and clean but frayed. His graying black hair neatly combed straight back, everything about him exuded determination—almost all of it focused on a son of about thirteen years.

Mendez wanted that son to move up in the world. Hectored him constantly about his schoolwork and had invested in a library of used classics that a college lecturer would not have found unworthy. Cicero, Caesar's *Gallic Wars.* Ovid. Herodotus, St. Augustine. You name it—he had it, including a nearly complete set of Cervantes and Shakespeare (in Spanish). In short, name almost any classic that had gone into the University of Chicago's Great Books series and Mendez had it tucked away in his humble hillside hideaway.

Since Mendez couldn't read well himself, he consulted educated Rubi regulars like Hector Morales, the patrón, or don Francisco. Once the books were acquired, his son read selections to him endlessly. Dad memorized amazing passages, and his boy was becoming a prodigy of sorts without even realizing it.

241

Whenever I had needed a classic for Mariquita in the summer of 1970, I got it from Mendez, carefully wrapped in plastic, and paid him a few pesos for each loan.

Once Mendez's son had begun to astonish his middle school teachers, they paid occasional visits, encouraging the young man to go on to "*La Prepa*," even borrowing books on occasion.

Over the years Mendez's fresh fish and lending library sent three kids to La Prepa. The son went on to the state university in Hermosillo and a *maestría* (master's) in the classics.

Canelo and I had been invited to his house for lunch in 1970 when Mendez discovered, through Rubi conversation, that I was an anthropologist. He sought me out, requesting consultations on books about the "history of Mexico." Of course, my first suggestion was Bernal Diaz del Castillo's history of the Conquest.

He had found a copy within a few weeks, inviting me back to inform his son of its value.

In "*El norte*," he explained, "one can still do things. Advance one's family." Exactly like the viejas, the north had drawn him from central Mexico as a young man. Much as California once drew Stateside dreamers to its "promised land."

Mendez was effusive when Mateo and I stopped by, and his library had grown. Life was good, his son headed for higher studies later in the summer. We sat under his shaded ramada, sipping cool mint tea. He'd heard from folks at the Rubi that I'd returned, was going to marry a "university girl" on the other side, and had continued my studies. He approved.

Born near the settlement of Teacapán, on the sea near the border of southern Sinaloa and Nayarit, he had come north as a young man. "Big dreams! My own little business. A house, garden—kids. Kids that would one day have more than I. Go to school. Read! Perhaps one even becoming a schoolteacher someday. Something important. Progressive. I have gained it all. Miraculous, Davíd, miraculous!"

Miracles, for most of us, are viewed on a grander scale. Stateside, we expect more, so ask for more. And are disappointed if we don't get more. But Sr. Mendez had "everything." Endless twelve-hour days, a fragile little house on a dusty hillside, but an extraordinary library of thumb-worn classics that had changed his family's fortunes. Every now and again you run into someone remarkable enough to generate their own miracles. Mendez was made of that stuff. One of the most satisfied men I ever knew.

Saturday continued to be a superb counterpoint to Friday's "burned coffee." After putting the chingas on the prick who would have become my moody, always pissed brother-in-law had his sister not cheated on me, I decided to celebrate. A lobster dinner at the Paradise seafood restaurant south of town hall seemed appropriate. I wanted company. Female. Mariquita and a friend or two—my own, final "bachelor's" dinner.

It was early enough that Chang's permission was granted. "Have them back by nine-thirty, Davíd!" So Mariquita, La Negra, and Burro joined me. We got front-window seating at my request. If folks were going to talk downtown about "La Flaca" and a big gob of spit on my boots, they might as well choke on our attention-getting foursome at the Paradise.

Mariquita looked spectacular in her formfitting little black dress. La Negra was, by comparison, merely lovely. Burro didn't mind. Shares in Burro's *movidas* (action, hustle), inherited from me and Lupita, were doubling on the street as we sat there in the window, taxis floating by every few minutes.

My last "date" as a bachelor, I told the assembled. Mariquita proposed a toast: "To the ferrocarrilero's daughter and her prometido. I will miss him so!" This loud enough that one of her rich, portly clients about three tables away nearly choked on his meal. She giggled.

At first Burro's mood was bittersweet. Subdued at losing his business partner to "a fate known only to God" on the other side, his mood didn't brighten until Negra winked at him and started toe stroking him under the table. Burro was clearly enchanted. Heck, he regularly became aroused and "indisposed" by something as simple as a cute chick's mid-calf dress half a block away.

Dinner over, Burro ran us back to the Zona, La Negra up front with him, Mariquita in the backseat with me. She was coy. "Francisca said I could not flirt with you, Davíd. You know she has been saving you for marriage, but I want one kiss."

Though I smiled and shook my head no, she kissed me anyway. Slowly... on the lips! The tip of her tongue delivered a heart-stopping caress. Ten thousand pesos a night? Cheap. Filene's Bargain Basement priced. "Our secret." She giggled as she jumped

243

out of the car, bounding up the steps to the Río Rita like a big-eyed doe.

Burro ran us back to the Rubi bar. Dice, a round of beers, Orange Crush for me, and another mad dash down that long, dark hallway. Then we were off to the Río Rita. Sixteen minutes till "showtime." Negro's Crown Vic, as always, drew the hoped-for shouts of "*¡Desgraciados!*" When I entered, there was the slightest pause, the cosmos's version of a quarter stutter.

Several pairs of eyes checked out my freshly polished Red Wings, already a brilliant two tone from Juanito's morning repairs. "Got to get these sticky gobs off, Güero," he had said, working them over with saddle soap. "What is this stuff, anyway?"

"Spit, Juanito. Just clean 'em up!"

"*¡Qué cochinada!* (What a mess!)" He drooled, apparently grossed out over Marta's bubbly, now solidified gobs of spit. Amazing, since he exuded about two quarts of snot daily—most of it winding up either on his smelly, stiffened sleeve or in extravagant foamy trails down the front of his shirt.

244

No matter, the Red Wings were as new again. Chang seated us at the front table. Premium. "No cover charge. Compliments of the girls, Davíd."

"Thank them for us, Chang." He grinned. "*¡Hecho!* (Done!)"

Francisca sat next to me. "This will be the last time, Davíd, won't it?" I looked uncertain, so she leaned in close and flat asked: "Have you changed your mind about La Güera on the other side?"

"No." I smiled. "I shall return Monday afternoon. We are to be married late Friday evening."

"A church wedding. White dress and all?"

"Yes, Francisca, modest but proper. Just as you have hoped for me."

"Tell me the hour, Davíd, I want to picture it. Can you describe the place?" I did. She smiled, the floor show already in progress. "Save an hour for us tomorrow, Davíd, two-thirty sharp!"

Twenty minutes later Mariquita was scheduled to dance. But there was a pause I didn't expect. Mariquita came to the stage still wearing her little black dinner dress, not her "signature" Catholic girls' school uniform. The announcer came to the stage. "Tonight and tonight only, La Mariquita dances in *black*. Her performance is dedicated to a special friend." Chang grinned again.

It took her nearly twenty minutes to slither out of that dress, millimeter by millimeter, staring blissfully as the crowd went nuts, screaming, "*¡Mucha ropa!* (Take it off!)" till they were hoarse.

Her eyes glistened as two hundred men fell in love with her again and one taut nipple emerged from the same brilliant black silk that had caressed it to erection. She finished, glistening with sweat, wearing only a jet-black silk G-string and patent leather stiletto heels.

As the lights faded, wadded-up bills hit the stage like a hailstorm. She stood there, took a bow, and sighed. Blissful. Dreamy-eyed.

Francisca had already slipped away. The girls made big money when Mariquita danced. As the lights came on again, Mariquita came to our table to shake hands, blow me a kiss, toss us a wink, then glided away to soak up the afterglow and cash from adoring fans.

I left with Canelo and Negro about one-thirty. A light meal at the Almita Restaurant downtown gave me a chance to say goodbye to Ana Maria López.

Back on the Rubi's terrace, I went up to my rocking chair and turned it toward the harbor. Paradise! Indigo sky, the malecón's old-fashioned streetlights reflected in the harbor. Creosote, salt air, processed shrimp, and the scent of warm concrete adding an indelible dimension to my panorama.

Downstairs I hung a wet towel over the table fan in my room, made myself comfortable, and wrote in my journals. Just like old times. The lonely baritone of a freighter's distant horn echoed into my window after bouncing off the shrimp-packing plant's high wall.

Several minutes later I heard the staccato exhaust of a pilot boat's diesel as it pulled away from Punta Lastre to guide the freighter in. Echoing across the water, the pilot boat sounded exactly like a huge Harley-Davidson. A mournful reminder that I'd soon cross over to the States. The trip "home" frightened me.

Compared to Guaymas, the States were lonely, competitive, antiseptic. Apart from the thud of tires on hot concrete and an occasional Greyhound bus, everything sounded different. In the States one heard garage door openers, lots of police sirens, and the smooth burble of expensive cars. In Albuquerque, where I lived, one often heard the muffled, sinister sound of gunfire echoing in the streets once the family crowd had gone home to watch television. That's when the creeps came out to play in the dark. In contrast to Guaymas, one heard no taco carts, no *chicle* (Chiclets/chewing gum) kids, shoe-shine boys, or ice cream vendors.

Even restaurants in the two countries sounded as if they had been constructed on two different planets. Mexican restaurants have a sharp, ringing clatter characteristic of hard-tiled surfaces and few curtains, upholstery, or wall hangings to soften the sound. Most Stateside restaurants tended toward the sedate. Hushed, soft lights, carpet, fat chairs. Somber—rather like funeral parlors where food happens to be served.

And as for smells, the States simply doesn't. Bland. Deodorized, except for occasional hints of Pine-Sol and gasoline. A nation that has, for some odd reason, given itself the equivalent of an olfactory hysterectomy. In short I was soon to reenter "the richest nation on earth," but one that sometimes came off as intent upon social and sensory deprivation. Was this a penance of sorts for becoming rich in spite of its Puritan beginnings? Whatever its origins, Stateside blandness represented a huge loss to me.

Lively downtown street scene. (Photo by Dan and Rachel Shaffer © 2004.)

Mexico is a world you can see, hear, smell, taste. You can even touch your friends—male or female—without everyone going creepy on you. Living each day with all of one's senses engaged can be downright addictive. And I was an addict. This line of thought wasn't putting me to sleep, so I turned off my brain, closed the window, and slept.

Sunday, my last full day in Guaymas, was bright, clear, and warm. A steady breeze from the Sea of Cortez created specks of foam in the outer harbor. Along the Serdan church bells toned, palm trees fluttered in courtyard gardens, and the pelicans dive-bombed, enjoying a waterside feast as roiling waters brought small fish to the surface. Each morsel a blinding flash of silver against the azure sky, only to be forever extinguished. The sea's own shooting stars.

Life. One brilliant flash. Then gone. Poof! Just like Lupita. I turned away from the malecón and the harbor. Time to refocus.

Next I walked the sitios. Cheerful. Goodbyes, cigarettes, parrot jokes. When I left the Serdan and ambled through the plaza on my way to see Gorda and Juanito, Mass was being said at San Fernando.

Men smoked and played checkers in the square. Kids ran, fell, or crawled in every direction, laughing, screaming, crying, and sleeping on the shaded benches as parents chatted nearby.

No one home at Gorda's. Odd. But it was Sunday. Perhaps the little guy had gotten her out of the house again, cane in hand. I left a note for Gorda, certain I'd see Juanito at the Colmenar Monday afternoon before I hit the road.

On a whim I wandered back to the main plaza, turning uphill to the little plaza of the Tres Pistolas, but lingered there only long enough to light a smoke, thinking about my one date with Indita. Too much emotion for me. I needed to disengage from Guaymas. Not continue to get lost in the memories, as I had done all week.

When a taxi drifted past, I half expected Indita to miraculously emerge with a picnic basket. She didn't, of course. But I grabbed the taxi anyway and headed to the Zona. It was already after 2 p.m. Couldn't be late for Francisca's lunch.

Francisca herself greeted me at the door, smiling. Wearing a demure linen suit, she walked me to the patio. "One of the taxistas from Miramar said he believed it may have been 'La Flaca' he took to the bus station—*muy madrugada* (early morning) on Saturday."

"*¡Ojalá!* (Lord, I hope so!)," I replied, wanting to believe that she was right. As at brunch the year before, I sat at her right, she at the head of the table. I was the only male invited that day. Topic. None.

The girls were playful—lots of chatter, punctuated by teasing about "getting married. Getting a job. Babies."

"No more sleeping on the beach and no *chupando* tequila (sucking down tequila) when I was out of sorts," ordered Francisca. "Okay, Mom!" I teased back.

Then it turned serious. La Negra produced a small box. "La Indita," she said. Huh! I already had an unopened box from La Indita and said so. "Yes, Davíd, this box was to have been given you last year. But we chose not, after...after..."

"*La mandadera*," Francisca butted in. "You were so sad then. This did not seem appropriate."

"And her other box—the one you already gave me?"

"She said you would return to Guaymas and we should hand it to you personally when you arrived."

"So why was I not supposed to open the other one? Were those her instructions as well?" "No." La Negra smiled. "We only knew that she believed you would have received this one first. Several of us had a difficult time with her requests. We were uncertain...the morphine, *sabes* (you know)."

249

I protested. "This does not make sense! And why am I to open it publicly?" Francisca took control again. "She asked it of you. And we are *not* in public. Sunday is *quite* private!" I hesitated, but Francisca insisted, "*¡Abrela!* (Open it!)" pushing it into my hands. I stared at it but didn't move. "Why not?" she asked.

"I want to open it alone, if I open it at all!"

"Very well," said Francisca, "*en tal caso* (in that case) we cannot give you the box." For a moment she was rigid...then relaxed. That's when Negra leaned over unexpectedly and tore it open anyway. Right in front of everyone!

Carefully withdrawing Indita's gold-and-jade nipple ring, she admired it for a moment, holding it up to the sunlight for all to see. Negra sniffled. "I loved her. So beautiful!"

Francisca reached over to Negra, comforting her, and gently took the ring. Holding it close to my face, she eyed me carefully. "Your eyes are moist, Davíd, *qué no*? Indita would be gratified. Perhaps I should tell you her story anyway!"

"I already know most of it," I protested again. Unmoved, Francisca continued.

"When she came to us, she was not a vieja, but *tierna*, pure of heart. Raised by the nuns, she had been turned out of the orphanage when she came of age. No place for her. Her only skill was embroidering altar cloths! Yet she was full of life and laughed easily." Negra and several others nodding, Francisca went on. "She smiled often, told everyone's fortune, made us happy. She never drank real liquor. Occasionally a beer, and never with a client. Then she became obsessed with the idea of this school for orphan girls...."

Now it was Francisca's turn to pause and dab her eyes, quiet for a few moments. "She could not make enough money as a fichera (from drink tokens) so she asked us what it was like to be with a man. How one made love with a client. Imagine, a virgin! Right here among us. She did not belong here. We tried to dissuade her from taking a client. Chang even reduced her rent. But she was obsessed with this school, calculating the cost of concrete, roofing tiles, benches."

She sighed. "So she took her first client. He paid her well and... la *descorchó* (took her cherry). But he hurt her and she was tormented, so she had this ring put in her *ceno* (breast) and prayed a lot. She went to the ermita almost daily. After that client she withdrew into herself. Became quiet, *impasible* (impassive), and no longer laughed, her face so still it was disquieting.

"Then she began to dream, tell her own fortune, assuring us that a fair-skinned man who knew her country would come for her. We thought she was merely indulging in the fantasies that many of us have had at one time or another. But she insisted it was so... and she was a fortune-teller.

"We did not know if she had gone slightly mad—raised by the nuns and tormented by her guilt. But as time went on, she both saved her money and no longer insisted that some young man would come to rescue her.

"That was about two years ago, perhaps a bit longer. Of course, she discreetly eyed every *güero* who passed. But none were Oaxaqueños. Rich boys from that area do not come here. They go to Acapulco or Mexico City *para divertirse* (to enjoy themselves), not Guaymas. She would maneuver and contrive to tell the fair one's fortunes, always trying to discover a connection to her homeland. To no avail.

"When you first visited us, she noticed you. But she was not looking for a gringo. The tourists were pleasant, most of them, but they were not of her vision.

"Then you came to our *cena* (formal meal) one Sunday and we discussed culture. We spoke of Aztec Mexico. You talked briefly about the Aztec language and calendar, using their word for 'rabbit.'"

251

"'Tochtli.'" Negra nodded. "Which you noted was 'Chi-lezú' among the Zapoteca. I mentioned to the girls that you knew some Nahuatl (Aztec) and Zapoteca. Indita reacted as if she had been struck, later confiding that she wished to tell your *buenaventura* (fortune). So she went with us on one of your excursions. Something happened on that day. She said nothing to you but reneged on telling us your fortune."

Francisca took over. "But you met her at the shrine...and later downtown." I started to protest. She raised her hand to stop me. "*La morfina* (the morphine), Davíd. She talked about *many* things as the narcotic coursed through her veins, including her date with you."

I shrugged. "It was a picnic, a casual date; she told me my fortune. She was very kind."

"And you to her...she cried one night after the injection, wishing you had come into her life before the gold ring. She was a bit delirious. Yet she cried."

Negra finished the story. "After you met her at the shrine, she removed the ring and never took another client. She wanted to tell you that after she was ill, but she feared you might not understand. She also feared that we would not understand . . . and we do not, fully. The details are not our business."

"Francisca, why was I told so little? I liked her!"

"She was dying, Davíd. She wanted love, not pity. She was strong in her soul, but her body failed her."

"And the ring?" I asked. "She wanted you to open the package," Francisca said.

"Well, Francisca, this all saddens me. She was a very special person—but I think her jewel should belong to someone who is free to love her always."

"I'd love to have it!" Negra sniffled again. I agreed. "Francisca, it belongs to Negra. She will light candles for Indita at the shrine. I am leaving tomorrow and will be married Friday. I had so hoped today would not be sad."

Francisca smiled at me while Negra strung Indita's gold ring on her chain and hung it around her neck. Negra's small gold crucifix and Indita's nipple ring hanging together. "It is sad, Davíd—one so young. So brave. So honorable. And born to such misfortune.

"But it is happy also. We worked so hard to save you for some señorita. Even Indita did not want that possibility taken from you. It is all destiny, Davíd. Our job is done. But do let Canelo know when you are married. We wish to have news of it."

I left them about twenty minutes later after some intentionally upbeat chatter to brighten the mood, handshakes, and a few hugs. Kisses on the forehead from both Francisca and Mariquita sent me on my way. La Negra was still off in a corner of the patio, clutching Indita's ring and crying softly. Love is where you find it.

Back at my hotel room, I opened Indita's "second" package. It contained a small embroidered square of moss green silk and

Dave and Cindy's wedding. (Photo by Paul Morgan © 1971.)

a note in the neat lettering of a Mexican schoolgirl. I am still in wonder at the visions I saw through her exquisite eyes. And I still have no explanations for any of it. All so senselessly sad. Destiny? And if so—why? No answers, of course.

My evening with Mercedes, Olga, and little Martha Aurora was warm, gentle. No sad stories there. That night I packed. Walked. Rocked and readied myself for the return to my homeland. On Monday, I lunched at the Colmenar, said goodbye to Juanito and Sr. Kiami, Canelo and Enrique. Burro was sad but resigned.

On Wednesday afternoon I reached Albuquerque. The ferrocarrilero's daughter was waiting—the light in her eyes intense. Love and joy enveloped her like "the splendor" of an angel.

"I was afraid you might not return." She beamed as she folded me into her arms.

"So was I," I admitted.

"Mexico," she whispered. "Do not leave me for it. Promise?"

We were married on Friday evening. Shortly after midnight, at the university's chapel. Friday, you see, was the thirteenth. After midnight made it the fourteenth. Yet the wedding certificate read Friday, June 13, 1971, anyway. On Tuesday, I phoned the hotel Rubi bar. "*Casado*, Canelo! Tell the others!"

My guess is that the news hit the Río Rita within a few hours. The sitios within a few minutes.

Love is where you find it. Not where you imagine it should be. And you simply must not make a woman guess. You must say it out loud—lessons I once learned the hard way from both a remarkable little girl and a beautiful young Indian woman.

254

chapter seventeen

LOS MOCHIS—MID-1970s

Time itself creates oddities. Life changed. Entire worlds became haunting memories and remembered faces became indistinct. I could still hear Lupita's voice whenever I dreamed of her—so very alive, "*¡Aay! Güero. Tenemos negocios!*" But I could no longer see her clearly in my dreams. Only the shaggy mop of hair and her searching eyes stayed with me. In shocking contrast my brain had fixed Marta's last portrait, every tragic detail of it stunningly vivid.

Why is it that we forget the faces of those most cherished, yet remember so clearly those we wish to forget? My wife, Cynthia, told me that I still spoke Spanish in my sleep. Mexico still worried her at times. It was the "other woman" in my love triangle. A spiritual ménage à trois of sorts.

Yet I'd done hard time, "black man's time" they called it in the South, while living in Florida. A professor of anthropology at age twenty-seven. Incongruous! Especially when listening to my colleagues lament at having to teach two, count 'em, TWO, courses per term, convinced they were being screwed over by life. Shafted by Fate.

Those conversations and the ironies they created, usually over fresh oysters and beers, always brought Mexico crashing back into my consciousness, secretly reopening the floodgates of my memory and emotion. One does not advertise the mistress, you know.

Letters still came from Mexico. Don Francisco. Mercedes. Felipe L. Others. One came to the Department of Anthropology from Burro after my wife and I returned to New Mexico, the two years of traditional academic exile served. Typed. As best I knew, Burro didn't write—and it was florid in style. Likely the work of a public scribe, still common in Mexico at that time. Short story— La Blanca at the Río Rita needed to see me. About Marta. *Un mandado!* (An order! A "must do!") In person. Confidential.

Okay, but what does one tell a young wife? "Uh, honey, got to go to Mexico to check up on the old mistress. A friend says she needs me." Chang's Rule of Silence seemed wiser.

So I pondered the problem—nothing happens immediately in Mexico—and Fate unexpectedly intervened. The solution presented itself! So "Mexico"! A flyer came to the Office of Contract Archeology, where I worked.

The annual Pecos Conference, held each August since it was founded in 1927 as a gathering of Southwestern archaeologists (several World War II year exceptions), was to be held in Kino Bay, Sonora, ninety miles north of Guaymas. Only six weeks away. I submitted a last minute paper. Made preparations.

Thus one August in the mid-1970s, I made my most poignant visit. I went first to Kino Bay for the Pecos Conference. A plane to Hermosillo, then to the small bus station for the bus to the coast. A repainted, cast-off U.S. school bus with no air-conditioning to leaven August's 110-degree-Fahrenheit afternoon temperature, the hard-cushioned third-class bus took me from Hermosillo. We crossed the same flat desert plain that Lupita and I had traversed in August 1970 while headed for our "vacation" to old Kino on the Sea of Cortez.

I had written a scholarly paper for the occasion. Once in Kino, however, I was immersed in nostalgia. The bittersweet memories of Lupita erupted when I visited a restaurant in new Kino. As I sat down to order, I looked up and there was Lupita's stuffed yellowtail! The countergirl was sweet. Seeing me stare at it, she told me of the "little Mexican girl" who had long ago come to town with one of my countrymen and caught it—all by herself.

The blue-green water, rocky reddish promontory, and deep-gray shadow of Tiburón Island were all overwhelming. It was beautiful, yet so sad. I could still see Lupita on the dock by the original fishing settlement, standing next to her trophy fish. Happy. Full of joy.

As I relaxed on the restaurant's elevated terrace, it struck me that she would then have been eighteen or nineteen. I wondered what she would have grown to look like. Would we still be selling fans and blenders, making buying trips to Tucson? Would she still be alive had I finally worked up the balls to tell her I loved her, then adopted her? And what would she be like had she lived?

257

Kino Bay was spread before me, its rugged beauty diminished by the pungent scent of remorse, like rotting kelp washed up from the sea.

Later that night the fog drifted in from Tiburón, so dense and turgid that one couldn't see ten feet. The town's electricity failed, smothered like me by the leaden mists. Black, wet, so quiet one couldn't even hear the sea. I simply could not bear it.

The next afternoon I handed my undelivered paper to a colleague at the seaside conference hotel, asking him to read it for me. I packed and stood out in the road, Panama in hand, waving a ride. The huge crowd of archaeologists were gathered on the shaded hotel patio thirty yards from me as I waited. Several turned heads and raised eyebrows let me know that I was slipping into the realm of the eccentric by hitchhiking.

A few minutes passed before one of the young hotel clerks stopped his Volkswagen Beetle for the waving hat and asked where I was headed. "Guaymas—I have family there."

"Me too!" he said. He turned out to be a nephew of Manuel, another taxista from the Sitio Rubi.

We drove down the narrow lane through old Kino, passing the little hotel where Lupita and I had once stayed. Then we turned, skirting the wall of the restaurant where we had celebrated Lupita's trophy fish. Five minutes later, after exploring "family ties," he asked, "You wouldn't be the one they called El Güero, would you?"

"Yes." I smiled.

"*¡Qué padre!* (Cool!)" He grinned. "Wait till I tell my friends. There are stories about you and the Zona and fayuca. What was it like then?" I told him.

258

He drove me right to the arched front door of the Rubi Hotel, the very same pleasant-faced lady still at its desk. But things were already changing. My old room and several near it had been converted into the offices of the Guaymas baseball team, Los Marineros. I settled for a room nearer the lobby, across the garden in the same wing. Not bad. I could still see the door to my old corner room.

Next, a taxi to the Río Rita. It was mid-afternoon and Chang wasn't there. I didn't know the bartender, so I simply asked for La Blanca and waited. She had aged a lot. Hard edges had crept into the once cute wrinkles of her face. No longer slim and sleek, she was downright skinny. Pale instead of light complected, with no flashes of youthful color left in her skin. Hooker time. They age at least two or three years for every one on the outside world.

Thankfully, her inner self still seemed intact. She was pleasant. To the point. "Davíd, you hoped La Flaca had returned to her family, as did we. But she did not. She merely fled to the Zona in Mochis (Los Mochis, northern Sinaloa). They say she has died.

It is rumored that no one claimed her body. And there is speculation she was buried a *fuera del camposanto* (outside of holy ground)
with her business name only."

"*¿Detalles, Blanca?*"

"Ask there, Davíd!"

"Are you certain, Blanca?" She nodded. "Please go and find
out. They say she has a friend there in the Zona, Selena or Serena
is her name. Club Marlin."

"Club Marlin," I commented, "is just down the block."

"There are Club Marlins all over the west coast and Baja—
same owner, they say *en la calle*. She must have a mass, a
rosary... her soul... it *must* be saved! We all fear this. If she is
dead and has been buried where the Virgin, even God himself, cannot find her, something must be done. And some say
you may know her Christian names. Is it not so?"

"Yes, it is so. I will go tomorrow."

"Good! *¡Amable!* You owe her nothing after..." I raised my
hand, palm out. "No need to explain. I shall go. I promised to
keep her name long ago." She nodded and gave me an address,
written on a scrap of paper.

Early the next afternoon, still thinking of Lupita and her fish,
I ordered a bowl of menudo at the bus station. The trip to Mochis
was hot and uncomfortable, the bus packed. We stopped in
Empalme, Obregón, and other nowhere places along the way. In
Mexico the huge, "deluxe" and "Pullman" class buses are wonderful but seats scarce at in between stops like Guaymas. Second
class is altogether another experience.

Besides, I didn't care for Mochis, such a shabby contrast to
the bright, interesting nearby fishing settlement of Topolobampo.
The sea and palms there soothe and soften. But Mochis had a
hard, battered edge to it.

I took a taxi to the red-light district, the driver making jokes
and recommendations. I told him I wasn't partying but came to

inquire about a friend. End of jokes. In fact, end of conversation, though he watched me furtively, glancing sideways in curiosity.

Unlike Guaymas, the red-light district in Mochis had nothing in particular to recommend it except plenty of shopworn hookers and lots of expensive beer. It was also on the edge of town—laid out along one wide, unpaved clay avenue. But there was no neat cage to contain the evil one.

Some of the nightclubs were elevated on crumbling concrete pedestals. Others simply sprouted from the clay as if by accident.

We pulled up in front of the Club Marlin. From "curbside" appearances a shithole, at peace with its decadence. I wondered, as Blanca had suggested, if there really was a Club Marlin in every sizable town along the Sea of Cortez.

Everywhere I had gone as a kid in Pennsylvania, West Virginia, and Ohio, there was a Dew Drop Inn less than two miles away. What a weird cultural parallel. All Dew Drop Inns looked alike, the lighted Budweiser and Iron City beer signs identical. The very same brand of urinals smelling of piss and "chew."

260

Well, Mochis's Club Marlin was certainly an unremarkable little place, just like the one in Guaymas. The taxi driver departed, even though I'd tipped him to wait. Cabrón! There was virtually no one in the red-light district at that time of day. It was hotter than blazes and the club's door was closed. I banged anyway.

When at last it opened, I was greeted by a short, dark burly Mexican guy who at first glance gave one the distinct impression that he enjoyed knocking people around if they crossed him. Perhaps it was his balled fists. Or his warm greeting, "*¿Qué quieres, puto?* (What do you want, faggot?)" Nice! So unlike the tone of things at the Río Rita.

I smiled, answering in Spanish that I "liked girls and had come to speak with one named Selena." Though surprised by the Spanish, he told me curtly that "La Selena doesn't receive clients at this time of day," and started to slam the door.

I replied, "*Un momento, señor. No soy cliente!* (One moment, sir. I'm not a client!) I have come on a *mandado* (errand or mission) sent by Chang and Brigido at the Río Rita in Guaymas. *¡Importante!*" He closed the door quietly after asking me to wait "*un momentito.*" As I gave up and turned to leave, the door opened on a crack. Good timing!

A young, thin-faced girl of about twenty stuck her nose out and called to me, "Señor?" I turned to ask if she was Selena. "I'm Selena. Has Chang really sent you?"

"Yes, I am *un socio.*"

"Aaay!" she responded. "The doorman regrets his comments."

"He should," I shot back. "*Inculto.* Chang will be insulted. He and I are family."

At this the puto hater stepped out, arms spread, palms out. Supplication. Time to close the deal. "If I get what I need—information and the most modest of assistance—all of us in Guaymas will be grateful." Like I said, Chang was a legend. So were the políticos who passed through the Río Rita's doors, their drivers waiting patiently and sweating in the heat. Mr. Warm and Cuddly nodded to the girl and withdrew into his shithole.

Now alone in the street, I explained, "I have come from Guaymas to talk to you about a friend of yours, La Marta, who, it is said, has died.

"*¿Porqúe?*" she asked. I answered, "La Blanca at the Río Rita referred you to me." She looked at me again, then down toward the aging Red Wings.

"You are not one of Chang's colleagues. You are the North American!"

I smiled. "*Pués.* I am a North American." She said, "No, *the* North American. Marta spoke of you. I was never certain that you were real. Are you he?" I nodded. "Yes, I am. May we talk? May I come in?"

"No," she said, "not here. Wait for me!"

A few minutes later she came out carrying a nylon net bag containing a large box. "Come on with me!" Young, she had either suffered bad acne or mild smallpox as a kid. Dark and slender, like Marta, she seemed nervous.

We walked to a little restaurant nearby that served the red-light district. I maneuvered for a spot in front of the fan. It was hotter than hell. She knew the manager and asked that we be left alone. I offered a beer. She didn't drink. Perhaps that's why Marta had picked her as a friend.

I had an Orange Crush. She a Coke. After wiping the sweat off, I pulled out my cigarettes, tapped a Pall Mall red on my thumbnail, and lit it. She asked to see the pack, studying it intently. Satisfied, she looked up again. "I have a sealed letter here for a North American and some other things. But you must first tell me who you are. I must know your name."

"My full name?" I asked.

262

"Yes."

I showed her my passport. She reached into the bag and, as I spoke, looked at her envelope. She studied my passport carefully and matched it to the envelope. I said, "My name is David Edward Stuart."

Selena smiled. "You've grown older and fatter. You have much less hair, but you smoke precisely as Marta described. And your boots . . . she talked of you many times, many nights. We shared a room when there were no clients. I never quite believed that you were real. She drank so much, you know." I asked softly, "Still the Ron Castillo?"

"Yes! You know all about it, then."

"I know some of it, but not all. I've come to ask you questions—has she died, as they hear in Guaymas?"

"Yes," she whispered. "Not long ago."

"Where is she buried?"

"Nearby, señor."

"*¿En camposanto, suelo sagrado?* (On holy ground?)"

"No!" Her eyes teared. "Last rites?" Again, "No."

"We'll fix all that," I reassured her.

After a long pause she looked up, managed a half smile, and handed me the faded envelope, a Mexican airmail addressed to me at the University of New Mexico—never sent. I asked Selena why Marta had never mailed it.

She hesitated. "La Flaca was mysterious about it. She told me only that she had to believe in something, one thing, just one thing—that she could no longer believe in more and that if it never reached your hands, it would be her punishment for having believed...and for...for...having spit on you."

The note inside was surprisingly short. It began with, *I am so sorry, Davíd....* The rest, well, as Chang would say, "It is forgotten." Still, she signed her full name, as if I might not remember it. She asked only one thing of me. The promise that had brought me there in the first place.

263

I thanked Selena, telling her that I had some business to undertake on Marta's behalf. "I'll help," she said, "and I have something else to show you." In the box, looking almost new, was Marta's blue dress, purchased in Jimmy Kiami's shop, El Capricho, in 1970. Selena wanted me to know that Marta had insisted again and again that she had never worn it for a client nor when she had been drinking.

I believed that—the dress had been worn only for her son on Sunday afternoons before she went to Club Guaymas. Selena looked up at me helplessly. "She never said what to do with it but keep it with the letter until you came. I knew about the dress. She took it out to show me and told me about the North American who had bought it for her."

So I asked why they hadn't buried her in it. Selena responded, "I asked her that once. You know she talked often about dying. The way she drank, one believed it. But she was adamant and told me she could not be buried in that dress, as a whore with no name."

"Well, I have come with her name. Do you know where she's buried?"

"Yes, señor."

"Selena, can you help me find a padre?"

"I think so," she said.

She hesitated. "Can you wait for me here un ratito? I will make arrangements. I need a hundred pesos."

I handed her the hundred, probably for a salida. I smoked and waited. When she returned, she had changed into street clothes. We hailed a taxi and went downtown to a small chapel in a poorer district.

The middle-aged padre there was decent. I asked, "What can we do?" He said "Well, we can go to the grave and I can offer a service. My guess is that the police had her buried with no formalities. But first, I'd like this young woman you've brought to give confession. You wait for me here." So I waited on the steps of the chapel near the door. Selena went into the confessional booth.

She came back after about fifteen minutes, looking down-cast. I asked, "What's the matter?" She blew it off. "Oh, it's just what he prefers and he's all that we have in the Zona." Fair or not, I pictured the padre jacking off in the confession booth as he listened to details of the young hooker's transactions.

Whatever transpired, the old boy came out, very pleasant, and talked to me for a few minutes. I asked, "Can we move her grave to holy ground?" He shook his head. "That will make it police business, but we can consecrate her grave, then give her a service. It's much less complicated than moving her, but I will need permission for the service. It's customary in these cases to make a donation to the church." So I made a donation of five hundred pesos, forty dollars. That seemed to satisfy him perfectly.

"Here is a card. Write me her full baptized names. Wait two hours. A colleague and I will need some time." Selena and I went

264

La Michoacana ice cream shop in Guaymas. (Photo by Dan and Rachel Shaffer © 2004.)

into an air-conditioned ice cream parlor nearby—La Michoacana. There seemed to be one of those in every sizable Mexican town.

When he reappeared, we didn't even need a taxi. The spillover graveyard was just one very long block down the street. At the still fresh grave a new wooden cross had been erected, her "street" name lettered on it. I stooped, scooped a bit of the soft earth from the base of her cross, and buried the folded-over church card with her full name on it. And a short note from me.

Then the padre delivered a brief service for her, saying her Christian names. Selena said that we ought to bury the dress with her. "No, you should keep it. Marta must have meant for you to have it. She grinned and said, "Oh, it is a beautiful dress, a very beautiful dress. You know, there are slippers to match." I sighed.... "Yes, I remember."

We left the graveyard and walked back up the street to the chapel, where the padre shook our hands. Selena was very quiet. I asked if he would give Marta's name in prayer next year at the same time and gave him another two hundred pesos. He said that it would be done. Then he had a word with Selena.

As we waited for a taxi to the Zona, Selena indicated that it was her dream to go back to a village near Culiacán and marry her "real" boyfriend who worked on a rancho (farm). She had only been in the Zona two years and still wrote her boyfriend often. He thought she was a maid in Los Mochis, trying to save enough money to return home and marry him.

I asked her if she had saved her money. She said she had, but it had been stolen out of the rooms several times and they thought it was the guy who I'd met at the door, but they could never prove anything. So she only had a few hundred pesos. It turned out that she had talked to the padre in the confessional, who scolded her to go back to the rancho near Culiacán and marry her farm boy.

266

I admitted that I'd misjudged the padre. She laughed, saying that if she'd had the good fortune to have worked in a club like the Río Rita, in Guaymas, she would have a few thousand pesos to buy a hectare (approximately two acres) of land and could go back home.

Out of the clear blue, I suggested, "If you can't go home without money to buy land, well, why don't you come back to Guaymas with me? I'll take you to the Río Rita and introduce you. Perhaps they can arrange something." She reacted, "Oh, how I would like to leave here! *Pues*, when would we go?"

"Tonight! Late bus," I suggested. It was then already dark, about eight-thirty in the evening. I had no reason to stay in Mochis and I was sad for Marta. I still wanted to know how Marta had died, but Selena was tight-lipped, even mysterious. "See the Cruz Roja (Red Cross), a guy named Manuel," she insisted.

We stopped at the Cruz Roja, where Manuel was out in the *ambulancia* (ambulance). Expected return about 10 p.m.

A taxi took us back to the Zona, waiting for us this time. Selena said she'd need another hundred pesos. The "salida" routine again? Once inside, I inquired about the stolen money, staring at Mr. Wonderful as if I owned neighboring Sonora. He conceded that they owed her some back wages and would see to it directly. I went on, "Chang wants a personal report. I am taking Selena with me. She will return in several days. Any problems?"

"¡No! No hay pedo, señor. (All cool—no "farts" [problems] here, sir.)"

"Good. If there are difficulties, I will send Brigido."

"No, señor. Everything is fine. Send our regards to Chang and the Río Rita's patrón."

I leered. "Señor X is in Guadalajara on business right now, but I will carry the message."

267

"Obligado, señor." Man, if I could control this bully with pure bullshit, Brigido could probably make him crap himself with just one close-up of those smallpox scars! If one is going to unfairly displace both guilt and anger, unloading on a bully is pretty satisfying.

Selena came out a side door, a case of belongings with her. She had to leave several things so it wouldn't be obvious that she was never coming back. Badass wasn't going to complain, but she had no way of knowing that. Even more miraculously, he had "found" part of her missing money and paid up for the fichas owed. She was giddy.

Back at the Cruz Roja, Manuel was in but scared shitless to talk to the "agente norteamericano" (U.S. agent). He was convinced I was bad news. Inexperienced at the Cruz Roja, Marta's death had rattled him anyway. So Selena got the story after I agreed to leave for the bus station. "Everything," I instructed her. She nodded, indicating she'd meet me at the bus station later.

I bought tickets, cool sodas, and tortas for the trip, wondering if Selena would really show for the late bus. She did, hurrying in with only a few minutes to spare and looking grim.

We had premium (front) seats right across from the driver. I asked for details. First, she told me that the girls in the Zona had tried to get Marta buried properly. But the cops were nasty. There had been a small collection, but the police would not release her body. She still had the money. About six hundred pesos ($48 US). Did I want it?"

"No, it's yours now."

"*Verdad?* (Really?)"

"Yes, for your dowry—land in Sinaloa. Now—details!"

I got them from Manuel's eyewitness account to her, then to me—on the late bus north from Mochis. I'd have been much better off not knowing. "We saw her there from the door of the club but dared not interfere—the police, you know." Selena sniffled....

Being a whore hadn't been easy. Still, she must have been drunk as hell to have died as she did. The August rains had come. A bottle of Castillo rum still clutched tightly in her fist, she drowned in six inches of filthy mud and water in that dismal Mexican port town, far from home. Goddamn her! She always did drink too much!

They found her not fifty yards from the door of the tawdry club where she screwed strangers, quickly and quietly, for a hundred pesos, then just as quickly spent her money on rum so she could forget what she had done.

Cradling her head against his chest, a young, light-skinned Cruz Roja medic kneels in the flooded "avenue" that announces the red-light district in Los Mochis. He wipes compulsively at her face, not noticing the streaks of dull orange mud, indelible as factory-made dye, that leave her death marks on his carefully starched white tunic.

Eyes wide open, she stares lifelessly up at her young attendant, who, transfixed, simply cannot force himself to look away. Watching from the ambulance, the driver looks disgusted, then pushes himself out into the cold rain. Burly and fortyish, his brilliantined hair glistens in the garish lights of a nearby nightclub.

"Come on, Manuelito. Vámonos." He grunts, grabbing the kid sharply. "Let her go!"

268

Still cradling her, the young medic whines back, "We should do something for her. We cannot just leave her here."

"Mira, look here, Manuel," the fat one says more softly, "you must become accustomed to all this. This one, poor thing, is only a vieja, a whore, and she is dead, Manuel. Dead! Do you understand me? This is police *business. We must leave her for the police—we do not want trouble with them, you and I ¿Verdad? Now be a compadre and put her back like you found her."*

Carefully propping her head up, Manuel lets her slide back into the muddy water. She lies there face upturned, childlike and serene. The rain washing away the last clumps of orange-brown mud clinging to her face and with them the final remnants of her self-hatred.

At last Death had forgiven her and erased her sordid memories. The bottle of Ron Castillo slipped from her grasp, no longer important.

When we reached Guaymas about 6 a.m., I sent Selena to the Río Rita by taxi and told her I'd come out the next afternoon. She was to ask for La Blanca. I went on to the Hotel Rubi. Exhausted, I slept till 1 p.m.

Late that afternoon I went out to the Río Rita, saw La Blanca and Selena. But there was discord. They didn't want her at the Río Rita. La Blanca wanted to talk to me alone, so we walked down the street to the restaurant where I had once drunk bitter coffee, waiting for Marta.

She said, "Look, this girl is a nice kid. But she's an amateur. There's no room for her here. There is no big money, like there once was. The old days are over. There is no room here for another girl. I think this one should go home. I talked with her early this morning and she would like to go home to Culiacán." I agreed.

Blanca continued, "The poor thing has only four hundred and some-odd pesos. They cheated her in Los Mochis where she

269

worked." I nodded, knowing she had a bit more, but chose not to argue it.

"Mira, Davíd, I took up a collection among the girls early this morning," Blanca went on, "We owe her something for her loyalty. We have gathered five hundred pesos and *pico* (change)."

"She thought she could go home if she had three thousand pesos. Now it's up to you. Maybe you could talk to Chang, Canelo, or Jacinto. Perhaps you can help a bit yourself. What do you think?"

I agreed. "We should send her home. I'll take her with me. I'll go downtown, I'll go to the Banco de Sonora. I'll see that she has a bus ticket and send her home with three thousand pesos."

"Thank God, Davíd! That would be a good thing. Life will be hard for her. She's going to marry some *campesino* (farm boy)."

"Yes," I said, "she told me."

"Besides, Davíd, she does not have the *purgaciones crónicas* (chronic clap)—she can still have babies. Many of us can't, you know. She can make a life for herself. It will be hard, but she can do it. She's not like us. She doesn't drink and she's a good person."

I commented, "It's odd, Blanca. Here we are doing something for this girl when I might have done something for Marta." She looked me right in the eye and said, "Don't blame yourself for that. All the money in the world couldn't have done anything for Marta. She hated herself so. This girl does not—yet. She should go home."

I took Selena downtown. She was a bit bummed that they couldn't make a place for her at the Río Rita but pleased that the girls had given her money. Francisca nodded at me from in front of the residencia as our taxi pulled away. The taxi waited for me at the Banco de Sonora, where I cashed two traveler's checks. I came out and we went on to the bus station. She was agitated, fearing that we were actually sending her back to Mr. Wonderful in Mochis.

Selena was in disbelief when I handed her a bus ticket to Culiacán and gave her another twenty-five hundred pesos. She still had Marta's blue dress and her own cardboard "suitcase." She had about four thousand pesos ($320 US) in hand—enough to buy a hectare or so (two to three acres) of hillside *milpa* (cornfield) out in the sticks. She asked how she could ever repay me.

"*¡Fácil!* (Easy!)" I said. "You may repay me by wearing the blue dress at your wedding and sending me a note," and I handed her my business card from the Office of Contract Archeology at the University of New Mexico.

She got into the bus before it really hit her. At her front window seat she pressed her lips to the glass, tears smearing both the window and her lipstick. Had she never written, the teary window kiss would have sufficed. But about three months later a note came to me at the university. Mexican airmail envelope.

¡Ya! Me casé por la civil! Vestido en puro azul. ¡Qué Dios le bendiga! Selena. (Done! I got married at the civil registry. Dressed all in blue. God bless you! Selena.)

271

La Indita. La Marta. La Selena. Viejas. Only one out of three survived to have a life. It could just as easily have been none. Both Indita and Selena had cheated the evil one, their souls safe. Marta's soul may still have hung in the balance. Who knew? But as I read the farm girl's note a second time, I grinned to myself and pictured the old horned bastard flicking his tail in frustration and rattling the bars of his dusty cage.

Later that day I walked up to the Newman Center on the university's campus and lit three candles. One for Lupita. One for Indita. One for Marta. On the street you have to take your victories as they are given you.

Part Three:
LIFE GOES ON

epilogue

1972–2003

In May of 1972, I again returned to Guaymas. Things were changing. I had already earned my Ph.D. in anthropology and brought the ferrocarrilero's daughter, Cindy, née Cynthia Morgan, as promised.

My twin brother, John, and his first wife accompanied us on that trip. All tourists but me, we booked seaside rooms upstairs at the Hotel Miramar, where Negro Jacinto still worked. The roof terrace where I had once danced and outrageously defended an errant fiancée's honor was, literally, overhead.

The palms and cascading buganvilla in varying shades of deep pink, red, and coral contrasted with the brown, coconut-thatched seaside palapas. The Miramar and the bay were a visual treat. New Mexico *is* dry. In contrast, Bacochibampo Bay and its soft, rhythmic surf was hypnotic. The Bohemias were ice cold, the "you-peel-'em" shrimp bountiful. The sweep of the bay and sunsets was majestic. All so picturesque.

But I was a creature of the Serdan. I'd lived on it, loved on it, lost on it, and had come of age in the society that breathed life into it.

And my gorgeous young wife wanted to meet those entangled in our unusual love triangle. She wanted to see the Serdan. Meet Canelo, Negro, and above all find out if people like Chang actually existed beyond the confines of my imagination.

As the others wiggled their toes on the beach, we started doing the Serdan. Greetings at the Sitio Medrano on Calle 19, then late lunch at the Colmenar. I introduced her to Mercedes, who was both gracious and pleased. We made a date to visit her on Sunday. Max, the restaurant's owner, also wanted us to visit his home and meet his mom, the widowed doña Adelpha. *Propio.*

Jimmy Kiami came by as word traveled. But Juanito didn't show. I reckoned I'd catch him later. Cindy loved the food, determined to sample every variety of freshly caught seafood available. If you like the local food in Mexico, smile, and shake hands, you're already halfway there.

Then we walked the Serdan, passing El Pollito and Kiami's El Capricho, where she bought a cute handmade top. It looked great on her, but what didn't? She was tall (five feet nine) with warm crinkly eyes, a huge dimpled smile, and long, wavy brown hair. The warmth and easy manner she naturally exuded made her *simpática.*

Next we went to the old city market. Stopped in the Almita. Said our hellos, shook hands, then hit the old curio and jewelry shops along the southern margins of the malecón. My wife found stuff she liked. Contributed to the local economy. Then we returned to Miramar and gathered the others for dinner at the Paradise seafood restaurant—at the time still in business and Guaymas's best.

Sitio Rubi and harbor. (Photo by Dan and Rachel Shaffer © 2004.)

Two lobsters with the trimmings were Cindy's request. Not a problem. In 1972 her two-lobster dinner cost all of $6.40 US. We sat at the same front table where I had once dined with Burro, Mariquita, and La Negra. Before that, I'd eaten there with Marta. And before Marta, my fiancée, Iliana.

As we stepped out of the Paradise, I spotted the facade of Casa Sagrestano across the street—a men's shop where both Edward Myers and I had bought guayaberas (volume 1) in '69 and '70.

After dinner we headed back to the Miramar. Drinks and a couple of dances later, I caught Negro's eye and we arranged to meet at the Rubi bar about ten-thirty. I borrowed my brother's Volvo and drove Cindy to the Rubi.

Canelo wasn't there—a big disappointment for her. He had recently been in a serious auto accident and, depending on who I asked, was either still in the hospital or already at the city jail. But Enrique was at the new bar, built in front of my old room block, adjacent to the lobby. This bar was upscale. Carpet, leather, and chrome, its side door opening right onto the sitio's taxi rank. No long block to walk in the summer heat for tourists and traveling businessmen.

Enrique, now married, was still Enrique—pleasant, effusive with Cindy, and as well turned out as ever. I drank Orange Crush, Cindy a Coke. We chatted, mixing some translations into the banter for Cindy's benefit. That's about the time don Francisco strolled in, walked to the bar, and ordered a drink. He didn't see me at first. So, Cindy in hand, I walked over and made the introductions.

As handsome and distinguished as ever, he was both culto and, to my surprise, stunningly bilingual. He told Cindy that I was both "a playboy and an astronaut." She laughed. "I know... but I have it under control." He laughed, charmed, responding in kind. They liked each other.

As he left a few minutes later (I think I knew where he was headed), he beamed at me, said, "Adiós," and, raising his eyebrows, gave me the "okay" sign. Cindy was easy to be around and had a *Vogue* cover girl's figure. Not that he noticed, of course.

Later we went down to the old Rubi bar, where Negro Jacinto was already waiting. Eva had joined him and we had beers. If Negro was happy for me, Eva was ecstatic. She not only got to "see" the ferrocarrilero's daughter, as promised, but she was sitting right there with her, over a beer, the two of them plotting. Negro and I translated a bit, but Cindy understood some Spanish (the beer helped) and Eva could speak much more English than I'd realized.

The conversation had turned to "visiting the Río Rita so as not to *desconocer* Davíd's friends there." This made Negro so nervous that he was actually sweating. I had my reservations too. It was Saturday night. Floor show in forty minutes. Not the time or place for discreet introductions and genteel tête-à-têtes.

But when two strong-willed women "decide" anything, it's going to happen. Yet in Mexico, one did not take one's señora into the Zona. Repeat. *Not!* I drove, Negro accompanied us—likely the single most valorous act of our long friendship. A "downtown" girl, Eva couldn't go but saw us to the door.

As we neared the Río Rita, Negro sweated more profusely and Cindy was quiet—displaying that smile women get when they are about to bust you for the bullshit you've laid on them. I imagined her thinking, *"Maybe there is a Zona!"* *"Possibly a joint called the Río Rita."* *"But none of the girls actually know him,"* and, *"No way is there a five-foot-tall, five-foot-round club manager named Chang...but I aim to find out!"* Her bullshit detector had fresh batteries in it.

But luck, and truth, were both on my side. The Volvo was just as square and chunky as the old '62 Rambler Classic. About twenty yards from the Río Rita's porch, the first of the girls saw the chunky car and started shouting, *"¡Descraciado!"* just as I warned her they might. Jacinto was either having a major panic attack or a mild coronary. I wasn't sure which.

When we emerged from the car and mounted the steps, my observant young wife looked up the street, surveying the bright lights of a half dozen other clubs. Several of the girls rushed us *"¡Davíd, bienvenidos! ¿Cuándo llegáste?* (Welcome! When did you arrive?)"

The three of us entered and headed toward the bar. There stood Chang, who moved forward quickly to deliver the ritual abrazos and shake hands. *Ha!* I thought. *Now call me a bullshitter!*

Five feet tall and fully five feet around the waist, Chang embraced me, sneaking a peek behind as we traded ritual shoulder pats and asked, *"¿Quién es la Güera altota?* (Who is the very tall gringa?)"

I grinned. "Señor Chang, meet my wife, Cynthia, the ferro-carrilero's daughter. Cindy, meet my friend Señor Chang." Chang should, of course, have shaken her hand but was, shall we say, momentarily "distracted."

Instead his fat arms rose, palms covering both sides of his plump face as he exclaimed loudly, "*¡Por Dios! ¡Es la esposa!* (Dear God, it's the wife!)" Nice work, Chang! At that pronouncement the band simply stopped, right in the middle of "Night Train."

For one moment all was still and very quiet. The familiar cosmic hiccup. The fart during a papal audience. Frankly, I think my wife has always cherished that moment. Her hubby may have been both eccentric and colorful but Chang, dammit, was round, real, and right in front of her. Who knew?

Chang recovered quickly, as impresarios usually do, and ushered us to a "reserved" front table. La Blanca hustled over to join us as did La Negra and another (not Marta) "La Flaca." I introduced them. Negro's impending infarct faded as he realized that Cindy was fine and the girls on the central committee had the situation in hand. The club returned to its normal pandemonium, accompanied by some rubbernecking, the only evidence of lingering awareness.

The girls approved of Cindy, chattering with her English and Spanish. Cindy leaned to me at one point, whispering, "This is cool. The girls are nice! I thought it would be rawer somehow."

"Nope, honey, not in the Río Rita. This is *old* Mexico. Nothing like a Stateside strip joint managed by some character called 'Ace.' Dance?"

As the floor show unfolded, the girls and Negro glanced at Cindy now and again, probably wondering if she'd finally "get it" and go nuclear in señora-like moral outrage. Chang came to sit briefly before Mariquita came onstage, asking obliquely if "your wife understands our business?"

"Totally, Chang. She wished to visit and meet those I have spoken of so often." Chang brightened. As if in response, the lights dimmed.

Mariquita! Oh, yeah! Halfway into her strip Cindy leaned close, whispering in my ear, "What would it cost to sleep with her?" I quoted the current rate. She paused, her brow knitting. "She's gorgeous! So why did you leave Mexico?" Cindy knew a lot, but she still knew nothing of Lupita, so I answered, very guy-like, "Sometimes I wonder!"

Later she needed to go to the women's room and asked me where it was. Totally stumped, as was Jacinto, I had to ask Blanca. Cindy ragged me. I countered, "Hey! Chang was real. What do you want? How the hell would I know where the women's john is in a cathouse?" Jacinto, who understood English, damn near split a gut.

281

The girls had a major laugh over that as Jacinto explained. They accompanied Cindy. Partly courtliness and, possibly, to make certain that none of the rich local men eyeing her made an indecent offer as she crossed the showroom floor.

Mariquita stopped by the table after the show. As did several of the waiters, like old Felipe L. Good old Brigido watched us from a distance. I waved. He nodded. Ah, Brigido was becoming downright effusive in his old age! Francisca was absent. She may have had a guest (don Francisco?) or she may have thought her presence inappropriate. But she would soon be briefed in detail.

As we left, Cindy thanked Chang for the great table, company, and floor show. La Blanca gave Cindy a squeeze, then told me that I "had gotten a jewel!" I'll bet the girls lit a candle for us at the shrine the next afternoon. They had saved me for a señorita. Mission accomplished.

This visit was already being transformed into street legend by Sunday as we lounged on the beach.

Later that day we went to visit Mercedes. Her small house near the main plaza was delightful. Breezy and bright with flowers both on the patio and a small balcony above, it was a happy place. There was no period of adjustment between her and my new wife. Mercedes was, and remains, warm, radiant, and emotionally accessible.

We had cafés con leche and played with baby Olga, then eighteen months old. Some of the kid's splotchiness had faded, but she squirmed as ever. Martha Aurora, the wolf pup, hid behind Mercedes, staring intently. Her nostrils twitched as before. When mom exited to bring the coffee, Martha was exposed. Vulnerable. She watched every move as I sipped my mug of steamed milk and coffee.

I forgot about her and sat cross-legged on the tiled floor, cradling Olga, still a miniature radiator. When I reached into my back pocket for a blue bandana to clear the sweat, my elbow bumped little Martha, who was hiding right behind me. I turned, reeled her in with one arm, and offered her a sip of the milky, sweet coffee. Contact!

Forever after, Martha Aurora and I shared our coffee ritual. As she grew, she always brought me the café con leche when I visited. I always let her drink some. Domestication, we call the process in anthropology. But over the years it became ever more difficult to tell just which one of us was in control of the process. This is the essence of bonding. Ours is deep—a private force field rich with understanding.

I saw Negro Jacinto in '71, '72, '77, '84, '92, '94, and in 1995, when he was driving a van for the Club Med at San Carlos. The lovely Miramar Hotel suffered a suspicious fire and was razed a number of years ago. Ever the anthropologist, I retrieved several of the tiles from its roof terrace. They remain in my storeroom.

I last saw him in November of 2003, when I gave him a copy of *The Guaymas Chronicles: La Mandadera*, first volume. By then he was driving a taxi at the Sitio del Puerto, not far from the plaza. Now in his late sixties, discussing the book that chronicled him and others, he summed it up nicely, his bedrock Guaymas values still on course. "*Vivimos. ¡Ya! ¡Ganamos!* (We live! We have won!)" He is still bubbly, gracious, kind, and wise. His life, like that of nearly every working stiff in Guaymas, has been one long series of daily battles. But he lives. He won.

I have seen Canelo, aka Jesse, even more frequently. By the 1990s the Hotel Rubi had been carved up into several businesses, its second story becoming government offices. So Canelo became a taxista, driving at the Medrano sitio on Calle 19.

He is still revered on the street. At age seventy-two and counting, he works every day, now driving a taxi at the sitio beneath the huge supermarket on the corner of Calle Diez (Ten) and the Serdan. He has a modest but very pleasant corner house, just several long blocks from my goddaughter Olga's place.

283

Canelo shares that home with his wife of many years, doña Ofélia. She is warm, pleasant, and works at a curio shop in San Carlos. They both love flowers, their dog, and, of course, a small parrot. From their front porch, one can see down the street to Ana Maria López's house. She of the Almita.

When I last visited Ana Maria with Canelo, in about 1995, she had matured into a very handsome woman. She talked of the "battles" of life, her eyes twinkling, the creases where the corners of her eyes meet her nose, still full of life. Now middle-aged, she remains sexy, interesting, and competent. The owner of the Almita in 1995, a son, Carlos, if I remember correctly, now runs the business. It's been several years since I ate there, but it was as good and as reasonably priced as I found it the first time I dined there in 1970.

Goddaughter Olga was both confirmed at San Fernando and well past the squirming stage by 1980. By 1988, at age eighteen, she had her passport, a visa obtained through the good offices of New Mexico's senior U.S. senator, Pete Domenici, and was living with my wife and me in Albuquerque, studying English at Albuquerque TVI. She returned to Mexico for a while, then came back to Albuquerque at age twenty-one, staying another year and a half.

On her first visit, young and homesick, she cried a few times. Besides, her father gone even before she was born, it was hard for her to accept the reality that I, her godfather, really was a gringo. The real, English-speaking pinche thing!

She had always teased me a bit about my mangled Spanish—as the years passed, my tongue no longer automatically went in the right direction when speaking Spanish, and I forgot words. But her nino—an honest-to-God gringo! At first it was a bit too much for her! Later, as she settled in, she asked perceptive questions:

"Nino, why is everyone traveling alone in their autos? Have they no family? Where are they going in such a rush anyway?"

"This is a rich country; why are the only people on the calle Central (Central Avenue) drunk or homeless?"

"If you liked the service the waitress gave us, why did you hide the tip under the plate—instead of thank her and hand it to her?"

"It is lonely here on the street. Must you know someone before you are permitted to say 'good afternoon'? Why do they look away when one greets them?"

And the coup de grace, "Why do they water such huge lawns here? Is it not a desert?"

Ah, yes, hmm! Frequently I found myself resorting to an all-purpose Guaymas-style answer, "*De costumbre* (custom), Olguita. *De costumbre.*"

Eventually my wife had the "women's power" conversation with Olga. I usually translated, but this one required none. My wife, pressing the theme one night, offered to buy Olga a small house in Guaymas as a wedding gift if she stayed in school and still had no babies at age twenty-three. Olga turned to me as I prepared to translate. "*¿Verdad? ¿Una casita a los veinte-tres?* (Truly? A small house at age twenty-three?)"

The sisterhood has simply miraculous methods of communication. Several years later she collected, within months of marrying Jesús Ramírez, a younger son of taxista Cocas Ramírez (chapter 1). They now have three kids, including a daughter, Cyndy, named after my Cindy—the ferrocarrilero's daughter. We are her godparents too. The second generation baptized at San Fernando. The little one, of course, is referred to as "Cyndy Chica" ("Little Cindy").

Jimmy Kiami, ever the visionary, opened new businesses out at San Carlos Yacht Basin and had died a short time before my 1995 trip. Many still living in San Carlos remember him fondly. His widow and family maintain businesses there to this day. You would have liked Jimmy. He was infectious.

The Rubi's patrón, Hector Morales, was very ill in the Sanchez clinic during my 1995 visit. He still lived in the house at the back corner of the hotel lot. That Victorian-style wood house had, I believe, once been assigned to the American consul in Guaymas. So important was Guaymas from about 1880 to 1940 that the U.S. consul was stationed there, rather than in Hermosillo.

The Hotel Rubi, as I've told you, changed greatly. A few rooms in the old block were still being rented in 2002. But it was no longer the gathering place it once had been. When the Hotel Rubi was downsized, Enrique Velarde and the others had to seek work elsewhere. In the '90s, I heard en la calle that he had gained some weight and worked at the shrimp-packing plant. I hope he is well. His life rich with family. Happy, healthy children. He was a prince.

By the time of my last visit, Max of the Colmenar had become something of a recluse. When Doña Adelpha died some years ago and the Pasaje Marvi was partially razed in a spasm of urban

285

renewal, it was hard on him. His mom and his restaurant were his life—he did right by both.

Ramon, El Huevón (volume 1), was still working at another hotel near Guaymas in 1995. He has since retired. Unlike fine wine, he did not improve with age. Are you surprised?

In the spring of 2002, as I finished chapter 13 of *La Mandadera*, this volume's predecessor, something truly remarkable happened—I received a card from my former fiancée, Iliana—thirty-two years after I put her on the bus to San Luis! She got my address from the last Christmas card I sent her family in 1994. I had sent cards for some years because of her sister, little Lisa—remember, rule one!

Iliana is fine. A mother of seven and grandmother, she lives far from Guaymas. I wrote back. I'd like to be at peace with her. When I first met her, she was lovely, happy, talkative. That changed, as those of you who read the first volume know.

I didn't see Burro again after the late '70s. They said en la calle that he had become addicted to the fayuca after helping me and Lupita with our movidas in 1970. Apparently he went on to grander levels of enterprise.

I can't confirm it, but on a 1984 trip, the story en la calle was that Burro had died, tangled in the wire fence that separates the United States from Mexico. No one claimed to know which side had started the fusillade of *balazos* (gunshots), but Burro was dead, still wearing his signature plaid shirt.

The plaid shirts are now as common as spit along the border. Nearly every self-styled badass gangbanger on both sides buys them at Wal-Mart by the dozen. The *cholos* and I simply don't get along. It's a "values" thing. And, of course, generational.

But I resent them most for having usurped what I consider Burro's trademark. Even though I know the current generation sporting plaid shirts has never even heard of Burro, I am irrational, taking it personally. It was *his* trademark, fellas!

And Burro wasn't a gangster. Just a guy with no family, a beat-up Chevy, and a desire to *elevarse* (move up in the world). Moral: Don't swim with sharks. Someone always gets eaten.

By the late '70s I also lost track of Gorda and Juanito. The family who were living in her room at the time of the Pecos Conference trip (and Marta's funeral service) were from Sinaloa. They knew nothing. My guess is that Gorda had died and he drifted away into the street again.

Some years ago I asked my comadre, Mercedes (of the Colmenar), if she remembered when she last saw Juanito. She thought it about the time her son, Benjamín, was born but wasn't sure. Mid-'70s. I wish I knew. The thought of him alone and vulnerable out there with no support system troubles me. Heroes deserve better.

287

In 1984 I discovered that Edward Meyers (volume 1) had died and Epifania returned to Guaymas. I saw her briefly. She told me they had some nice years that "lit up her life." Edward had done right by her in his will. She was busy being a grandmother and matriarch of her extended family. In the late '80s she took her family back to west-central Mexico to be with the rest of her original clan, her own mother homesick and near the end of her days.

Time passed. My job became more consuming, and the trips to Guaymas became less frequent. The Zona was closed, in part or completely, depending on whose version one accepts, sometime in the '80s. A spasm of self-conscious, "We've got to clean this up." "Old-fashioned. Unseemly," apparently swept through much of Mexico. NAFTA mentality. Guaymas wasn't spared.

In 2003 the only "club" operating on the margins of the old Zona was a cantina called El Serenita (the Little Siren). It was just another cheap cantina in a down-at-the-heels barrio. No girls, no floor show, no band. Just cold beer and a jukebox.

Once the Zona was closed and many of its buildings were razed, people scattered. The nearby barrio went downhill—no big service industry remained to support it. The makeshift front room *tienditas* (little stores) that had once supported so many families were long gone by 2003, the families gone with them.

Francisca, it is said, never returned to Mexico City and died in Guaymas a few years ago. Chang died in the '80s, Brigido a bit later. La Blanca bought several more houses nearby and, remarkably, morphed completely into Tía X, leaving behind her old identity after she packed and crossed the Zona's wide clay perimeter one last time. She is alive. A value to the community where she now resides (not in the old Zona barrio) and, wonder of wonders, both respected and respectable.

La Negra, they say en la calle, returned to Oaxaca, still wearing her cross and jade-beaded gold ring. I don't know more but imagine her living, if she is still alive, somewhere near Indita's grave. Under Mexico's social conventions of 1970 she could not openly declare her love for Indita while alive but was free to love her and keep her memory in death.

Mariquita moved to central Mexico many years ago and became a force in the nation's entertainment industry. I last saw her in the early '90s. Handsome. Still a fine figure. She is rich, powerful, and now a brunette. Cover, you know! As little Lupita would have put it, "security issues" prevent me from disclosing more. Trust me on this one—her dreams came true.

The dean of the Rubi's waiters, Felipe L., sent Christmas cards for some years, then mine went unanswered. He was probably sixtyish in 1970. I must remember to ask Canelo about him when I visit again.

With the destruction of the Zona, it passed into legend. By the late '80s, taxi drivers' full-grown sons would occasionally ask me to tell them about the fabled Río Rita, just as had happened on my way from Kino Bay to Guaymas in the '70s when Marta died.

In 1994, when I visited with my friend Rory Gauthier, who coauthored *Prehistoric New Mexico* with me, the grandson of a taxista at the Medrano asked all the same questions. By then the rest of the Zona had been bulldozed and the era I spent in Guaymas had become a fabled golden age where the shrimp harvests were immense, the town clean and well kept, and an ordinary taxista could earn a *"pinche rollote de lana"* (frigging huge roll of cash) in one Saturday night ferrying customers to the Río Rita and nearby clubs.

On the same trip I went to visit Lupita's grave but couldn't find it. Her wooden cross was obviously long gone. The graveyard where she was buried is much changed since 1970. At the time of her death I never saw any paperwork. I never even asked about it!

At age twenty-five and in shock, I wasn't thinking about plot "numbers" and "in perpetuity" arrangements. I never even saw her death certificate. What would they have used for her last name? I simply do not know. In '94 that merely reignited my guilt over her death. Some readers of volume 1 have wanted to visit her grave and leave flowers. I'm touched.

All I can suggest is that the next time a scrawny, shaggy-mopped, dark-skinned nine-year-old hustles you on the street in Mexico, why not buy them a taco instead of shoo them away? My mandadera would, I suspect, be honored to know that some kid like her or Juanito got a meal in her memory. She so wanted to be "a great woman someday!" Heck, she might even vibrate from on high, as she did when she "felt happy."

But Lupita, you see, is not dead—she is merely *reposando.* Meanwhile she lives on in my heart, in my capacity to love, and

289

in volume 1 of these chronicles (*La Mandadera*). Truth be told, you can find such kids in every large Mexican town, hustling chicles or competing to wash your windshield.

On the same 1994 visit I managed to locate Eva, through Canelo. She was then a "manager" at the "Tejano Club" (fake name) out on Route 15. She had attained at least a piece of her dream. Remarkably, already past age fifty, she was still quite an eyeful. Rory and I sat at the bar and had a beer. Eva offered to send over a cute, slender, dark-haired girl "if you want company, Davíd."

I declined, reminding her that she was one of the ones who had urged me to be faithful if I married. "But that was at least twenty years ago, Davíd! Are you still with her?" "Yes." I nodded. "And you have not cheated?"

"No! Not once." I don't know whether or not she actually believed me, but the beer was on the house. I haven't seen her since.

Now that the old ambiente as known in the Zona of 1970 simply no longer exists, club life as depicted at the Río Rita is gone. Northern Mexico's late night street life and demimonde have transformed. Unregulated, unhealthy, and rather alien to old-timers.

There are no longer weekly clinics. No Changs to impose decorum. No Brigidos to watch over the girls. No wide, red clay streets to contain the damage. And no weekly cleansing at the Shrine of the Virgin.

In other ways time itself has been hard on Guaymas. Just as in the States, most big stores are now owned not by local families, but by the multinationals like Kmart and Wal-Mart, only slightly disguised so as not to seem too "gringo."

Population growth and huge migrations from southern and central Mexico to El Norte have taxed Guaymas's infrastructure.

290

Canelo, Jacinto, and the author. Jacinto is holding a copy of *The Guaymas Chronicles*. (Photo by Cynthia M. Stuart © 2003.)

Even the old plaza area changed dramatically after many of the great founding families moved to Miramar and San Carlos, the Guaymas equivalent of upscale, Stateside bedroom communities.

It is not for me to judge these trends, especially when they strike me as suspiciously "American." But the compact, pastel-colored late colonial Guaymas of 1970 is much changed. The Almita restaurant now competes with Pizza Hut. Sunday strolls on the plaza compete with Hollywood Video, and the "public" beach at Miramar is now walled off—private. No playa left for ordinary working folks.

The ubiquitous street sweepers of the 1970s who once emerged each morning by 6 a.m. to keep Guaymas picture-perfect are also gone. So is the custom of saying, "*¡Buenas tardes!*"

Martha Aurora's wedding party. (Photo by Cynthia M. Stuart © 2003.)

to everyone you pass. The compartments of social life that once protected dignity, sanity, and civility have begun to rupture.

Heck, you know the story—just ask your grandparents what it was like in the States when Eisenhower was president. Men tipped their hats then. Wore ties to baseball games. Never used the f word in public.

But in Guaymas, the essential spirit of ordinary folks on the street hasn't changed. The warmth and goodness still in individual control hasn't eroded. Canelo is still Canelo. Negro is still Negro, and Mercedes is still Mercedes—none of them or their acquaintances diminished one iota by the constant batallas of life.

This was utterly clear in November of 2003, when I returned with my wife to participate in Martha Aurora, the wolf pup's, wedding. She had vacationed with us often in the States

Shot 2, wedding party. Mercedes and author on right. Sr. Muñoz, the groom's father, on left. (Photo by Cynthia M. Stuart © 2003.)

after she came of age and obtained her own passport. But she waited to marry. Always intent on either the right husband— or no husband. The wolf pup wouldn't settle for less.

The events leading to the wedding began for me at an early reading of *The Guaymas Chronicles: La Mandadera* at The Reader's Oasis, a bookstore in Tucson. As the reading wound down, one of the guests asked whether I'd maintained any connections with Guaymas, a doubtful tone in her Spanish-accented voice.

I explained that I'd returned to Guaymas to baptize Mercedes' daughter, Olga, then Olga's daughter a generation later. Originally from Mexico, the reader was still doubtful. So I related my long-term relationship with Mercedes' family, talking about Mercedes' daughter Martha Aurora—just as she walked in the door and rushed over to give me a hug!

View of Armida Hotel. (Photo by Cynthia M. Stuart © 2003.)

294

The doubter had about the same look on her face as my wife had displayed about five minutes before she saw Chang with her own eyes in 1972. In Guaymas, relationships last forever.

Martha's presence stunned the doubter. Yet Martha's mission wasn't to stand up for me at a reading. That would not even have made sense to her. Instead she came to introduce me to the man she intended to marry. She had finally found "Mr. Right." Her own dad already dead, I was next in line. Of course, I approved. Any Mexican guy who would make a long bus trip to the States simply to meet some gringo his fiancée considered "like a godfather" had to be a-ok.

Rafael Muñoz Correa and Martha Aurora Monteverde C. de Muñoz were married in November of 2003 at the church of Sagrádo Corazón. I walked her down the aisle and gave her in marriage to a big, handsome teddy bear of a guy who was kind, patient, attentive, smart, a hard worker, and *bien educado*

Second view of Armida Hotel. (Photo by Cynthia M. Stuart © 2003.)

(properly raised). Rock-solid Guaymas/Sonoran personality and values.

Their wedding was one of the happiest days of my life. With no daughter of my own, I'd simply borrowed several of Mercedes' girls over the years. Godfathers do that. And like any "dad," I had to blot my eyes during the ceremony.

After the wedding came photos in the garden of the lovely Hotel Armida, not a hundred yards from the obelisk/statue that had once defined the limits of Lupita's world.

The wedding party afterward took place at the Naval Club's relatively new pavilion across the bay at Las Playitas—almost exactly where I had once lounged by my old gray Rambler, smoking and checking out Mariquita in her bathing suit as the viejas played on the beach.

The wedding fiesta was de costumbre—the relatives, including my wife and me, marching in a circle, our names announced as we were "presented" to the several hundred assembled guests. Food. Beer. Music. And dancing—all in a pavilion by the sea.

I could even look straight across the harbor to the steeples of San Fernando, see city hall, and wistfully remember the spot where I had once danced at the long-gone Chapultepec Pavilion before most of the wedding guests had even been born.

Guaymas is constantly changing, but the fundamental rhythm of life goes on. By the time you read this, I will have held Martha Aurora and Rafael's baby son (born July 22, 2004) in my arms. And I will likely smell just as exotic to him as I did to his mom so long ago.

As for me, I went into academics, mostly because it keeps me near young people. My wife and I never managed to have kids, so it turned out to be great work after all. But Guaymas habits remain imbedded in the fabric of my daily life.

I still invest in the Albuquerque version of Serdaneando, walking Route 66/Central Avenue near campus, doing the coffee shops, bookstores, and restaurants. It's one way to make a family. Mannie's Restaurant, on the corner of Girard and Central, where I lunch, even sells my books at their cash register. Here in the Southwest things are mellow. Spanish is widely spoken, as are many Indian languages. It suits me.